THEORY OF COMPUTATION

Formal Languages, Automata, and Complexity

The Benjamin/Cummings Series in Computer Science

Almasi/Gottlieb, *Highly Parallel Computing*

Booch, *Software Engineering with Ada, Second Edition*

Booch, *Software Components with Ada: Structures, Tools, and Subsystems*

Brookshear, *Computer Science, An Overview, Second Edition*

Etter, *Problem Solving with Structured FORTRAN 77*

Etter, *Structured FORTRAN 77 for Engineers and Scientists, Second Edition*

Etter, *Problem Solving in Pascal for Engineers and Scientists*

Etter, *WATFIV: Structured Programming and Problem Solving*

Fischer/LeBlanc, *Crafting a Compiler*

Helman/Veroff, *Intermediate Problem Solving and Data Structures: Walls and Mirrors*

Helman/Veroff, *Walls and Mirrors: Intermediate Problem Solving and Data Structures—Modula II Edition*

Kelley/Pohl, *A Book on C: An Introduction to Programming in C*

Kelley/Pohl, *C by Dissection: The Essentials of C Programming*

Kelley/Pohl, *Turbo C: The Essentials of C Programming*

Kerschberg, editor, *Expert Database Systems: Proceedings from the Second International Conference*

Luger/Stubblefield, *Artificial Intelligence and the Design of Expert Systems*

Maekawa/Oldehoeft/Oldehoeft, *Operating Systems: Advanced Concepts*

Maier/Warren, *Computing with Logic: Logic Programming with Prolog*

Preas/Lorenzetti, *Physical Design Automation of VLSI Systems*

Savitch, *Pascal: An Introduction to the Art and Science of Programming, Second Edition*

Savitch, *TURBO Pascal: An Introduction to the Art and Science of Programming, Second Edition*

Savitch, *TURBO Pascal 4.0/5.0: An Introduction to the Art and Science of Programming*

Sebesta, *Concepts of Programming Languages*

THEORY OF COMPUTATION

Formal Languages, Automata, and Complexity

J. Glenn Brookshear
Marquette University

The Benjamin/Cummings Publishing Company, Inc.
Redwood City, California • Fort Collins, Colorado
Menlo Park, California • Reading, Massachusetts • New York
Don Mills, Ontario • Wokingham, U.K. • Amsterdam • Bonn
Sydney • Singapore • Tokyo • Madrid • San Juan

Sponsoring Editor: Alan Apt
Associate Editor: Mark McCormick
Production Coordinator: Janet Vail
Production, Text, and Cover Design: Linda Seals, B. Vader Design/Production
Copy Editing: Anna M. Huff
Illustrations: Sharon Van Court
Composition: Graphic Typesetting Service

The basic text of this book was designed using the Modular Design System, as developed by Wendy Earl and Design Office Bruce Kortebein.

LIBRARY OF CONGRESS CATALOGING-IN-PUBLICATION DATA
Brookshear, J. Glenn.
  Theory of computation.

  Bibliography: p. 317
  Includes index.
  1. Machine theory.   2. Computational complexity.
I. Title.
QA267.B76 1989   511   88-26232
ISBN 0-8053-0143-7
BCDEFGHIJ-DO-8932109

The Benjamin/Cummings Publishing Company, Inc.
390 Bridge Parkway
Redwood City, California 94065

To Earlene and Cheryl

PREFACE

I designed this book to serve as a text for a one-semester introductory course in the theory of computation. It covers the traditional topics of formal languages, automata, computability, and computational complexity. Thus, the book would be a suitable text for such courses as CS16 in the ACM Curriculum '87 and CO3 in the ACM Liberal Arts Computer Science Curriculum (Communications of the ACM, March, 1986).

UNDERLYING PHILOSOPHY

My goal in writing this book was to present the foundations of theoretical computer science in a format accessible to undergraduate computer science students. I wanted students to appreciate theoretical ideas as the foundation on which real problems are solved, rather than viewing them as unuseable abstractions.

I approached this task by adopting two underlying principles. The first was to emphasize the relationship between the theoretical topics being presented and the applied topics with which students at this level are familiar. Without this emphasis, students whose background consists of programming, software engineering, and data structures find it difficult to relate to automata theory, formal languages, and recursive function theory. Consequently, the theoretical topics in this book are closely associated with practical issues. For example, the hierarchy of automata theory and formal languages is developed in the context of constructing well-designed parsing routines for a compiler. As another example, the subject of computability is related to the question of what structures are required within a programming language to insure that any algorithmically solvable problem can be solved by a program in that language.

The other principle to which I subscribed when writing this book was to avoid becoming sidetracked by less important topics. This is a text for a one-semester introductory course, not a definitive encyclopedia of the subject. I want students to appreciate the forest, not become bogged down in the study of trees. This view is lost if, for example, one tries to introduce all the topics associated with regular languages before moving on up the language hierarchy. If the progression is too slow, students lose their perspective of the subject.

Thus, I chose to avoid those topics that do not contribute directly to the overall picture and are not required background for topics to be discussed later in the book. This left ample material for a one-semester course but allowed the text to keep moving quickly enough so that its plot is not buried in the details. More details can be covered in a later course or courses. In short the text covers:

- regular, context-free, and general phrase-structure languages along with their associated automata,
- computability in the context of Turing machines, partial recursive functions, and simple programming languages, and
- complexity theory with an introduction to some of the open classification problems relating to the classes P and NP.

PEDAGOGICAL AIDS

I classify pedagogical aids as being either implicit or explicit. In the category of implicit aids, I have tried to do more explaining than proving. I have, of course, provided rigorous proofs throughout the text, but I have also provided a significant amount of intuitive motivation and dialogue. My goal is to teach the material, not just present it. Thus, the text has more informal exposition than is found in a formal definition–theorem–proof format.

Under the category of explicit pedagogical aids, I have closed each chapter with a section called "Closing Comments," in which I review the material and discuss the interrelationships. I have also provided numerous exercises throughout the text. Each section (after the introductory chapter) ends with a few exercises designed to review the material just discussed. After each chapter, I have provided a variety of problems. These problems not only review the material in the chapter, but also relate the material to other chapters and point to concepts not covered in the text.

ACKNOWLEDGEMENTS

There are numerous people who contributed to this book; I thank all of them. In particular, the following people served as reviewers: J. Mack Adams, Eric Bach, T. M. Phillips, Donald Friesen, Tim Long, Matthias Stallmann, George Struble, and Allen Tucker. In addition, Richard Iltis taught from an early version of the manuscript and supplied a wealth of helpful comments, and discussions with Walter Savitch helped remove several rough spots from the final manuscript.

I also thank Paul Bankston, Mark Barnard, Phillip Bender, Madhu Deshpande, Douglas Harris, Gary Krenz, John Moyer, Francis Pastijn, John Simms, and Michael Slattery. All are members of my department at Marquette University who contributed their time and ideas to this project. They are a great bunch of colleagues; otherwise, they would have long ago started closing their office doors when they heard me coming down the hall.

A big thank you also goes to those students who took courses based on the early versions of my manuscript and gave me their comments. Many of these students demonstrated uncanny ability (and joy) in pointing out my mistakes. Their enthusiasm has made this a better book.

Finally, I recognize the patience of my wife Earlene and daughter Cheryl, to whom this book is dedicated.

CONTENTS

CHAPTER 0

Preliminaries

Fundamental to the science of computing is the notion of a computational process, also called an algorithmic process or algorithm. It is by executing such processes that computers are able to solve problems; conversely, a problem that does not have an algorithmic solution cannot be solved by a computer. Thus, any limitation on the capabilities of computational processes is also a limitation on the capabilities of computational machines.

This text is an introduction to the study of computational processes. Our goal is to explore the scope of such processes using rigorous, mathematical methods, while at the same time relating theoretical results to practical concerns. We begin with a theoretical study of pattern-recognition techniques that we relate to the practical issues of language processing in general, and to compiler construction in particular. This will lead us to apparent bounds on the powers of computational processes and hence to a theoretical study of computability. Here again we will not address theoretical issues alone. We will find there are many problems that are theoretically solvable by algorithms, yet they do not have practical algorithmic solutions. More precisely, many problems that are algorithmically solvable in theory require such massive resources (in terms of time or storage space) that they remain unsolvable from any practical point of view. Thus, our study will conclude with an investigation of current research efforts aimed at identifying those problems that have practical solutions.

To motivate our study of computability further, let us compare a physicist who solves problems using the physical laws discovered by Isaac Newton and a computer programmer who solves problems by expressing their solutions in a programming language. There are many problems the physicist can solve within the Newtonian framework. However, there are also problems for which the physical laws of Newton are too restrictive; to solve them the physicist must use the more comprehensive laws of Einstein's theory of relativity. The very science of physics embodies the search for more powerful laws with which to explain increasingly complex physical phenomena. Regardless of the fundamental principles on which their study is based, however, there would appear to be a limit to the questions physicists can ultimately answer. For instance, if we assume the big bang theory is true, it is highly unlikely that physicists will ever be able to explore that portion of the universe that lies beyond the distance traveled by light since that explosion.

By comparison, there are numerous problems the computer programmer can solve using a particular programming language, but the language being used may impose limitations on the problems the programmer can solve. Can such limitations be overcome by developing more powerful programming languages? Moreover, as in the case of the big bang theory, is there a point at which attaching additional features to a programming language or changing to another language will not increase the programmer's problem-solving power? Such questions are at the core of our study.

0.1   REVIEW OF SET THEORY

Much of our study will involve the basic concepts of set theory, so let us review these ideas before proceeding.

Basic Definitions

Intuitively, a **set** is a collection of objects. These objects are usually called **elements** (or **members**) of the set. We often use bracket notation when describing a set. For example, we may write $A = \{a, b, c\}$ to indicate that A is the set whose elements are a, b, and c. Another example is $W = \{x: x$ is a positive integer$\}$, read "W equals the set of all x such that x is a positive integer," which indicates that W is the set of all positive integers. A somewhat special case is the **empty set,** denoted by $\{\ \}$ and also by $\varnothing$. It contains no elements.

A set may also be called a collection or a family. We may refer to a set of numbers, a collection of numbers, or a family of numbers. Another term often used is **class**, although class is technically a more general term than set. Indeed, the concept of a class was developed to avoid such paradoxes as "the set of all sets that are not members of themselves." (Would such a set contain itself or not?) However, we need not concern ourselves with such details. We will simply use the term class in those cases where it is customary to do so.

A set that arises often in the following chapters is the set of **natural numbers,** also known as the set of nonnegative integers $\{0, 1, 2, 3, \cdots\}$, which we represent with the symbol $\mathbb{N}$. Unfortunately, the definition of natural numbers varies somewhat. Some people do not consider 0 to be in the set of natural numbers. Instead, they define the natural numbers as the set of positive integers $\{1, 2, 3, \cdots\}$. We will represent this set as $\mathbb{N}^+$. Such a distinction is only a minor inconvenience, however. The trend to include 0 as a natural number reflects the fact that computer scientists find it convenient to start counting with 0 rather than 1.

The symbol $\in$ is read "is an element of." Thus, $x \in X$ means x is an element of X. Conversely, $\notin$ is read "is not an element of."

The **union** of two sets A and B, denoted by $A \cup B$, is the collection of all the elements that are in either A or B. Thus, $A \cup B = \{x: x \in A$ or $x \in B\}$. The **intersection** of two sets A and B, denoted by $A \cap B$, is the collection of objects that are elements in both A and B; therefore, $A \cap B = \{x: x \in A$ and $x \in B\}$. For example, if $A = \{a, b, c\}$ and $B = \{b, c, d\}$, then $A \cup B$ would be $\{a, b, c, d\}$ and $A \cap B$ would be $\{b, c\}$.

We use a minus sign to denote set subtraction. That is, $\{a, b, c\} - \{a, c\} = \{b\}$, and $\{a, b\} - \{d, e\} = \{a, b\}$. The set $A - B$ is called the **complement** of B relative to A. In certain cases the elements of all the sets being considered are understood to belong to some large, universal set. In these cases we refer to the complement of a set X relative to this universal set as simply the complement of X. Thus, in a discussion concerning natural numbers, the complement of the set $\{1, 5\}$ would be understood to mean the complement of $\{1, 5\}$ relative to $\mathbb{N}$; in a discussion regarding alphabetic symbols, the complement of $\{a, b, c\}$ would be the set of symbols other than a, b, and c.

We say set A is a **subset** of set B, written $A \subseteq B$, if all elements of A are also elements of B. (Thus, the empty set is a subset of any set.) Set A is a **proper subset** of B if $A \subseteq B$ and $B - A \neq \varnothing$. The sets A and B are equal if both $A \subseteq B$ and $B \subseteq A$.

The **Cartesian product** of two sets A and B, denoted by $A \times B$, is the set of all ordered pairs of the form (a, b), where $a \in A$ and $b \in B$. (Note that, in general, $A \times B \neq B \times A$ since the arrangement of the components in an ordered pair is significant.) The concept of the product of sets can be generalized to obtain the product of more than two sets. For example, $A \times B \times C = \{(a, b, c): a \in A, b \in B,$ and $c \in C\}$. It is customary to use the shortened notation A^2 to represent $A \times A$, A^3 to represent $A \times A \times A$, and in general, A^n to represent the collection of all n-tuples of elements in A.

Given two sets A and B, a **function** from A to B is a subset of $A \times B$, such that each element of A appears as the first component of one and only one ordered pair in the function. We say such a function **maps** A into B. If f is a function from A to B, we call A the **domain** of f and say that f is a function on A. The set of elements that appear as the second component in the ordered pairs of a function is called the **range** of the function. If every element in B is in the range of f, we say f is a function from A **onto** B (or f maps A onto B). If each member of the range of f is associated with only one element in the domain, we say f is a **one-to-one** function, or simply f is one-to-one.

We usually think of the elements of a function's domain as inputs to the function and the elements in the function's range as the output values. This concept of input and output motivates the notation $f:A \to B$, which denotes a function f from A to B. Given a function $f:A \to B$, we denote the output value associated with the input x as $f(x)$.

For example, suppose $f:\mathbb{N} \to \mathbb{N}$ is the function consisting of the ordered pairs of the form (n, n^2), that is, $f(n) = n^2$ for each $n \in \mathbb{N}$. This function is one-to-one, but it is not onto $\mathbb{N}$ since the range of f contains only perfect squares.

Proof by Induction

At times we will want to prove that some statement holds for a sequence of integers. For example, if $\mathcal{P}(X)$ represents the **power set** of X (that is, the collection of all subsets of X) and $|X|$ represents the number of elements in the set X, we may want to prove that

$$|\mathcal{P}(X)| = 2^{|X|}$$

for all finite sets X of size one or greater.

Figure 0.1 confirms this formula for sets of size one, two, and three by exhaustively listing all the subsets in each case. (Note that what names we give the elements in the sets is not significant. Here, we use the notation $\{1, 2, \cdots, n\}$ to represent a generic set of size n.) However, this explicit case-by-case approach can never prove that the formula we are considering is true for all cases, since there are infinitely many cases to test. What we need is a general argument that covers all cases at once.

In our example, we can obtain such an argument by identifying a generic method of constructing the collection of subsets of the set $\{1, 2, \cdots, n + 1\}$ from the collection of subsets of the set $\{1, 2, \cdots, n\}$. In particular, having

The set X	All subsets of X	
{1}	{ }	{1}
{1, 2}	{ }	{2}
	{1}	{1, 2}
{1, 2, 3}	{ }	{3}
	{1}	{1, 3}
	{2}	{2, 3}
	{1, 2}	{1, 2, 3}

Figure 0.1   Sets of cardinality 1, 2, and 3 together with all their subsets

generated all the subsets of the set {1, 2, ⋯, n}, we can generate all the subsets of {1, 2, ⋯, n, $n + 1$} by listing all the subsets found in the preceding case (in a column) and then repeating this list (in a second column), inserting the additional element, $n + 1$, in each subset. (This was the technique used to construct Figure 0.1.) From this general observation we conclude that there are twice as many subsets of a set of size $n + 1$ as there are subsets of a set of size n. That is, for any $n \in \mathbb{N}^+$,

$$|\mathcal{P}(\{1, 2, \cdots, n + 1\})| = 2|\mathcal{P}(\{1, 2, \cdots, n\})|$$

The important point here is that this is a generic conclusion, because it does not rely on a specific value of n: It is just as valid for the value $n = 3$ as it is for $n = 153$ or any other $n \in \mathbb{N}^+$. Hence, if we could show by a specific argument that $|\mathcal{P}(X)| = 2^{|X|}$ for a set X, this generic statement would imply that the equation could be extended to each larger finite set, without actually validating each case by a separate argument. Indeed, if there are always twice as many subsets of a set of size $n + 1$ as there are subsets of a set of size n and if $|\mathcal{P}(X)| = 2^{|X|}$ for some finite set X, then for any set Y with $|Y| = |X| + 1$ we have

$$|\mathcal{P}(Y)| = 2|\mathcal{P}(X)| = 2(2^{|X|}) = 2^{|Y|}$$

Thus, if we confirm the equation $|\mathcal{P}(X)| = 2^{|X|}$ for the case of a set of size one (as we have done in the first row of Figure 0.1), then the equation must be valid for any set with size $n \in \mathbb{N}^+$.

This technique is known as proof by **induction**; it is useful when we wish to prove some statement about a sequence of integers. Rather than attempting a case-by-case argument, which would never be complete in instances where there are infinitely many cases, we provide a specific argument that covers the smallest value being considered (called the **base case**), and then give a generic argument that shows that if the statement should hold for any case, then it must also hold for the next larger case.

We have used the power set example here because the formula obtained will be useful in later discussions. For an example more closely associated with the programming environment, let us apply induction to show that the recursive procedure sort, as outlined in Figure 0.2, returns the sorted version of its input list. We will proceed by induction on the number of entries in the input list.

We first confirm that sort performs correctly for the base case, in which the input list contains no entries (the empty list), by explicitly tracing the execution of the procedure in that case. We then assume that the procedure correctly returns the sorted version of inputs with n entries, where n is a generic positive integer, and argue that it must therefore return the sorted version of any list containing $n + 1$ entries.

To this end we note that a request of the form sort(InputList), where InputList is a list containing $n + 1$ entries, will result in the execution of the then portion of the procedure. There, another activation of sort produces the sorted version of the sublist that consists of those entries that follow the first entry in the original InputList. Since this sublist contains only n entries, this activation of sort will perform its task correctly (by our assumption about lists with only n entries), and thus our original input list will appear as the original first entry followed by the sorted version of the remaining list. Consequently, the next instruction in the procedure, which moves the first list entry to its proper place among the others, will complete the task of sorting the entire list. We conclude that if the procedure sort correctly sorts lists of n entries, then it must also correctly sort lists with $n + 1$ entries. Combining this with our previous conclusion—that sort performs correctly when given the empty list—implies that the procedure sort will sort finite lists of any size.

Countable and Uncountable Sets

Let us now consider the intuitive notion of the number of elements in a set. At first there seems to be nothing complicated about the concept. Clearly, the number of elements in the set $\{a, b, c\}$ is three, and the number of elements in $\{x, y\}$ is two. But how many elements are in the set $\mathbb{N}^+$? The layperson would probably say "infinity," but for our purposes this is far too simplistic. Infinity is not a number in our normal counting system. Instead, the term infinity reflects the concept of a set having more elements than can be represented by any traditional number. Moreover, we are about to see that sets containing infinitely many elements, called **infinite sets,** do not all contain the same amount of elements. The sizes of two infinite sets can be different just as the sizes of two finite sets can be different. Thus, there are levels of infinity, with some infinite sets being larger than others.

Because there are no numbers in our traditional counting system to represent the size of an infinite set, it is necessary to extend our system to

```
procedure sort (list);
begin
     if (list not empty) then
          begin
               sort (portion of list following first entry);
               move first entry to its proper place within
                    the following portion of the list
          end
end;
```

Figure 0.2   An outline for the procedure **sort**

account for such sets. In this extended system we refer to the size of a set as its **cardinality.** The cardinality of a finite set corresponds to our traditional notion of the number of elements in the set, but the cardinality of an infinite set is not a number in the usual sense. Rather, the cardinality of an infinite set is a number, called a **cardinal number,** that exists only in our extended number system. We represent the cardinality of a set A by $|A|$.

To complete our cardinality system we need to establish a way of comparing the cardinalities of different sets, that is, we need to define what it means for one cardinality to be less than another. To this end we agree to say the cardinality of the set X is less than or equal to the cardinality of the set Y, written $|X| \leq |Y|$, if and only if each element of X can be paired with a unique element of Y. In other words, $|X| \leq |Y|$ if and only if there is a one-to-one function mapping X into Y. Note that if X and Y are finite sets, this definition of less than or equal to corresponds to the traditional definition: $|\{x, y\}| \leq |\{r, s, t\}|$ because x can be paired with the element r while y can be paired with s.

Next we say the cardinality of the set X is equal to the cardinality of the set Y, written $|X| = |Y|$, if and only if there is a one-to-one function mapping X onto Y. (The Schröder–Bernstein Theorem, whose details need not concern us, confirms that these definitions agree with our intuition. It states that if $|X| \leq |Y|$ and if $|Y| \leq |X|$, then $|X| = |Y|$.) Note that $|\mathbb{N}| = |\mathbb{N}^+|$, where a suitable one-to-one function is the function that associates each x in $\mathbb{N}$ with the number $x + 1$ in $\mathbb{N}^+$. Finally, we define $|X| < |Y|$ to mean $|X| \leq |Y|$ and $|X| \neq |Y|$.

In our discussion, the relationship between a set and its power set is extremely important. In the case of a finite set X, we have already shown that there are more elements in $\mathcal{P}(X)$ than in X. (In fact, if X contains n elements, then $\mathcal{P}(X)$ will contain 2^n elements.) The following theorem extends this relationship between a set and its power set to infinite sets.

THEOREM 0.1
If X is any set, then $|X| < |\mathcal{P}(X)|$.

PROOF
Clearly, $|X| \leq |\mathcal{P}(X)|$ because the function mapping each element x in X to the set $\{x\}$ provides the required one-to-one function. (If X is empty, then every element in X can be mapped to an element in $\mathcal{P}(X)$ because there are no such elements in X.)

Our task, then, is to show that $|X| \neq |\mathcal{P}(X)|$. We can do this by showing that there is no function mapping X *onto* $\mathcal{P}(X)$. Suppose f is any function from X to $\mathcal{P}(X)$ and consider the set $Y = \{x: x \in X$ and $x \notin f(x)\}$. Note that Y is a subset of X and therefore an element in $\mathcal{P}(X)$. Thus, if f is onto $\mathcal{P}(X)$, there must be some y in X such that $f(y) = Y$.

If such a y exists, however, then either $y \in f(y)$ or $y \notin f(y)$—both of which lead to contradictions. If $y \in f(y)$, then the definition of Y would imply that $y \notin Y$, which contradicts our claim that $f(y) = Y$. Likewise, if $y \notin f(y)$, then the definition of Y would imply that $y \in Y$, which also contradicts the assumption that $f(y) = Y$.

We conclude that there is no $y \in X$ such that $f(y) = Y$. Consequently, f cannot be *onto* $\mathcal{P}(X)$ and hence $|X| < |\mathcal{P}(X)|$.

∎

We are now in a position to support our claim that infinite sets can have different cardinalities. We need merely select any infinite set X and compare its cardinality to that of its power set $\mathcal{P}(X)$. By Theorem 0.1, the cardinality of the latter must be greater than that of the former. In fact, the process of forming power sets leads to a hierarchy of infinite sets because the cardinality of $\mathcal{P}(\mathcal{P}(X))$ must be greater than the cardinality of $\mathcal{P}(X)$, and so forth. That is,

$$|X| < |\mathcal{P}(X)| < |\mathcal{P}(\mathcal{P}(X))| < \cdots$$

A consequence of this hierarchy is that there is no largest infinite cardinal. Given any infinite set, its power set will always be larger.

There is, however, a smallest infinite cardinal. It is the cardinality of $\mathbb{N}$. This claim agrees with our intuitive feeling that if X is an infinite set then we should be able to extract elements one at a time without exhausting the set; that is, we could extract a "zero" element, then a "first" element, followed by a "second," etc., and hence X must contain at least $|\mathbb{N}|$ elements. However, this intuitive argument is based on a case-by-case approach which, as we agreed in our discussion of induction, fails to provide valid proof. Therefore, we present the following formal theorem and proof. It is based on the Axiom of Choice, which states that given any collection of nonempty sets there is a function g whose domain is the collection of sets, and for each set X in the collection, $g(X) \in X$. That is, when given a set X from the collection as input, the function will return an element of X as its output.

THEOREM 0.2

The cardinality of the set of natural numbers is less than or equal to the cardinality of any infinite set.

PROOF

We must show that given any infinite set X, there is a one-to-one function f from $\mathbb{N}$ into X. For this purpose we let g represent a function whose domain is the collection of nonempty subsets of X, and for each nonempty subset Y of X, $g(Y)$ is an element of Y. (The existence of such a function is based on the Axiom of Choice.) Based on this association between nonempty subsets of X and elements, we now define the function f by induction. We define $f(0)$ to be $g(X)$. Then, if n is a natural number for which $f(n)$, $f(n-1)$, $\cdots$, $f(0)$ have been defined, we define $f(n+1)$ to be the element $g(X - \{f(0), f(1),$ $\cdots$, $f(n)\})$. Note that according to our definition of g, $f(n+1)$ is chosen from the set $X - \{f(0), f(1), \cdots, f(n)\}$, which is nonempty since X is infinite and $\{f(0), f(1), \cdots, f(n)\}$ is finite. Therefore, $f(n+1)$ must be distinct from $f(0)$, $f(1)$, $\cdots$, $f(n)$. Thus f is a one-to-one function from $\mathbb{N}$ into the set X. We conclude that the cardinality of the natural numbers is not greater than that of X.

∎

Theorem 0.2 shows that the set $\mathbb{N}$ is one of the smallest infinite sets. We say it is *one* of the smallest because there are many sets of this same size (just as there are many sets of size three). For example, we have already seen that $\mathbb{N}^+$ is the same size as $\mathbb{N}$.

Finally, we should introduce the concepts of countable and uncountable sets as promised earlier. Here it is helpful to recall the process we normally refer to as counting. To count the elements of a set means to assign the values 1, 2, 3, $\cdots$, to the set's elements. We may even pronounce the words "one, two, three, $\cdots$" as we point to the objects we are counting. In short, the counting process assigns positive integers to the elements of a set. We have seen, however, that there are infinite sets with more elements than there are positive integers. Thus, these sets cannot be counted, because there are not enough positive integers to go around. Such sets are said to be **uncountable.** In contrast, any set whose cardinality is less than or equal to that of the positive integers is said to be **countable** (also **enumerable**). The set of natural numbers is countable; its power set is not. In fact, Theorems 0.1 and 0.2 combined imply that *the power set of any infinite set is uncountable.*

One way to show that an infinite set is countable is to demonstrate that there is a process for listing its elements as a sequence in such a way that each element in the set will ultimately appear in the list. Such a listing is a way of counting the elements: the first entry in the list is assigned one, the second is assigned two, the third is assigned three, etc.

As an example, let us show that the set $\mathbb{N}^+ \times \mathbb{N}^+$ is countable. We do this by describing a listing of all the elements in $\mathbb{N}^+ \times \mathbb{N}^+$. This list consists of all the pairs whose components add to two, followed by pairs whose components add to three, followed by those pairs whose components add to four, etc. We arrange the pairs within each of these groupings in the order corresponding to their first components. Thus, the list has the form $(1, 1), (1, 2), (2, 1), (1, 3), (2, 2), (3, 1), \cdots$. (See Figure 0.3.) Note that this list will ultimately contain each element of $\mathbb{N}^+ \times \mathbb{N}^+$. (The pair (m, n) will appear as the mth entry in the portion of the list that contains the pairs whose components add to $m + n$.) Finally, we observe that this listing is actually a counting of the elements of $\mathbb{N}^+ \times \mathbb{N}^+$—we have assigned one to $(1, 1)$, two to $(1, 2)$, three to $(2, 1)$, etc. Consequently, we can conclude that $\mathbb{N}^+ \times \mathbb{N}^+$ is countable.

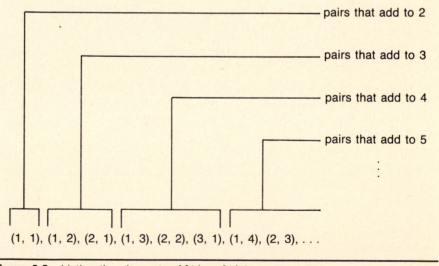

pairs that add to 2

pairs that add to 3

pairs that add to 4

pairs that add to 5

$(1, 1), (1, 2), (2, 1), (1, 3), (2, 2), (3, 1), (1, 4), (2, 3), \ldots$

Figure 0.3   Listing the elements of $\mathbb{N}^+ \times \mathbb{N}^+$ in a sequence

So What?

Let us close this section by relating our discussion to a typical computing environment. Suppose we have a program ready to run on an actual computer. The program is designed to accept some input (perhaps a list of names to be sorted) and produce some output (such as the sorted list). Regardless of what the input and output are, each is merely a string of bits from the machine's point of view. Thus, we can consider the input and output as natural numbers represented in binary notation. (We can imagine an additional 1 placed at the leftmost end of these bit strings so that any leading 0s in the original strings will be significant.) From this perspective, the program accepts an input number and, based on the value of that number, produces an output number. That is, the action of the program is to compute a function from $\mathbb{N}$ to $\mathbb{N}$. In turn, each function from $\mathbb{N}$ to $\mathbb{N}$ suggests a program we may at some time wish to write.

How many such functions are there? Clearly there are no more functions from $\mathbb{N}$ to $\{0, 1\}$ than there are functions from $\mathbb{N}$ to $\mathbb{N}$, since the latter provides more potential output values. But there are as many functions from $\mathbb{N}$ to $\{0, 1\}$ as there are elements in the power set of $\mathbb{N}$. Indeed, for each subset X of $\mathbb{N}$ there is a function f, called the **characteristic function** of X, from $\mathbb{N}$ to $\{0, 1\}$ defined by

$$f(n) = \begin{cases} 1 \text{ if } n \in X \\ 0 \text{ if } n \notin X \end{cases}$$

We conclude that there are at least as many functions from $\mathbb{N}$ to $\mathbb{N}$ as there are elements of $\mathcal{P}(\mathbb{N})$. Thus, there are uncountably many functions for which we may want to write programs.

Now, consider your favorite programming language. There are a finite number of symbols from which any program in that language is constructed. Let us establish an "alphabetical" order for these symbols. Then, we could list all programs in the language that have a length of one symbol (if there are any) in alphabetical order; following this we could list all the programs of length two in alphabetical order; then, all programs of length three in alphabetical order; etc. Such a listing would ultimately contain any program that could be written in the language. Thus, this listing procedure implies that the set of all programs that can be written in the language is countable.

What have we shown? There are only countably many programs that can be written in your favorite programming language, but there are uncountably many functions that you may want to compute with a program. Because each program computes only one function, you are bound to come up short. Thus, there are problems you might want to solve using a computer, but for which no program in your favorite programming language can be written!

What are some of these problems? Could you solve such a problem by changing to a different programming language? Could such problems be solved if we built a bigger computer? Even if you are able to produce a program for solving a problem, will today's machine be able to execute it fast enough to produce an answer in your lifetime? Would tomorrow's computer be able to produce an answer in your children's lifetime? These are some of the questions addressed directly or indirectly in the following chapters.

0.2   GRAMMATICAL BASIS OF LANGUAGE TRANSLATION

Much of the early part of our study will be based on problems dealing with language processing. We therefore take this opportunity to review some of the concepts and terminology associated with the language translation process.

First, we should clarify the terms **formal language** and **natural language.** The two can be differentiated with the question, "Which came first, the language or its grammatical rules?" In general, a natural language is one that has evolved over time for the purpose of human communication. Examples include English, German, and Russian. Such languages continue to evolve without regard for formal grammatical rules. Any rules associated with the language are developed after the fact in an attempt to explain the language's structure rather than to determine it. As a result, natural languages rarely conform to simple or obvious grammatical rules. This nonconformance is a thorn in the side of grammarians, many of whom would like us to believe that our way of speaking is incorrect rather than accept the possibility that they have not found the correct set of rules, that their rules are no longer valid, or that there are no such rules to be found.

In contrast to natural languages, formal languages are defined by, and hence rigorously conform to, pre-established rules. Examples include computer programming languages and mathematical languages such as algebra and propositional logic. It is because of this adherence to rules that the construction of efficient computerized translators for programming languages is possible, whereas it is the lack of adherence to established rules that makes it difficult to construct a translator for a natural language.

To underscore the role of grammar in the translation process, let us review the steps followed by a typical language translator such as a compiler for a programming language. A fundamental task of such a translator is to recognize the individual building blocks of the language being translated. At its lowest level this involves recognizing that certain strings of symbols in the program being translated (the **source program**) should be considered as representing a single object. For example, the variable name LIST must be recognized as a single identifier instead of a string of four separate letters, the string of digits 524 must be recognized as a single number, and the string := (used in several programming languages) must be recognized as the single operation of assignment.

The process of identifying such multisymbol sequences within the source program is handled by a portion of the compiler known as the **lexical analyzer.** This is essentially a submodule that accepts the source program as a string of symbols and produces a string of **tokens,** where each token represents a single object that may have been represented by more than one symbol in the input string. (A token might be represented as an integer value that can be stored in a single cell of a machine's memory.)

Having reduced each multisymbol sequence that represents a single object to a token, the translator's next task is analyzing the pattern of tokens. At this point a typical compiler might need to recognize that the tokens for if, then, and else together represent an if–then–else structure, or that the string lying between a repeat token and its matching until token represents the body of a loop structure. Such analysis is called **parsing** and is done by a module within the compiler known as the **parser.**

As the parser recognizes various structures in the program, it requests the services of another module called the **code generator** to produce the translated version of that particular part of the program. As these translated portions are formed, the translated version of the program (the **object program**) takes shape.

In summary, the translation process consists of three basic components: lexical analysis, parsing, and code generation, as represented in Figure 0.4. The first two of these lean heavily on the ability to recognize patterns. If the patterns to be recognized are based on grammatical rules, the recog-

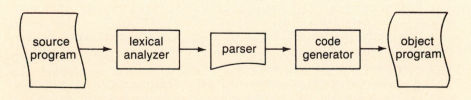

Figure 0.4   The basic translation process

nition process can also be based on these rules. Such is the case when processing a formal language. If, however, the language being translated does not strictly adhere to well-defined grammatical rules, the construction of a program segment for parsing the language would be very difficult.

0.3 HISTORICAL BACKGROUND

Most of today's scientific knowledge is the result of many years of research, often performed in seemingly unrelated subjects. This is true even in such a young field as computer science. Many of the results in the following chapters were discovered in the early part of the twentieth century by mathematicians working in such areas as axiomatic systems and logic. A brief introduction to this mathematical period is therefore relevant to our study.

The beginning of the twentieth century found mathematics on the threshold of discovery. The developments of the next 40 years were destined to shake the very foundations of mathematics and have far-reaching consequences in the field of computer science, which at that time was yet to be born. To understand this period of transition, let us consider the axiomatic approach to mathematics—a subject that received major attention at the turn of the century.

Simply stated, the axiomatic method calls for a collection of basic statements, called **axioms,** that describe the fundamental properties of the system to be studied. From these axioms additional statements, called **theorems,** are derived by applying finite sequences of **inference rules.** These rules are designed so that any theorem that might be derived must be a statement that logically follows from the axioms. For example, a well-known inference rule is modus ponens, which states that from two statements of the form

$$\text{if } X \text{ then } Y$$

and

$$X$$

we can derive the statement Y. It is modus ponens that allows us to conclude "the wind is blowing" from the statements "the trees are moving" and "if the trees are moving then the wind is blowing."

One advantage of the axiomatic method is that it provides a model of deductive reasoning in which all assumptions are isolated in the initial axioms and inference rules. Any statement later derived within such a system is assured to be a consequence of these and only these assumptions.

Thus, the axiomatic method provides an important tool with which scientific inquiries can be undertaken.

In the early 1900s many mathematicians believed all of mathematics could be based on a single axiomatic system. The goal was to find the right set of axioms and inference rules. Then, any theorem in mathematics could be derived from the axioms merely by applying some finite sequence of inference rules. In this manner mathematics would be reduced to a computational system in which the truth or falseness of any mathematical statement could be determined algorithmically.

A startling breakthrough came in 1931 with the publication of Kurt Gödel's incompleteness theorem. This theorem essentially states that for any valid axiomatic system that is rich enough to describe that part of mathematics that consists of the natural numbers along with the operations of addition and multiplication, there must be mathematical statements that can be neither proved nor disproved from within the system. That is, the axiomatization of mathematics was doomed to fail.

Gödel's theorem generated tremendous interest in the powers of axiomatic methods and computational processes. If there is no general algorithm for proving theorems in mathematics, then exactly what can be accomplished by algorithmic means? To answer this question, mathematicians began to design theoretical computational machines (this was before technology was able to provide actual machines) and to study the capabilities and limitations of these machines. The results of this work form the core of the subject known as the theory of computation, which today encompasses such subtopics as formal language theory, computability theory, and complexity theory—the subjects of our study.

It is not surprising, then, that theoretical computer science has a strong mathematical flavor. The questions of computability faced by theoretical computer scientists are actually the questions of provability faced by mathematicians, and vice versa. The distinction is essentially a matter of one's point of view.

0.4 PREVIEW OF THE REMAINING TEXT

We conclude this preliminary chapter with a short summary of the remaining chapters. In chapters 1 through 3 we study three classes of theoretical machines—finite automata, pushdown automata, and Turing machines—each of which is more powerful than the preceding class. We consider the powers of these machines within the context of solving pattern-recognition problems. That is, we will be interested in identifying the types of symbol patterns that can be recognized by the various classes of machines.

As we have already seen, problems of pattern-recognition are at the core of language processing systems such as the compilers for today's high-level programming languages. Thus, it is not surprising that the material discussed in the next three chapters provides the theoretical foundation of modern compiler construction—a relationship between theory and practice that we will explore.

The material covered in chapters 1 through 3 also applies to the field of natural language processing. We will learn that the hierarchy of machines studied in the coming chapters corresponds to a hierarchy of languages discovered in the 1950s by the linguist N. Chomsky, who was interested in establishing a formal foundation for linguistic studies. Thus, our study of pattern-recognition machines is a close cousin of linguistics.

The next three chapters will also lead us to an apparent bound on the computational abilities of machines. No one has been able to design a class of machines (actual or theoretical) that has more computational power than the class of Turing machines. In fact, a generally accepted conjecture known as Turing's thesis says that Turing machines possess the power to solve any problem that is solvable by computational means. It is within the context of Turing's thesis that we will formulate our study of computability.

In Chapter 4 we explore evidence that supports Turing's thesis. With this as our goal we consider other areas of research that have exposed apparent limitations of computational processes and show that these bounds agree with those of Turing machines. The early sections of Chapter 4 introduce the subject of recursive function theory, a topic in which the apparent bound on computational powers is identified by a conjecture known as Church's thesis. Then, we show that Church's thesis is equivalent to Turing's thesis. As further evidence, we consider the bounds of computational processes within the context of programming language design, and once again find a limit that agrees with Turing's thesis.

Finally, in Chapter 5 we consider the question of computability from a practical point of view rather than a theoretical one. Here we discuss some of the challenges that face researchers attempting to classify problems in terms of the resources required to solve them by algorithmic means. We will find that the algorithmic solutions to many problems require such massive amounts of time or storage space that the problems remain unsolvable in any practical sense, even though their solutions lie within the theoretical capabilities of computational processes. We will also find that the classification of many other problems still eludes researchers. Hence, the question of whether or not these problems have practical solutions remains unresolved.

In short, the following chapters present a broad range of topics. We study such abstract issues as the computational power of theoretical machines and the ultimate capabilities of computational processes. We also consider the relationship between these abstract ideas and such down-to-earth concerns as compiler construction techniques, the computational power of programming languages, and questions concerning the practicality of solving certain problems by computers.

Chapter Review Problems

1. Show that the following equalities (known as DeMorgan's Laws) hold for any three sets X, Y, and Z. (To show that $A = B$, prove that $A \subseteq B$ and $B \subseteq A$.)

$$(X - Y) \cap (X - Z) = X - (Y \cup Z)$$
$$(X - Y) \cup (X - Z) = X - (Y \cap Z)$$

2. Prove that for any three sets X, Y, and Z:
   a. $X \cap (Y \cup Z) = (X \cap Y) \cup (X \cap Z)$
   b. $X \cup (Y \cap Z) = (X \cup Y) \cap (X \cup Z)$

3. Suppose that $X = \{x: x \in \mathbb{N} \text{ and } x \text{ is odd}\}$, $Y = \{y: y \in \mathbb{N} \text{ and } y \text{ is prime}\}$, and $Z = \{z: z \in \mathbb{N} \text{ and } z \text{ is a multiple of three}\}$. Describe each of the following sets.
   a. $X \cap Y$ b. $X \cap Z$
   c. $Y \cap Z$ d. $Z - Y$
   e. $X - Y$ f. $X - (Y \cap Z)$
   g. $(Y \cap Z) - X$ h. $(X \cap Y) \cap Z$
   i. $X \cup Y$ j. $X \cup (Y \cap Z)$

4. List all of the elements in each of the following sets.
   a. $\{x, y\} \times \{a, b, c\}$
   b. $\{a, b, c\} \times \{x, y\}$
   c. $\{x, y\} \times \{k\} \times \{a, b\}$
   d. $\{x, y\} \times \{\}$

5. Find examples of nonempty sets for which each of the following statements is true.
   a. $X - Y = Y$ b. $A \times B = B \times A$ c. $P - Q = Q - P$

6. a. Define a function $f: \mathbb{N} \rightarrow \mathbb{N}$ that is one-to-one but not onto.
   b. Define a function $f: \mathbb{N} \rightarrow \mathbb{N}$ that is onto but not one-to-one.

7. Prove that $0 + 1 + 2 + \cdots + n = \dfrac{n(n + 1)}{2}$ for all values of n belonging to $\mathbb{N}$.

8. Prove that $1^2 + 2^2 + \cdots + n^2 = \dfrac{n(n + 1)(2n + 1)}{6}$ for all values of n that belong to $\mathbb{N}^+$.

9. Prove that $1^3 + 2^3 + \cdots + n^3 = \dfrac{n^2 (n + 1)^2}{4}$ for all values of n that belong to $\mathbb{N}^+$.

10. Prove that $2^2 + 4^2 + \cdots + (2n)^2 = \dfrac{2n(n + 1)(2n + 1)}{3}$ for all values of n that belong to $\mathbb{N}^+$.

11. Prove that $1 + 2 + 2^2 + \cdots + 2^n = 2^{n+1} - 1$ for all values of n that belong to $\mathbb{N}$.

12. Show that $x^n - y^n$ is divisible by $x - y$ for all n in $\mathbb{N}^+$.

13. Show that if x is a nonnegative number, then $(1 + x)^n - 1 \geqslant nx$ for all values of n in $\mathbb{N}$.

14. Prove that $\dfrac{1}{2} + \dfrac{1}{6} + \cdots + \dfrac{1}{n(n + 1)} = \dfrac{n}{n + 1}$ for all values of n that belong to $\mathbb{N}^+$.

15. List all the elements of $\mathcal{P}(\{x, y\})$. Then, list all the elements of $\mathcal{P}(\mathcal{P}(\{x, y\}))$. Show that $|\{x, y\}| \leqslant |\mathcal{P}(\{x, y\})| \leqslant |\mathcal{P}(\mathcal{P}(\{x, y\}))|$ by identifying one-to-one functions from $\{x, y\}$ into $\mathcal{P}(\{x, y\})$ and $\mathcal{P}(\{x, y\})$ into $\mathcal{P}(\mathcal{P}(\{x, y\}))$.

16. Show that the cardinality of the set of people registered with the United States Social Security system is no greater than the set of integers from $1,000,000,000$ to $1,999,999,999$.

17. Show that the cardinality of $\mathcal{P}(X)$ is equal to the cardinality of the set of all functions from X into $\{0, 1\}$.

18. Suppose that $f_1, f_2, \cdots$ is a countably infinite list of functions from $\mathbb{N}^+$ to $\mathbb{N}^+$. Define the function $f: \mathbb{N} \to \mathbb{N}$ so that $f(n) = f_n(n) + 1$ for each $n \in \mathbb{N}^+$. Prove that the function f is not one of the functions in the original list.

19. a. Give an example of two disjoint, nonempty sets A and B such that $|A| < |B| < |A \cup B|$.

    b. Give an example of two disjoint, nonempty sets A and B such that $|A| < |B| = |A \cup B|$.

    c. Give an example of two disjoint, nonempty sets A and B such that $|A| = |B| = |A \cup B|$.

20. Pick your favorite programming language and identify the first three programs that would appear in the listing described in the closing paragraphs of Section 0.1.

21. Show that there are at most countably many sentences in the English language.

22. Show that $|\mathbb{N}| = |\mathbb{N} \times \mathbb{N} \times \mathbb{N}|$.

23. Show that the set of even natural numbers has the same cardinality as the set of odd natural numbers.

24. Show that the cardinality of the set of prime numbers is the same as the cardinality of $\mathbb{N}^+$.

25. Give examples to show that the intersection of two uncountable sets can be:
    a. finite
    b. countably infinite
    c. uncountable

26. Show that if X is an uncountable set and Y is a countable set, then $X - Y$ must be uncountable.

27. Show that the union of two countable sets is countable.

28. Show that a set can have the same cardinality as a proper subset of itself.

29. Show that the set of all finite subsets of $\mathbb{N}$ is countable.

30. Show that the set of all real numbers is uncountable.

31. Show that any countably infinite set has uncountably many infinite subsets of which any two have only a finite number of elements in common.

CHAPTER 1

Finite Automata and Regular Languages

In this chapter we define and study the class of theoretical machines known as finite automata. Although they are limited in power, we will find that these machines are capable of recognizing numerous symbol patterns, which we identify as the class of regular languages.

Finite automata and regular languages are the lowest level of a hierarchy of machines and languages that we will study in the next three chapters. This foundational role establishes the importance of these machines and languages from a theoretical perspective, but their significance is not limited to theory. The concepts illustrated by finite automata and regular languages are of fundamental interest in most applications that require techniques of pattern-recognition.

One such application is compiler construction. For instance, a compiler must be able to recognize which strings of symbols in the source program should be considered as representations of single objects, such as variable names, numeric constants, and reserved words. This pattern-recognition task is handled by the lexical analyzer within the compiler. In this chapter we consider the basic principles that govern the construction of lexical analyzers; these principles will become the foundation on which much of our remaining study will be based.

1.1 LEXICAL ANALYSIS

Let us consider one problem faced by a compiler—that of detecting whether or not a given string within a source program represents an acceptable variable name. In a typical programming language these names begin with a letter followed by an arbitrary (but finite) mixture of letters and digits. Thus, X25, *BetsyRoss*, and *x2y3z* would be acceptable names whereas 25, *x.h*, and *Betsy-Ross* would not. Also, any lexical structure in a programming language ends with one of a set of symbols that is recognized as terminating the structure. We will call such symbols **end-of-string markers.** In the case of variable names, these markers might include spaces, semicolons, and carriage returns.

Transition Diagrams

Our first step toward developing a program unit that will recognize occurrences of variable names might be to represent the structure of an acceptable name in some concise, unambiguous manner. For this purpose we might use the pictorial form of a **transition diagram** (also called a **state diagram** or, in the field of natural language processing, a **transition network**), as represented in Figure 1.1. A transition diagram is a finite collection of circles, which we may label for reference purposes, connected by arrows called **arcs.** Each of these arcs is labeled with a symbol or symbol category (such as "digit" or "letter") that might occur in the input string being analyzed. One of the circles is designated by a pointer and represents an initial or starting position. Moreover, at least one circle is represented as a double circle. These double circles designate positions in the diagram at which a valid string has been recognized.

We say that a string of symbols is accepted by a given transition diagram if the symbols appearing in the string (from left to right) correspond to a sequence of labeled arcs that leads from the circle designated by the pointer

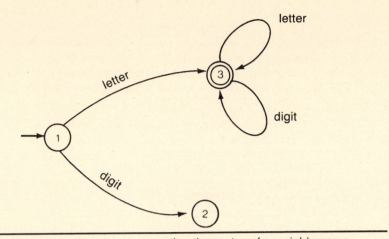

Figure 1.1 A transition diagram representing the syntax of a variable name

to a double circle. Thus, when analyzing the string *X*25 using Figure 1.1, we leave the starting circle following the arc labeled "letter" (since the string starts with *X*). From circle 3 we traverse the arc labeled "digit" twice (once for the 2 and again for the 5) and find ourselves at the double circle 3. In contrast, using the string 25 we again begin at the starting circle, but this time we follow the arc labeled "digit" and find ourselves at a dead end. We conclude that *X*25 is an acceptable variable name, whereas 25 is not.

Note that the circles in a transition diagram represent positions, or states, in which we might find ourselves while testing a string of symbols. Referring to Figure 1.1, we see that circle 1 can be identified as the state of starting the analysis of a string, circle 2 represents the state of having found a digit to be the first symbol in the string, and circle 3 represents the state of having found a string that starts with a letter. It is therefore customary to call the circles in a transition diagram **states.** The starting circle is called the **initial state,** and the double circles are called **accept states.**

Once we have developed a transition diagram that accepts exactly those syntactic structures that constitute valid variable names, a program segment that recognizes such structures is not far away. For example, the diagram of Figure 1.1 suggests the program segment shown in Figure 1.2. Observe that the basic structure of the algorithm produced is that of a single case statement that directs activities according to the current state. For each state, the possible options are handled with further conditional structures such as the nested if–then–else statements. In the case of an unacceptable string, the program segment exits to an error routine that, by means of a parameter,

```
State : = 1;
Read the next symbol from input;
While not end-of-string do
   Case State of
   1: If the current symbol is a letter then State : = 3,
      else if the current symbol is a digit then State : = 2,
      else exit to error routine;
   2: Exit to error routine;
   3: If the current symbol is a letter then State : = 3,
      else if the current symbol is a digit then State : = 3,
      else exit to error routine;
   Read the next symbol from the input;
End while;
If State not 3 then exit to error routine;
```

Figure 1.2   An instruction sequence suggested by the transition diagram of
Figure 1.1

can be used to print an appropriate message such as "Variable name must begin with a letter" or "Illegal identifier."

We see, then, that transition diagrams can be used as design tools for producing lexical analysis routines in much the same way that data flow diagrams and structure charts are used by software engineers. However, code generated directly from a transition diagram does not necessarily represent the best solution to the problem. A more elegant solution is obtained through the use of transition tables.

Transition Tables

A **transition table** is a two-dimensional array whose entries provide a summary of a corresponding transition diagram. To construct such a table we first build an array, with a row for each state in the transition diagram and a column for each symbol or symbol category that might occur in the input string. The entry found in the mth row and n^{th} column of the table is the state that would be reached in the transition diagram by leaving state m via an arc labeled n. If there is no arc labeled n leaving state m, then the corresponding entry in the table is marked as an error state. To complete the transition table we add an extra column labeled "EOS" for end-of-string. The entry in the EOS column contains the value "accept" if the row corresponds to an accept state in the diagram, or the value "error" otherwise. Figure 1.3 represents a transition table obtained from the transition diagram of Figure 1.1.

Designing a lexical analyzer based on a transition table is quite simple. All we must do is initialize a variable to the initial state and then repeatedly

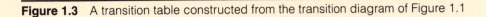

	letter	digit	EOS
1	3	2	error
2	error	error	error
3	3	3	accept

Figure 1.3   A transition table constructed from the transition diagram of Figure 1.1

```
State : = 1;
Repeat
     Read the next symbol from the input stream;
     Case symbol of
         letter: Input : = "letter";
         digit: Input : = "digit";
         end of string marker: Input : = "EOS";
         none of the above: exit to error routine;
     State : = Table[State, Input];
     If State = "error" then exit to error routine;
  until State = "accept"
```

Figure 1.4   A lexical analyzer based on the transition table of Figure 1.3

update this variable from the table as the symbols are read from the input string, until we reach the end of the string being analyzed. For example, a lexical analyzer based on the table in Figure 1.3 is presented in Figure 1.4.

As a further example, figures 1.5, 1.6, and 1.7 show a transition diagram, a transition table, and a lexical analyzer, respectively, for recognizing strings that represent positive real numbers in either decimal or exponential notation, such as 35.7, 2.56E10, or 34.0E-7. Note that the structure of Figure 1.7 is essentially that of Figure 1.4, the only difference being in the routine that classifies the input symbol. Indeed, the fundamental algorithm for analyzing a string using a transition table is the same for any lexical structure.

In conclusion, we have presented rather simple techniques for developing lexical analyzers. Now we need to discover the extent to which these techniques can be applied. Can program segments constructed on the basis of transition diagrams be used to analyze any syntactic structure, or are there structures that cannot be recognized by such diagrams? If there are limits to these techniques, what is required to handle the more complex cases? We pursue these questions in the remaining sections of this chapter and continue our quest through chapters 2 and 3 as well.

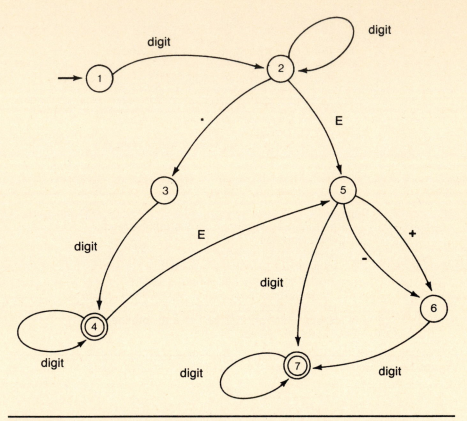

Figure 1.5   A transition diagram representing the syntax of a real number

	digit	•	E	+	–	EOS
1	2	error	error	error	error	error
2	2	3	5	error	error	error
3	4	error	error	error	error	error
4	4	error	5	error	error	accept
5	7	error	error	6	6	error
6	7	error	error	error	error	error
7	7	error	error	error	error	accept

Figure 1.6   A transition table constructed from the transition diagram of Figure 1.5

```
State : = 1;
Repeat
   Read the next symbol from the input stream;
   Case symbol of
      0 through 9: input : = "digit";
      End of string marker: input : = "EOS";
      • ,E, + , – : Input : = symbol;
      None of the above: exit to error routine;
   State : = Table[State, Input];
   If State = "error" then exit to error routine;
until State = "accept"
```

Figure 1.7   A lexical analyzer based on the transition table of Figure 1.6

Exercises

1. Design a transition diagram for recognizing arithmetic expressions of arbitrary length that involve positive integers separated by addition, subtraction, multiplication, or division signs.

2. Write a lexical analyzer directly from the following transition diagram.

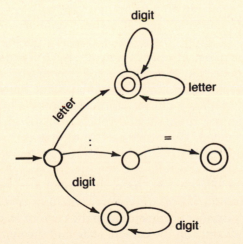

3. Build a transition table from the diagram in Exercise 2 and write a lexical analyzer based on that table.

4. Show that a transition diagram that contains an arc labeled by a symbol string of length two or more—meaning that to traverse the arc requires that entire string rather than a single symbol—can be modified to con-

tain only arcs labeled by single symbols, but in such a way that it still accepts exactly the same strings as before.

1.2   DETERMINISTIC FINITE AUTOMATA

We concluded the previous section by asking whether transition diagrams provide a tool powerful enough to develop programs for recognizing syntactic structures of arbitrary complexity. In this section we pursue this question by formalizing the process of recognizing structures via transition diagrams more precisely. Our goal is to identify the pertinent characteristics of a pattern-recognition system built on the principles of transition diagrams, so we can study the powers of that pattern-recognition system in a generic manner rather than approaching each example as an independent case.

Basic Definitions

To begin this formalizing task, we recognize that the strings that must be analyzed in any application are constructed from a set of symbols. In the case of a lexical analyzer within a compiler, these strings are usually made up of the symbols available on a computer terminal's keyboard. However, within a modern digital computer, all of these symbols are represented by patterns of 0s and 1s. From this more elementary perspective, any string consists of a combination of only two symbols. Thus, depending on the point of view, the collection of symbols used to construct strings varies. In each setting, however, we find that the symbol set is finite. Therefore, our first step toward formalizing our recognition process is to hypothesize the existence of a nonempty, finite set of symbols from which the strings to be analyzed are constructed. We call this set an **alphabet.**

Next we note that each string to be analyzed is received as a sequence of symbols, one symbol at a time. We refer to the source of this sequence as the **input stream** (Figure 1.8). As each symbol arrives from the input stream, our recognition process involves switching from one of a finite number of states to another or remaining in the current state. What the new state will be depends only on the current state and the symbol received. To emphasize this point, observe that once the recognition process has reached state 5 in Figure 1.5, its next state will not rely on whether it reached state 5 from state 2 or from state 4. Rather, the next state will be determined solely by the next symbol received and the fact that the process is now in state 5. The fact that recognition systems built from such transition diagrams cannot remember how they got where they are will prove very important in later discussions.

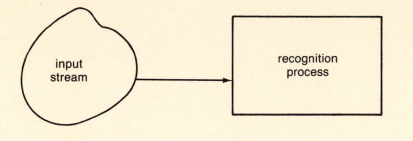

Figure 1.8   An input stream as a symbol source

We solidify our thoughts thus far by defining a conceptual machine known as a **deterministic finite automaton.** Such a machine consists of a device that can be in any one of a finite number of states, of which one is an initial state and at least one is an accept state. Attached to this device is an input stream on which symbols from a given alphabet arrive sequentially. The machine has the ability to detect the symbols as they arrive and, based on the current state and the symbol received, execute a (state) **transition** that consists of either switching to another state or remaining in the current state. Exactly which transition occurs as each symbol is received is determined by a **control mechanism** within the machine that is programmed to know what the new state should be, given any current state and input symbol combination.

We should emphasize that the program within a deterministic finite automaton, just as a program for any computer, must not contain ambiguities. This is an important point that we will discuss in more detail shortly. For now we note that it is the reason for the word "deterministic" in the name "deterministic finite automaton." The word "finite" refers to the fact that the machine has only a finite number of states. At times you will hear these machines called deterministic finite state automata.

A deterministic finite automaton is traditionally envisioned as in Figure 1.9. The machine's control mechanism is represented by a rectangle containing a type of clock face. The possible states are represented around the circumference of this clock and a pointer points to the current state. The machine's input stream appears as a strip of tape that is divided into cells, each cell capable of holding a single symbol. We envision the tape as having a left end but extending indefinitely to the right. The machine is able to read the symbols on this tape from left to right by means of a read head whose position is indicated in Figure 1.9 by an arrow. Each time a symbol is read, the read head moves to the next position on the tape. Thus, the resting position of the read head is always over the next cell to be read.

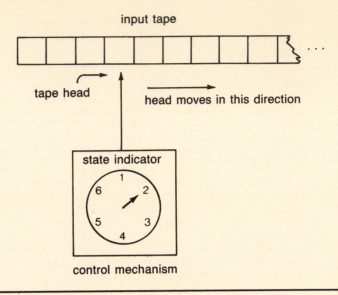

Figure 1.9   A representation of a deterministic finite automaton

To represent a program within the control mechanism, we use a transition diagram in which the diagram states represent the machine states and each arc represents a potential machine transition. In this context the initial and accept states in the diagram correspond to the initial and accept states of the automaton.

We say that a deterministic finite automaton accepts its input string if, having started its computation in its initial state with its tape head over the first symbol of the input, the machine shifts to an accept state upon reading the last symbol of the string. (See Figure 1.10.) If reading the last symbol of the string does not leave the machine in an accept state, we say the string is rejected. Thus, a deterministic finite automaton is essentially a string analyzing machine that accepts those strings accepted by its internal transition diagram and rejects all others.

A somewhat distinct case arises if the machine reaches the end of its input before reading any symbols (i.e., the input begins with an end-of-string marker). In this case, we say that the input is the **empty string** (the string containing no symbols). Unfortunately, the empty string does not show up well on the printed page, so we represent it with the symbol λ. We emphasize that the empty string contains no symbols; therefore, a deterministic finite automaton will accept λ if and only if its initial state is also an accept state.

Finally, we should note that the technology of tapes, read heads, and clock faces in which we have described deterministic finite automata is not

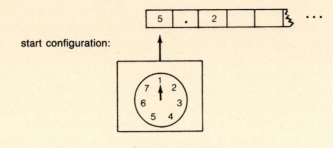

start configuration:

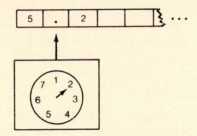

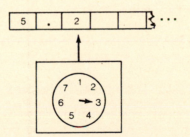

accept configuration:

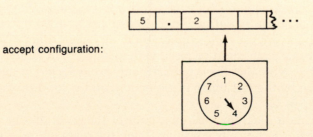

Figure 1.10 The steps performed by a deterministic finite automaton (programmed by the diagram in Figure 1.5) while processing the string "5.2"

critical to our definition. Rather, this implementation is merely an informal model that helps us remember the properties of deterministic finite automata. Machines with these same computing properties can be constructed using a variety of technologies, as we will see at the end of this section, and each of these machines should be recognized as a deterministic finite automaton. Thus, we now summarize our discussion with a precise, formal definition of deterministic finite automata that identifies the pertinent features of such machines and can serve as a decisive reference.

A deterministic finite automaton consists of a quintuple $(S, \Sigma, \delta, \iota, F)$, where:

a. S is a finite set of states.
b. Σ is the machine's alphabet.
c. δ is a function (called the **transition function**) from $S \times \Sigma$ into S.
d. ι (an element of S) is the initial state.
e. F (a subset of S) is the set of accept states.

The interpretation of the transition function δ of a deterministic finite automaton is that $\delta(p, x) = q$ if and only if the machine can move from state p to state q while reading the symbol x. Thus, a transition diagram for a deterministic finite automaton is merely a pictorial representation of the machine's transition function. It follows that the automaton $(S, \Sigma, \delta, \iota, F)$ accepts the nonempty string $x_1 x_2 \cdots x_n$ if and only if there is a sequence of states $s_0, s_1, \cdots, s_n$ such that $s_0 = \iota$, $s_n \in F$, and for each integer j from 1 to n, $\delta(s_{j-1}, x_j) = s_j$.

Deterministic Transition Diagrams

The requirement of determinism places certain restrictions on the transition diagrams that can appear as programs for deterministic finite automata. In particular, each state in such a diagram must have only one arc leaving it for each symbol in the alphabet; otherwise, a machine arriving at that state would be faced with a choice of which arc to follow. Moreover, such a diagram must be **fully defined** in the sense that from each state there must be at least one arc for each symbol in the alphabet; otherwise, a machine arriving at that state could be faced with a situation in which no transition is applicable. Note that these requirements are reflected in our formal definition, first by the fact that δ is a function, and second by the fact that its domain is $S \times \Sigma$.

A transition diagram satisfying both of these conditions is said to be **deterministic.** Technically speaking, then, the diagram in Figure 1.1 is not deterministic since it is not fully defined: it does not represent what action should occur if a letter or a digit is received while in state 2. The diagram in Figure 1.5 has similar problems. Among other things, it does not describe what should happen if a period is received while in state 1. However, both these diagrams have no more than one arc for each symbol leaving each state and can therefore be modified to conform to the requirements of determinism. We first add an additional state that will play the role of a catch-all state. Then, for each symbol in the alphabet, we draw an arc, labeled by that symbol, that both originates and terminates at this new state. Finally, we add arcs from other states to the new state until every state is the origin for an arc for each symbol in the alphabet.

Figure 1.11 shows the result of applying this technique to the transition diagram of Figure 1.5. The new state is number 8. Observe that in the original diagram the occurrence of an unacceptable string caused an error by requesting the traversal of a nonexistent arc. In the modified diagram,

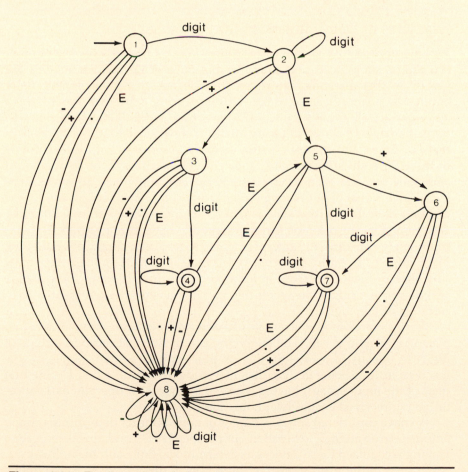

Figure 1.11   The "completion" of the diagram in Figure 1.5

an unacceptable string causes the machine to traverse an arc to state 8, where it remains until the end of the input string is reached. At this point the string would be rejected since state 8 is not an accept state. Thus, the two diagrams are equivalent in that they accept the same strings. They differ merely in the way they arrive at their conclusions.

Figure 1.11 also demonstrates why, when drawing deterministic transition diagrams, we are tempted to avoid representing all the transitions. Indeed, including all the transitions easily leads to cluttered diagrams that obscure the significant structure of the automaton being represented. Consequently, one often draws partial, or skeletal, versions of deterministic transition diagrams in which the catch-all state and its related arcs are omitted. Such is the case in figures 1.1 and 1.5.

Examples of Deterministic Finite Automata

We have approached deterministic finite automata from the context of modern digital computers, and thus it is not surprising that our models are geared in that direction. However, the concept of a deterministic finite automaton is not restricted to the traditional computer environment. Such automata are all around us. Consider a typical vending machine that dispenses a person's choice of candy after it has received a total of 30 cents in nickels, dimes, and quarters. In this case, the automaton's alphabet consists of three different sizes of coins, a state of the machine is the total amount of money that has been received since the last candy was dispensed, the initial state is that of not having received any coins since the last candy was dispensed, and an accept state is that of having received at least 30 cents. Assuming that the machine is not designed to make change and will therefore merely consume any overpayment, its transition diagram would look like Figure 1.12. An input string is accepted if it leads to the accept state (the state of having received at least 30 cents). In this state, the machine will dispense a candy bar when the operator pushes the button that indicates his or her choice.

We encounter another example of a deterministic finite automaton when placing a telephone call. The telephone is a device that receives strings of digits by means of a rotating dial or push-button system. States in this machine include being in long-distance mode (the result when 1 is the first digit of the input string), having received a request for operator assistance, or having received a valid telephone number.

We have considered these examples of noncomputer deterministic finite automata in an attempt to broaden our perspective beyond lexical analyzers. Having recognized these devices as deterministic finite automata, however, we are led to the realization that the action of these devices is essentially

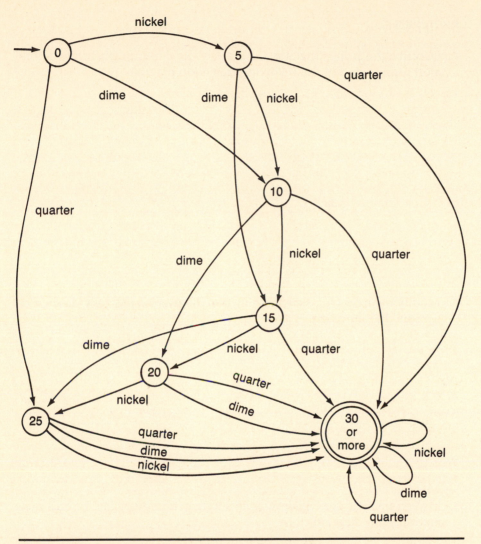

Figure 1.12   A transition diagram for a vending machine

that of lexical analysis. The vending machine analyzes strings of coins; the telephone analyzes strings of digits. Thus, by abstracting the essential ingredients of lexical analysis found in a compiler, we are led to insights in other settings that might otherwise go undetected. Although this particular example is far from earth-shattering, it exemplifies the power of abstract theories.

Exercises

1. Describe the strings that are accepted by the deterministic finite automaton represented in the following transition diagram.

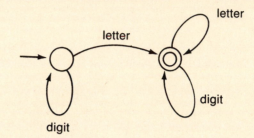

2. Modify the following skeletal transition diagram so it is fully defined yet accepts the same strings as before.

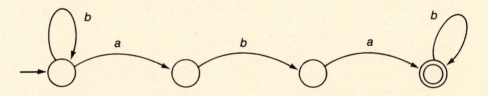

3. Identify another deterministic finite automaton in everyday life and draw its transition diagram.

1.3   THE LIMITS OF DETERMINISTIC FINITE AUTOMATA

To this point we have introduced the class of machines known as deterministic finite automata and have discussed their association with lexical analyzers. Our problem now is to determine the extent to which string-recognition algorithms can be constructed from these principles. In particular, we now ask ourselves whether the use of transition tables, as presented in Section 1.1, provides enough flexibility for general string processing.

Deterministic Finite Automata as Language Accepters

Let us reconsider the task that we are asking deterministic finite automata to perform, which is to accept those strings and only those strings that conform to certain compositional rules. In other words, each deterministic finite automaton can be thought of as dividing the class of all potential input strings into two groups: those strings that are acceptable and those that are not.

To characterize this task in more formal terms, we first define the length of a string w to be the number of symbols in it and denote this value by $|w|$. Thus, $|xy|$ is two and $|xyx|$ is three. Next, we consider the collection of all strings of finite length (including the empty string) that can be constructed from the alphabet being used. Assuming that the alphabet is denoted by Σ, this set of strings is represented by Σ^*. Thus, if Σ were $\{a, b\}$, then Σ^* would be $\{\lambda, a, b, aa, ab, ba, bb, aaa, aab, \cdots\}$.

A subset of Σ^* is called a **language** (over the alphabet Σ), as motivated by our traditional use of the term. Indeed, if Σ contains all letters, punctuation marks, and digits, as well as a blank, then all sentences in the English language would constitute a subset of Σ^*, while another subset would consist of all Latin sentences. Of course, there would also be subsets of Σ^* that do not satisfy our intuitive definition of a language, but for our purposes such subsets will be considered languages nonetheless. Thus, the set of strings $\{a, ab, b\}$ will be considered a language over the alphabet $\{a, b\}$.

If M is the deterministic finite automaton $(S, \Sigma, \delta, \iota, F)$, the collection of strings it accepts constitutes a language over Σ. We denote this language by $L(M)$, which we read as "the language accepted by M." We emphasize that $L(M)$ is not merely any collection of strings accepted by M, but *the* collection of *all* strings accepted by M, no more and no less. A language of the form $L(M)$ for some finite automaton M is called a **regular language.**

Examples of regular languages are abundant. To obtain one we need merely draw a transition diagram for a deterministic finite automaton and then identify the language it accepts. For instance, Figure 1.13 presents a

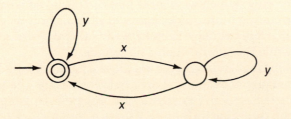

Figure 1.13 A transition diagram for a deterministic finite automaton that accepts exactly those strings of xs and ys that contain an even number of xs

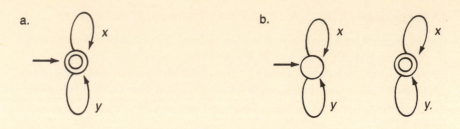

Figure 1.14   Transition diagrams for deterministic finite automata that accept
a.) the language {*x*, *y*}* and b.) the language ∅

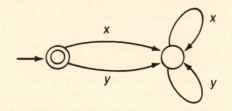

Figure 1.15   A transition diagram for a deterministic finite automaton that accepts
the language {λ}

transition diagram that accepts exactly those strings of *x*s and *y*s that contain an even number of *x*s and any number of *y*s. Hence, this language (over the alphabet {*x*, *y*}) is regular. A somewhat special pair of regular languages is the collection of all strings of finite length over an alphabet Σ, which we already represent as Σ^*, and the collection containing no strings, known as the **empty language**, which we represent by ∅. Figure 1.14 presents transition diagrams for these languages over the alphabet {*x*, *y*}.

Still another example of a regular language is the language consisting of the empty string, which we denote by {λ}. This is the language accepted by the deterministic finite automaton whose transition diagram is shown in Figure 1.15. Note the distinction between {λ} and ∅: the former contains one string, while the latter contains no strings.

Note that the regular languages are those languages for which the lexical analysis techniques of Section 1.1 are applicable. Thus, the following theorem, which establishes the existence of nonregular languages, is relevant to our question regarding the power of these techniques. In short, the lexical analysis techniques of Section 1.1 are not flexible enough for general string processing.

THEOREM 1.1

For any alphabet Σ, there is a language that is not equal to $L(M)$ for any deterministic finite automaton M.

PROOF

Since any arc in a deterministic finite automaton that is labeled by a symbol outside of Σ would have no effect on the processing of a string in Σ^*, we can consider only machines with alphabet Σ. But, the collection of deterministic finite automata with alphabet Σ is countable since we can systematically list all possible machines with one state, followed by all machines with two states, followed by those with three states, etc. On the other hand, the number of languages over alphabet Σ is uncountable since the infinite set Σ^* has an uncountable number of subsets. Thus, there are more languages than there are deterministic finite automata. Consequently, since each deterministic finite automaton accepts only one language, there must be languages that are not accepted by any such machine.

■

Theorem 1.1 tells us there are sets of strings that cannot be identified by deterministic finite automata, and therefore cannot be recognized by our lexical analysis techniques. The fact that deterministic finite automata cannot solve all such recognition problems, however, is only the tip of the iceberg. We will learn that any algorithmic process has similar limitations.

A Nonregular Language

Let us now demonstrate a specific example of a language that is not regular. Such examples will indicate how the lexical analysis techniques of Section 1.1 can be improved to allow for a broader range of string structures.

With this as our goal, consider the problem of analyzing arithmetic expressions in which parentheses are used to clarify the order of execution or to override the normal precedence of operators, as in the expressions $(a + b) \div c$ and $a + (b \div c)$. In such expressions there must be the same number of left and right parentheses. Furthermore, when an expression is scanned from left to right, the number of right parentheses encountered must never exceed the number of left parentheses encountered. Based on these observations, our intuition tells us that the analysis of such arithmetic expressions requires the ability to remember how many left parentheses have been encountered and not yet matched with a right parenthesis. Because a deterministic finite automaton has no way of saving such a count for later reference, we might guess that the analysis of arithmetic expressions that contain parentheses is a task beyond the powers of finite automata. To prove this, however, requires a few preliminaries.

First, we introduce the notation w^n, where w is a string in Σ^* and n is a nonnegative integer. This is a short way of representing a string of n copies of the pattern w. Thus, if $\Sigma = \{x, y\}$ then $x^4 = xxxx$, $x^2y^2 = xxyy$, $(xy)^3 = xyxyxy$, and $y^0 = \lambda$ (the empty string).

Next, we need the following theorem.

THEOREM 1.2

If a regular language contains strings of the form $x^n y^n$ for arbitrarily large integers n, then it must contain strings of the form $x^m y^n$ where m and n are not equal.

PROOF

Suppose M is a deterministic finite automaton such that $L(M)$ contains $x^n y^n$ for arbitrarily large n. Then, there must be a positive integer k that is larger than the number of states in M and such that $x^k y^k$ is in $L(M)$. Since there are more symbols in x^k than there are states in M, the process of accepting $x^k y^k$ will result in some state in M being traversed more than once before any ys in the string are reached. That is, in reading some of the xs a circular path will be traversed in the machine's transition diagram. If j is the number of xs read while traversing this path, then the machine can accept the string $x^{k+j} y^k$ by traversing this path an extra time (see Figure 1.16). Hence, there is a positive integer m (namely, $k + j$) that is not equal to k, such that $x^m y^k$ is in $L(M)$.

■

An immediate consequence of Theorem 1.2 is that the language $\{x^n y^n : n \in \mathbb{N}\}$ is not regular. A more subtle consequence is that the powers of deterministic finite automata are not great enough to analyze arithmetic expressions that involve parentheses. If a deterministic finite automaton did accept such expressions then it would have to accept expressions of the form $(^n)^n$ for arbitrarily large integers n. However, Theorem 1.2 tells us that such an automaton must also accept expressions in which the number of left parentheses does not equal the number of right parentheses. Thus, such a machine would accept incorrect expressions as well as correct ones.

In closing we should note that although deterministic finite automata are restricted in their power, they are not useless. If you review the syntax

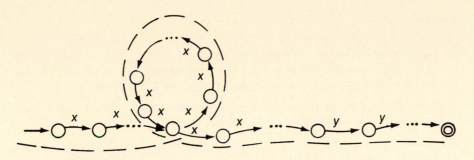

a. The path traversed when accepting $x^k y^k$

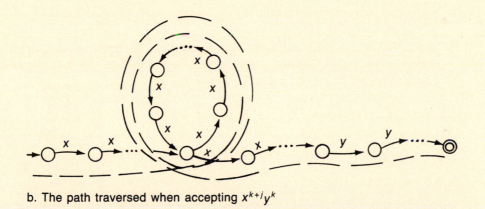

b. The path traversed when accepting $x^{k+j} y^k$

Figure 1.16   The portion of a transition diagram that accepts both $x^k y^k$ and $x^{k+j} y^k$

of your favorite high-level programming language, you will probably find that all the details of its program structure cannot be recognized by a finite automaton since, among other things, the language probably allows the use of parentheses in arithmetic expressions. On the other hand, you will also find that the structure of building blocks such as reserved words, variable names, and operation symbols can be processed by finite automata. The simplicity at this level of the language is no accident: It allows the lexical analyzer within a compiler to be constructed using simple techniques such as those presented in this chapter.

Exercises

1. How can the deterministic finite automaton $M = (S, \Sigma, \delta, \iota, F)$ be altered to obtain a machine that accepts the language $\Sigma^* - L(M)$? (Thus, the complement of a regular language [relative to Σ^*] is regular.)

2. List all the deterministic finite automata based on the alphabet $\{x, y\}$ with one state and then those with two states.

3. Show that if a deterministic finite automaton is capable of accepting an infinite number of strings, then it must accept a string that consists of the concatenation of three segments such that any repetition of the middle segment (which is nonempty) will result in another acceptable string. (This is known as a **pumping lemma** because it implies that other acceptable strings can be generated by "pumping up" a single acceptable string.) Hint: Reconsider the proof of Theorem 1.2.

4. Show that there is no deterministic finite automaton M such that $L(M) = \{x^n y^n z^n : n \in \mathbb{N}\}$.

5. Show that a deterministic finite automaton can be used to recognize strings of balanced, nested parentheses if the depth of the nesting is guaranteed not to exceed a particular value.

1.4   NONDETERMINISTIC FINITE AUTOMATA

Having realized the limitations of deterministic finite automata, let us examine modifications that might increase their powers. Our approach here, and in the following chapters as well, is to consider loosening restrictions we have imposed on the machines. After all, intuition tells us a more flexible machine should be able to perform more varied tasks and thus might accept a language that could not be accepted by the more restricted versions. However, we are about to see that our intuition is not always correct.

In our study thus far, we have insisted that the transition diagrams of the automata under consideration be deterministic. From any state there could be one and only one arc labeled with a given symbol. Our motivation for this was that we planned to develop programs from these machines, and a program that behaves in a nondeterministic manner would be of little use. Now that we are faced with the problem of extending the power of our techniques, it seems reasonable to reconsider this restriction; if nondeterminism is beneficial, we might be able to design a program to handle multiple options by applying backtracking techniques.

With this in mind, let us consider another conceptual machine known as a **nondeterministic finite automaton.** Such a machine is much like a deterministic finite automaton in that it analyzes strings constructed from a finite alphabet and can take on only a finite number of states, some of which are accept states, while one is the initial state. In contrast to a deterministic finite automaton, however, the transition to be executed at a given stage in a nondeterministic finite automaton can be uncertain. This may be the result of either more than one transition being applicable or perhaps no transition being applicable, as in the case of a machine that is not fully defined.

As an example, consider the transition diagram in Figure 1.17, which is intrinsically different from the diagrams we have drawn in the past. More precisely, the fact that an input string begins with a digit does not tell us exactly which arc should be taken from the initial state, since there are two possibilities. One leads to the section of the diagram that describes the

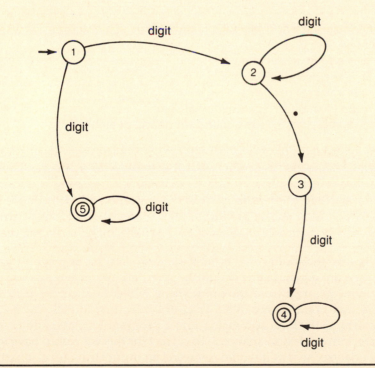

Figure 1.17 A transition diagram that accepts either strings representing integers or strings representing real numbers in decimal notation

structure of a real number in decimal notation; the other leads to a description of an integer. Thus, a finite automaton programmed with this diagram would be nondeterministic.

Recall that in the case of a deterministic finite automaton, we say a string is accepted if its analysis leaves the machine in an accept state. However, in the case of nondeterministic finite automata, any single attempt to test a string might result in failure merely because incorrect choices were made at points where multiple options were provided. (If we made a wrong choice at the first step of analyzing the string 352 using Figure 1.17, we would not reach an accept state, even though the string in question is compatible with other paths through the diagram.) Thus, we say that a string is accepted by a nondeterministic finite automaton if it is *possible* for its analysis to leave the machine in an accept state.

As in the case of deterministic finite automata, the set of all strings accepted by a nondeterministic finite automaton M is a language that we denote by $L(M)$ and refer to as the language accepted by M.

In summary, we formally define a nondeterministic finite automaton as follows:

A nondeterministic finite automaton consists of a quintuple $(S, \Sigma, \rho, \iota, F)$, where
a. S is a finite set of states.
b. Σ is the machine's alphabet.
c. ρ is a subset of $S \times \Sigma \times S$.
d. ι (an element of S) is the initial state.
e. F (a subset of S) is the collection of accept states.

The subset ρ in this definition represents the possible transitions of the machine. That is, the tuple (p, x, q) is in ρ if and only if the automaton can pass from state p to state q while reading the symbol x from the input string. Thus, a nondeterministic finite automaton $(S, \Sigma, \rho, \iota, F)$ accepts the nonempty string $x_1 x_2 \cdots x_n \in \Sigma^*$ if and only if there is a sequence of states $s_0, s_1, \cdots, s_n$ such that $s_0 = \iota$, $s_n \in F$, and for each integer j from 1 to n, (s_{j-1}, x_j, s_j) is in ρ.

Note also that both (p, x, q_1) and (p, x, q_2) can be in ρ even though q_1 and q_2 are not equal. If this should happen, an option would occur when the symbol x is read from the input string while the machine is in state p: The machine could move to either q_1 or q_2. In turn, directly translating a nondeterministic finite automaton into a program format could produce a nondeterministic lexical analyzer. To correct for this we would have to modify the analyzer so that it would not reject an input string until it had tested all possible paths through the transition diagram and found that each led to failure. Such a backtracking system would add to the complexity of the analyzer and would only be worth the effort if we gained more processing power as a result. Thus, Theorem 1.3 explains why we would not want to use a nondeterministic finite automaton as a basis for a lexical analyzer.

To motivate this theorem, we imagine the approach we might take if we were using a nondeterministic transition diagram to analyze a string. In such a case, we might forgo committing ourselves to a single possibility and attempt to follow each of the options in parallel. Hence, we would find ourselves traversing more than one path through the transition diagram at the same time. As each symbol was consumed from the input, each of these paths would advance independently. In this context, we would accept a string if any one of the paths terminated in an accept state when the end of the input was reached. The other paths would merely represent choices that, had we committed ourselves to them, would have led to failure and the need to backtrack to pursue other options.

When following such a parallel processing approach, our state at any time would no longer be represented by a single state in the transition diagram, but rather by the collection of current states from all the paths under consideration (see Figure 1.18). Furthermore, if K is this collection

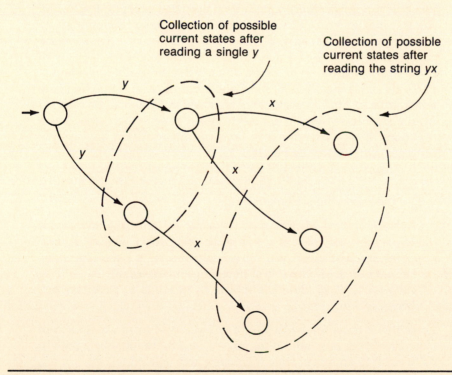

Figure 1.18 Analyzing a string using a nondeterministic finite automaton by pursuing options in parallel

of current states, then reading some symbol x from the input stream would result in a new current state represented by the collection of states that could be reached from some state in K over an arc labeled x.

Note that this parallel approach, which moves from collections of states to collections of states, eliminates the need to make decisions when multiple choices are presented—we merely follow all of the choices in parallel. Thus, it would appear that the nondeterminism in a finite automaton could be overcome by such a parallel approach. It is this observation that motivates our proof of the following theorem.

THEOREM 1.3

For each nondeterministic finite automaton there is a deterministic finite automaton that accepts exactly the same language.

PROOF

Assume that M is the nondeterministic finite automaton defined by the quintuple $(S, \Sigma, \rho, \iota, F)$. Our task is to demonstrate the existence of a deterministic finite automaton that accepts exactly the same strings as M. To this end we define another automaton M' by the quintuple $(S', \Sigma, \delta, \iota', F')$ where $S' = \mathcal{P}(S)$, $\iota' = \{\iota\}$, F' is the collection of subsets of S that contain at least one state in F, and δ is the function from $S' \times \Sigma$ into S' such that for each x in Σ and s' in S', $\delta(s', x)$ is the set of all s in S such that (u, x, s) is in ρ for some u in s' (that is, $\delta(s', x)$ is the set of all states in S that can be reached from a state in s' over an arc labeled x). Observe that, since δ is a function, M' is a deterministic finite automaton. (For an example of this construction, see Figure 1.19.)

It remains to show that M and M' accept exactly the same strings. To this end we apply an induction argument to show that for each $n \in \mathbb{N}$ the following statement holds.

> *For each path in* M *from state* ι *to state* s_n *traversing arcs labeled* w_1, w_2, $\cdots$, w_n, *there is a path in* M' *from state* ι' *to state* s'_n *traversing arcs labeled* w_1, w_2, $\cdots$, w_n *so that* $s_n \in s'_n$; *and conversely, for each path in* M' *from* ι' *to* s'_n *traversing arcs labeled* w_1, w_2, $\cdots$, w_n *and each* $s_n \in s'_n$, *there is a path in* M *from* ι *to* s_n *traversing arcs labeled* w_1, w_2, $\cdots$, w_n.

From this it must follow that for any path in M from ι to an accept state traversing arcs labeled w_1, w_2, $\cdots$, w_n, there must be a path in M' from ι' to an accept state traversing arcs labeled w_1, w_2, $\cdots$, w_n, and vice versa. Thus, M and M' must accept the same language.

We begin our induction by considering the case of $n = 0$. In this

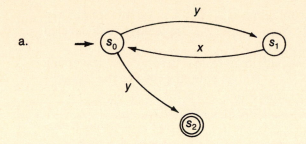

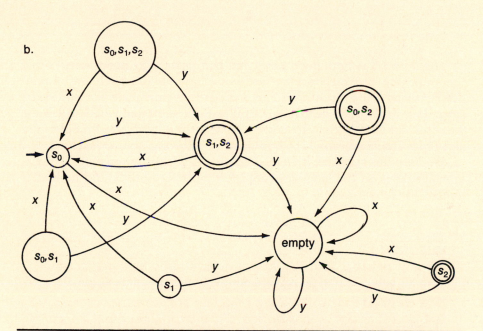

Figure 1.19 a. A transition diagram for a nondeterministic finite automaton
b. The transition diagram for the equivalent deterministic finite automaton as constructed in the proof of Theorem 1.3

case s_n must be ι and s_n' must be $\iota' = \{\iota\}$, so the statement holds trivially.

Next we assume the statement holds for some $n \in \mathbb{N}$ and consider a path in M from ι to some s_{n+1} traversing arcs labeled $w_1, w_2, \cdots, w_{n+1}$. Let s_n be the next to the last state of M along this path. Thus, $(s_n, w_{n+1}, s_{n+1}) \in \rho$. By our induction hypothesis there is a path in M' from ι' to some s_n' traversing arcs labeled $w_1, w_2, \cdots, w_n$ such that $s_n \in s_n'$. Since $(s_n, w_{n+1}, s_{n+1}) \in \rho$, there is an arc in M'

labeled w_{n+1} to a state containing s_{n+1}. Let s'_{n+1} be this state. Then there is a path in M' from ι' to s'_{n+1} traversing arcs labeled $w_1, w_2, \cdots, w_{n+1}$ so that $s_{n+1} \in s'_{n+1}$.

Conversely, consider a path in M' from ι' to some s'_{n+1} traversing arcs labeled $w_1, w_2, \cdots, w_{n+1}$, and let s'_n be the next to the last state along this path. Then, by induction, for each $s_n \in s'_n$ there must be a path in M from ι to s_n traversing arcs labeled $w_1, w_2, \cdots, w_n$. But, $\delta(s'_n, w_{n+1}) = s'_{n+1}$ so s'_{n+1} is the set of states s in M such that $(s_n, w_{n+1}, s) \in \rho$. Hence, for each s in s'_{n+1}, there is a path in M from ι to s traversing arcs labeled $w_1, w_2, \cdots, w_{n+1}$, as required.

■

Theorem 1.3 is both good news and bad news. The good news is that the branching and backtracking that would be required to convert a nondeterministic finite automaton into a progam segment are not necessary, since there is always a deterministic finite automaton that will do the same job. The bad news is that the power of our techniques based on deterministic finite automata cannot be improved by allowing nondeterminism.

We close this section with a theorem that explicitly summarizes the relationship between the languages accepted by deterministic and nondeterministic finite automata.

THEOREM 1.4
For any alphabet Σ, $\{L(M): M$ is a deterministic finite automaton with alphabet $\Sigma\}$ = $\{L(M): M$ is a nondeterministic finite automaton with alphabet $\Sigma\}$.

PROOF
The fact that the languages accepted by nondeterministic finite automata are also accepted by deterministic finite automata is merely a restatement of Theorem 1.3. Conversely, if $M = (S, \Sigma, \delta, \iota, F)$ is a deterministic finite automaton, then the nondeterministic finite automaton $(S, \Sigma, \rho, \iota, F)$, where $(p, x, q) \in \rho$ if and only if $\delta(p, x) = q$, accepts exactly the same language.

■

Because of Theorem 1.4, many authors do not distinguish between deterministic and nondeterministic finite automata when discussing language acceptance. Instead, they merely refer to finite automata; we shall often do the same.

Exercises

1. Identify the points of nondeterminism in the following transition diagram.

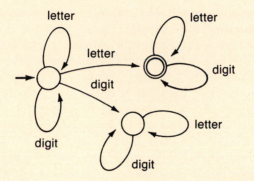

2. Using intuitive methods, modify the transition diagram in Figure 1.17 so that it accepts the same strings as before but no longer involves nondeterministic branches.

3. Show that each deterministic finite automaton $(S, \Sigma, \delta, \iota, F)$ is a nondeterministic finite automaton, by showing that the transition function δ can be represented as a subset of $S \times \Sigma \times S$.

4. Using the techniques presented in the proof of Theorem 1.3, draw a transition diagram for a deterministic finite automaton that would accept the same strings as the nondeterministic finite automaton that is represented by the following transition diagram.

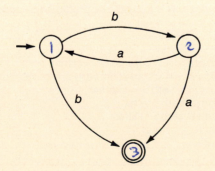

1.5   REGULAR GRAMMARS

Our goal in the remainder of this chapter is to learn more about regular languages. In this section we analyze their grammatical structure, and in the next we consider their algebraic composition. We begin with the general concept of a grammar.

It is helpful to motivate our discussion with examples from natural languages, where grammatical rules are used to distinguish those strings of symbols that constitute acceptable sentences from those that do not. For example, we might describe a simple English sentence as a structure with a subject followed by a predicate. The subject might take the form of a single noun, while the predicate might be an intransitive verb or perhaps a transitive verb followed by an object. This top–down decomposition could continue until we reached the level of detail in which we would describe the literal symbols that actually appear in English sentences. For instance, we might describe a transitive verb as the word "hit" or the word "likes." Such a decomposition is shown in Figure 1.20.

There are several points to be made regarding Figure 1.20. First, you will note that some terms are enclosed in brackets while others are not. Terms that do not appear in brackets are called **terminals.** These are the symbols that may actually appear in a sentence. The terms enclosed in brackets are called **nonterminals.** One of these nonterminals (in Figure 1.20, it is <sentence>) is considered the **start symbol.** Each line in Figure 1.20, consisting of a left and right side connected by an arrow, is called a **rewrite rule.** The right side of each such rule represents a more detailed description of the left side. For instance, the first rewrite rule of Figure 1.20 indicates that a <sentence> has the structure of a <subject> followed by a <predicate> followed by a <period>. A more detailed description of these non-

<sentence> → <subject> <predicate> <period>
<subject> → <noun>
<noun> → John
<noun> → Mary
<predicate> → <intransitive verb>
<predicate> → <transitive verb> <object>
<intransitive verb> → skates
<transitive verb> → hit
<transitive verb> → likes
<object> → <noun>
<period> → .

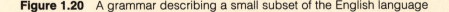

Figure 1.20   A grammar describing a small subset of the English language

terminals appears later in the figure. Thus, Figure 1.20 describes the structure of a sentence in a hierarchical manner, beginning with the start symbol <sentence>.

Such a finite collection of nonterminals and terminals together with a start symbol and a finite set of rewrite rules is called a **grammar,** or more precisely a **phrase-structure grammar,** since it is based on the composition of strings in terms of "phrases" with each phrase represented by a nonterminal. More formally, a grammar is defined as a quadruple (V, T, S, R), where V is a finite set of nonterminals, T is a finite set of terminals, S (an element of N) is the start symbol, and R is a finite set of rewrite rules. In general, the left and right sides of a grammar's rewrite rules can be any finite combination of terminals and nonterminals as long as the left side contains at least one nonterminal. Moreover, the right side of some rewrite rules may consist of the empty string (in which case the rule means that the pattern represented by the right side of the rule may be the empty string). Such a rule is called a **λ-rule.**

The use of brackets to distinguish nonterminals from terminals helps prevent confusion. For example, in a grammar describing the structure of English sentences, the term *sentence* might appear both as a nonterminal representing the start symbol and as a terminal representing a word in a sentence. In this case the use of brackets allows us to distinguish between dual uses of the term. In our study, however, we will distinguish between nonterminals and terminals with a less cumbersome notational system. Unless otherwise specified, we will denote nonterminals by upper case letters and terminals by lower case letters. Thus, a rule of the form $S \rightarrow xN$ will mean that the nonterminal S can be refined as the terminal x followed by the nonterminal N.

A grammar is said to generate a particular string of terminals if, by starting with the start symbol, one can produce that string by successively replacing patterns found on the left of the grammar's rewrite rules with the corresponding expressions on the right, until only terminals remain. The sequence of steps in this process is called a **derivation** of the string. For example, the string (the sentence)

Mary likes John.

can be generated from the grammar in Figure 1.20 through the derivation in Figure 1.21. As another example, Figure 1.22 shows another grammar, with start symbol S, and a derivation showing how that grammar can generate the string xyz.

If the terminals of a grammar G are symbols in an alphabet Σ, we say that G is a grammar over the alphabet Σ. In such a case the strings generated by G are actually strings in Σ^*. Thus, a grammar G over an alphabet Σ specifies a language over Σ that consists of the strings G generates. This

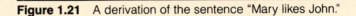

<sentence>

⇓

<subject> <predicate> <period>

⇓

<noun> <predicate> <period>

⇓

Mary <predicate> <period>

⇓

Mary <transitive verb> <object> <period>

⇓

Mary likes <object> <period>

⇓

Mary likes <noun> <period>

⇓

Mary likes John <period>

⇓

Mary likes John.

Figure 1.21   A derivation of the sentence "Mary likes John."

$S \rightarrow XSZ$

$S \rightarrow Y$

$Y \rightarrow yY$

$Y \rightarrow \lambda$

$X \rightarrow x$

$Z \rightarrow z$

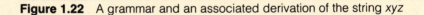

$$S \Rightarrow XSZ \Rightarrow xSZ \Rightarrow xyYZ \Rightarrow xyZ \Rightarrow xyz$$

Figure 1.22   A grammar and an associated derivation of the string xyz

$S \rightarrow 0T$	$T \rightarrow 0T$	$U \rightarrow 0V$	$V \rightarrow 0V$
$S \rightarrow 1T$	$T \rightarrow 1T$	$U \rightarrow 1V$	$V \rightarrow 1V$
$S \rightarrow 2T$	$T \rightarrow 2T$	$U \rightarrow 2V$	$V \rightarrow 2V$
$S \rightarrow 3T$	$T \rightarrow 3T$	$U \rightarrow 3V$	$V \rightarrow 3V$
$S \rightarrow 4T$	$T \rightarrow 4T$	$U \rightarrow 4V$	$V \rightarrow 4V$
$S \rightarrow 5T$	$T \rightarrow 5T$	$U \rightarrow 5V$	$V \rightarrow 5V$
$S \rightarrow 6T$	$T \rightarrow 6T$	$U \rightarrow 6V$	$V \rightarrow 6V$
$S \rightarrow 7T$	$T \rightarrow 7T$	$U \rightarrow 7V$	$V \rightarrow 7V$
$S \rightarrow 8T$	$T \rightarrow 8T$	$U \rightarrow 8V$	$V \rightarrow 8V$
$S \rightarrow 9T$	$T \rightarrow 9T$	$U \rightarrow 9V$	$V \rightarrow 9V$
	$T \rightarrow .U$		$V \rightarrow \lambda$

Figure 1.23   A regular grammar that generates strings representing rational numbers in decimal notation

language is denoted $L(G)$. You may wish to confirm that the language generated by the grammar in Figure 1.22 is $\{x^m y^n z^m : m, n \in \mathbb{N}\}$.

We now define a **regular grammar** as a grammar whose rewrite rules conform to the following restrictions. The left side of any rewrite rule in a regular grammar must consist of a single nonterminal, and the right side must be a terminal followed by a nonterminal, or a single terminal, or the empty string. Thus, rewrite rules of the form

$$Z \rightarrow yX$$
$$Z \rightarrow x$$
$$W \rightarrow \lambda$$

would be allowed in a regular grammar, whereas rules of the form

$$yW \rightarrow X$$
$$X \rightarrow xZy$$
$$YX \rightarrow WvZ$$

would not.

Figure 1.23 presents a regular grammar that generates strings representing rational numbers in decimal notation, and Figure 1.24 presents a regular grammar that generates strings consisting of one or more copies of the pattern xy. In both examples the start symbol is S. You will note that neither of these grammars uses a rule whose right side consists of a single terminal. Although allowed by the definition of a regular grammar, rules of this form are actually not needed. Indeed, any rule of the form

$$N \rightarrow x$$

in a regular grammar could be replaced by the pair of rules

$$N \rightarrow xX$$
$$X \rightarrow \lambda$$

where X is a nonterminal that does not appear elsewhere in the grammar, without altering the set of strings that could be generated by the grammar.

$$S \rightarrow xX$$
$$X \rightarrow yY$$
$$Y \rightarrow xX$$
$$Y \rightarrow \lambda$$

Figure 1.24   A regular grammar that generates strings consisting of one or more copies of the pattern xy

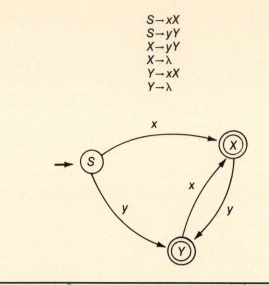

$$S \to xX$$
$$S \to yY$$
$$X \to yY$$
$$X \to \lambda$$
$$Y \to xX$$
$$Y \to \lambda$$

Figure 1.25   A regular grammar G and a transition diagram for a finite automaton M such that $L(G) = L(M)$

The significance of regular grammars is that the languages they generate are exactly the languages that are recognized by finite automata, as shown by Theorem 1.5.

THEOREM 1.5

For each alphabet Σ, $\{L(G):\ G$ is a regular grammar over $\Sigma\} = \{L(M):$ M is a finite automaton over $\Sigma\}$.

PROOF

If G is a regular grammar over Σ, we can convert it to a regular grammar G' that generates the same language but does not contain rewrite rules whose right sides consist of a single terminal (see comments preceding Theorem 1.5). We can, then, define M to be the nondeterministic finite automaton $(S, \Sigma, \rho, \iota, F)$, where S is the collection of nonterminals in G', ι is the start symbol in G', F is the collection of nonterminals of G' that appear on the left side of some λ-rule, and ρ consists of the triples (P, x, Q) for which G' contains a rewrite rule of the form $P \to xQ$. Conversely, if M is the nondeterministic finite automaton $(S, \Sigma, \rho, \iota, F)$, then we can define G' to be the regular grammar over Σ for which the nonterminals are the states in S, the start symbol is ι, and the rewrite rules are of the form $P \to xQ$ if (P, x, Q) is in ρ and $Q \to \lambda$ if Q is in F.

Syntax diagrams   Rewrite rules

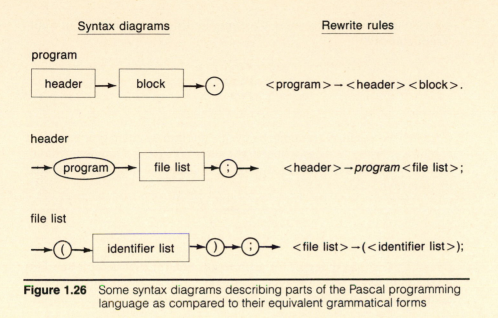

program

$<$program$> \rightarrow <$header$> <$block$>$.

header

$<$header$> \rightarrow$ *program* $<$file list$>$;

file list

$<$file list$> \rightarrow (<$identifier list$>)$;

Figure 1.26 Some syntax diagrams describing parts of the Pascal programming language as compared to their equivalent grammatical forms

In either case $L(M) = L(G')$ since a derivation of a string based on the grammar G' corresponds directly to a path in the transition diagram of M that leads from the initial state to an accept state, and vice versa. As an example, see Figure 1.25.

The significance of the grammatical approach to language specification becomes clear in the next two chapters, where we will see that the use of grammars leads to a classification scheme for various types of languages. For now, you might compare the composition of grammars to that of the syntax diagrams that are often used today when describing the syntax of programming languages such as Pascal, Modula-2, or Ada. You will find that these syntax diagrams are essentially another way of representing the rewrite rules of a grammar (see Figure 1.26).

Exercises

1. List all the sentences generated by the grammar in Figure 1.20.
2. Show that the grammar below (with start symbol S) can be modified to be a regular grammar without changing the language it generates. Which

exercise in a previous section is essentially this same problem in a different context?

$$S \rightarrow xyX$$
$$X \rightarrow xxX$$
$$X \rightarrow yY$$
$$Y \rightarrow \lambda$$

3. Convert the regular grammar below to another regular grammar that contains no rewrite rules whose right sides consist of a single terminal, and yet generates the same language. Describe the language generated in your own words.

$$S \rightarrow xS$$
$$S \rightarrow y$$
$$S \rightarrow z$$

4. Draw a transition diagram for a finite automaton that accepts the language generated by the regular grammar (with start symbol S) shown below. Describe the language in your own words.

$$S \rightarrow \lambda$$
$$S \rightarrow xX$$
$$S \rightarrow yY$$
$$Y \rightarrow yY$$
$$Y \rightarrow \lambda$$
$$X \rightarrow xX$$
$$X \rightarrow \lambda$$

5. Present a regular grammar that generates the language accepted by a finite automaton whose transition diagram is shown below.

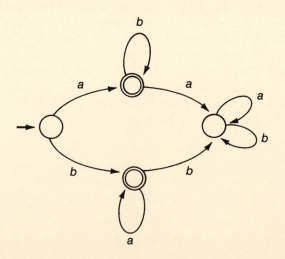

1.6   REGULAR EXPRESSIONS

We have defined regular languages as those that are recognized by finite automata and have shown that they are also those languages that are generated by regular grammars. In this section we develop another characterization of regular languages that provides still more insight into their composition.

Our approach is to show how regular languages can be constructed from simple building blocks. We begin by considering the simplest languages that could be formed from an alphabet Σ. That is, we are interested in the simplest subsets of Σ^*. You might conjecture that these would be the subsets which consist of single strings of length one, and indeed we will use these languages as some of our building blocks. After all, if $\Sigma = \{x, y\}$, then the languages $\{x\}$ and $\{y\}$ would appear to be natural building blocks from which to construct other languages over Σ.

There are, however, two languages that we would not be able to build using these blocks. One is the language $\{\lambda\}$; the other is $\varnothing$. For reasons that will be clear in a moment we do not use $\{\lambda\}$ as one of our building blocks. Rather our chest of building blocks contains the empty language and all the languages of single strings of length one.

With this foundation established, we turn our attention to ways in which more complicated languages can be constructed from these basic ones. Perhaps the most straightforward technique is to combine two languages into one by forming their set theoretic union. We denote this operation with the traditional set union symbol, $\cup$. Thus, if L_1 were the language $\{x, xy\}$ and L_2 were $\{yx, yy\}$, then the language $L_1 \cup L_2$ would be $\{x, xy, yx, yy\}$.

Is the union of any two regular languages a regular language? To answer this question we consider the diagrams in Figure 1.27a. One of these accepts the language consisting of zero or more xs followed by a single y while the other accepts zero or more ys followed by a single x. To construct a diagram that accepts the union of these languages, one may be inclined to identify the initial states of the two diagrams as shown in Figure 1.27b. However, the resulting diagram accepts the string $xyxyx$, which is not in the union of the two original languages.

The problem here is that this simple method of combining the original diagrams allows more interaction between them than we can afford. We need a combination technique that produces a diagram that commits us to one or the other of the original structures without letting us switch back and forth. The answer lies in introducing a new initial state from which we can transfer into one of the original diagrams without being able to return, as shown in Figure 1.27c. The general construction is as follows: Draw a new initial state. Declare this new state to be an accept state if and only if one of the original initial states was also an accept state. To each state that is the destination of an arc from one of the original initial states, draw an

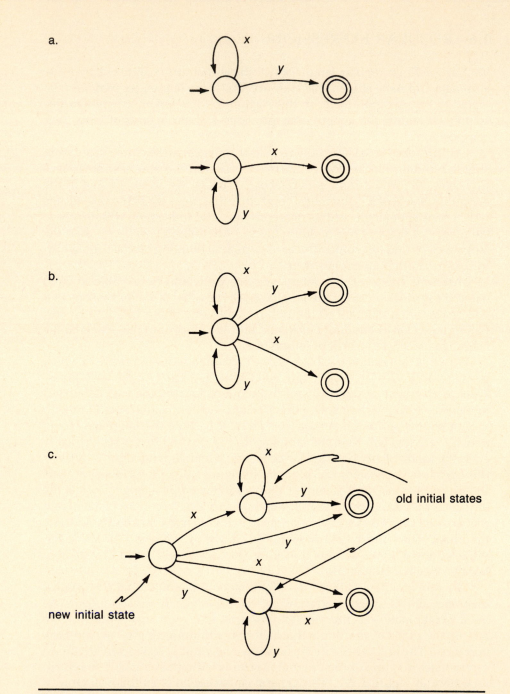

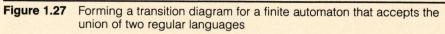

Figure 1.27   Forming a transition diagram for a finite automaton that accepts the union of two regular languages

arc with the same label from the new initial state. Cancel the initial status of the original initial states.

When applied to any pair of transition diagrams for finite automata, this process will produce another transition diagram for which any computation is a copy of a computation that could have been performed by one of the original machines, and vice versa. Thus, *the union of any two regular languages is regular.*

Another technique for combining two languages is to collect all those strings formed by concatenating a string from the first language with a string from the second. The collection of strings formed in this manner is called the **concatenation** of the two languages. The operation of concatenation is denoted by a small circle, $\circ$. Thus, if L_1 were again the language $\{x, xy\}$ and L_2 were the language $\{yx, yy\}$, then the language $L_1 \circ L_2$ would be $\{xyx, xyy, xyyx, xyyy\}$. Note that $L_1 \circ L_2$ is not the same as $L_2 \circ L_1 = \{yxx, yxxy, yyx, yyxy\}$. That is, the concatenation of languages is not commutative.

Suppose we are given transition diagrams T_1 and T_2 that accept languages L_1 and L_2, respectively, and we wish to construct a transition diagram that accepts $L_1 \circ L_2$. We could proceed as follows: From each accept state of T_1, draw an arc to each state of T_2 that is the destination of an arc from the initial state of T_2. Label each of these arcs with the label of the corresponding arc in T_2. Allow the accept states in T_1 to remain accept states if and only if the initial state in T_2 is also an accept state. Remove the initial state designation from the initial state in T_2. (As an example, see Figure 1.28.) Note that a string can be accepted by such a combined diagram if and only if it is the concatenation of two substrings, the first defining a path from the initial state of T_1 to an old accept state of T_1, and the second defining a path from this old accept state to an accept state of T_2. Hence, the language accepted by the combined diagram will be $L_1 \circ L_2$. In turn, *the concatenation of any two regular languages is regular.*

The final operation we consider is known as the **Kleene star** (named for S. C. Kleene) and differs from the previous ones in that it enlarges a single language rather than combining two. This is done by forming all concatenations of zero or more strings from the language being enlarged. (Since we include the concatenation of zero strings the empty string will be a member of the enlarged language.) We denote this operation by a superscript asterisk, *. (Note that we have already met the Kleene star when using Σ^* to represent the set of all finite strings that can be formed from the alphabet Σ.)

For example, if L_1 is the language $\{y\}$, then L_1^* would be the language consisting of all finite strings of ys including the empty string, or if L_2 is the language $\{yy\}$, then L_2^* would be all strings consisting of an even number of ys including the empty string. Furthermore, since λ is a member of the

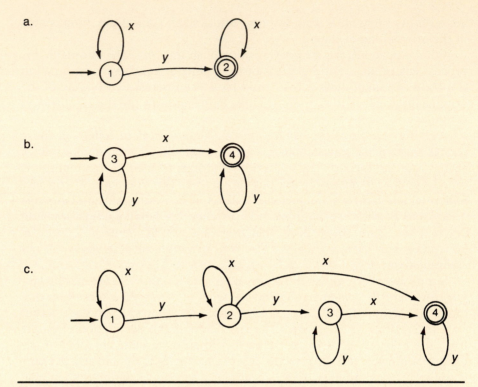

Figure 1.28 Forming a transition diagram for a finite automaton that accepts the concatenation of two regular languages

Kleene star of any language, it must be a member of $\varnothing^*$. Thus, $\varnothing^* = \{\lambda\}$. (The fact that $\{\lambda\}$ is generated from $\varnothing$ via the Kleene star is why we did not include $\{\lambda\}$ as one of our building blocks.)

Intuition tells us that constructing a transition diagram to accept the Kleene star of a regular language involves concatenating the original transition diagram back into itself. In this case our intuition is correct except for one small detail—the new transition diagram must accept the empty string. To accomplish this, our intuition might tell us merely to designate the original initial state as a new accept state, but the problem is not so easily solved. For example, designating the initial state of Figure 1.29a as an accept state would not only allow the acceptance of the empty string but would also allow the acceptance of strings such as *xxxx*.

Consequently, our first step toward modifying a transition diagram so that it accepts the Kleene star of the language originally accepted is to draw a new initial state and connect it to the original diagram in much the same manner as in the case of the union operation: To each state that was the destination of an arc from the initial state in the original diagram, we draw

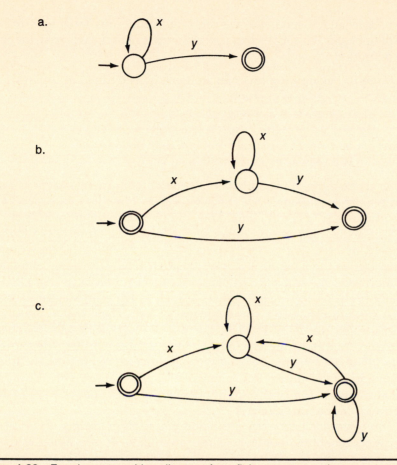

Figure 1.29 Forming a transition diagram for a finite automaton that accepts the Kleene star of a regular language

an arc from the new initial state with the same label. Then, we designate the new initial state as an accept state also (see Figure 1.29b).

Once the new initial state has been added, our next task is to modify the diagram so that we can cycle back to the "beginning" of the diagram from the accept states. This is done by adding an arc from each accept state to each state that is the destination of an arc from the initial state. Each of these new arcs is labeled with the same label as the corresponding arc from the initial state. The result is a transition diagram that accepts a nonempty string if and only if that string is the concatenation of strings accepted by the original diagram. (For an example, see Figure 1.29c.) We conclude that *the Kleene star of any regular language is regular.*

Given a particular alphabet and using the three operations union, concatenation, and Kleene star, we can build numerous languages from our building blocks. To convey this process more precisely, we make the following definition.

A **regular expression** (over an alphabet Σ) is defined as follows:
a. $\varnothing$ is a regular expression.
b. Each member of Σ is a regular expression.
c. If p and q are regular expressions then so is $(p \cup q)$.
d. If p and q are regular expressions then so is $(p \circ q)$.
e. If p is a regular expression then so is p^*.

As an example, if the alphabet Σ were $\{x, y, z\}$, then $(x \cup (z \circ y))$ would be a regular expression since $(z \circ y)$ would be a regular expression by Rule d, and hence $(x \cup (z \circ y))$ would be a regular expression by Rule c.

Each regular expression r over some alphabet Σ represents a language, denoted by $L(r)$, that is constructed from our building blocks. More precisely, $L(\varnothing)$ is the language $\varnothing$, and for each $x \in \Sigma$, $L(x)$ is the language $\{x\}$. Furthermore, if p and q are regular expressions, then $L((p \cup q)) = L(p) \cup L(q)$, $L((p \circ q)) = L(p) \circ L(q)$, and $L(p^*) = L(p)^*$. For example, the expression $(x \cup (z \circ y))$ represents the language $\{x, zy\}$. That is, it represents the language generated by forming the union of $\{x\}$ with the language obtained by concatenating $\{z\}$ and $\{y\}$. In a similar manner, the expression $((x \circ y)^* \cup z^*)$ (obtained by applying Rule d to x and y, then Rule e to $(x \circ y)$ and z, and finally Rule c to $(x \circ y)^*$ and z^*) represents the language that consists of strings of zero or more copies of the pattern xy in addition to strings of zero or more zs.

Thus, regular expressions provide yet another means, in addition to transition diagrams, automata, and grammars, of specifying languages. Theorem 1.6 shows why we are interested in languages that are represented by regular expressions.

THEOREM 1.6
Given an alphabet Σ, the regular languages over Σ are exactly the languages that are represented by regular expressions over Σ.

PROOF
First we must show that the language represented by any regular expression is regular. We have already seen that the language $\varnothing$ is regular as well as any language containing a single string. Moreover, we have seen that the union and concatenation of two regular languages is always regular, and that the Kleene star of any regular language is regular. Thus, this first step of our proof is complete.

Next, we show that any language accepted by a finite automaton can also be represented by a regular expression. We assume that T

is a transition diagram for some finite automaton and show, by induction on the number of states in T that are not initial or accept states, that there is a regular expression that represents the language accepted by T. The diagrams we will consider are slightly more general than traditional transition diagrams in that their arcs can be labeled by regular expressions. (To traverse such an arc requires that the machine read a pattern compatible with the expression.) If the languages accepted by such generalized diagrams can be represented by regular expressions, then any language accepted by a traditional transition diagram for a finite automaton can also be so represented.

Our induction process assumes that T has only one accept state. Otherwise, for each accept state we could make a separate copy of T in which only that state was an accept state, find regular expressions associated with each of these diagrams, and then form the union of these expressions to obtain the desired expression for T.

To begin our induction process, then, let us assume that T is a generalized transition diagram with only one accept state, and that every state in T is an initial state or an accept state. There are two possibilities: Either T contains only one state that is both the initial state and the accept state, or T contains two states of which one is the initial state and the other is the accept state. In the former case, the desired expression is merely the Kleene star of the union of the labels that appear on the arcs in the diagram.

The latter case is a bit more complex. If there are multiple arcs connecting the same states in the same direction, we replace them with a single arc labeled by the regular expression that represents the union of the original labels. At this point T can contain at most four arcs: one from the initial state back to the initial state, one from the initial state to the accept state, one from the accept state back to the accept state, and one from the accept state to the initial state. Let us denote these arcs with the labels r, s, t, and u, respectively (see Figure 1.30).

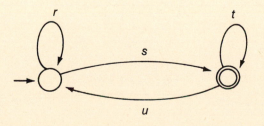

Figure 1.30 The possible arcs in a transition diagram with two states—one an initial state and the other an accept state

If the arc labeled s is not present in the diagram, then the associated regular expression is $\varnothing$ since there would be no way to reach the accept state from the initial state. Otherwise, the structure of the associated regular expression depends on the absence or presence of the arc labeled u. If this arc is not present, then the expression

$$((r^* \circ s) \circ t^*)$$

is the desired regular expression, where r and t are replaced by $\varnothing$ if the corresponding arc is not present in the diagram. If there is in fact an arc from the accept state to the initial state, then the expression

$$(((r^* \circ s) \circ t^*) \circ (u \circ ((r^* \circ s) \circ t^*))^*)$$

is the desired expression, where again r and t are replaced by $\varnothing$ if the corresponding arc is not present in T.

Let us now suppose that $n \in \mathbb{N}$, and that the language accepted by any generalized transition diagram with no more than n states that are not initial or accept states can be represented by a regular expression. For any generalized transition diagram having $n + 1$ states that are not initial or accept states, we proceed as follows (refer to Figure 1.31): Select a state s_0 in T that is not an accept state or an initial state. Remove this state and all its incident arcs from T. For each pair of removed arcs—one leading to s_0 from another state and the other leading away from s_0 to another state, labeled p and q, respectively—draw an arc from the origin of the arc la-

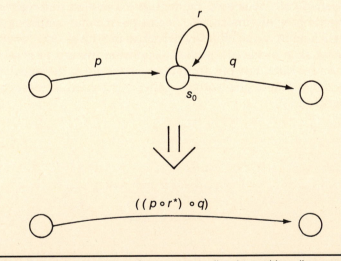

Figure 1.31   Removing a state s_0 from a generalized transition diagram for a finite automaton

beled p to the destination of the arc labeled q, and label this new arc $((p \circ r^*) \circ q)$, where r is either the union of the labels of those arcs that originally went from s_0 to s_0, or $\varnothing$ if there were no such arcs. The resulting diagram is another generalized transition diagram that will accept the same language as T and has only n states that are not initial or accept states. Thus, by our induction hypothesis, the language in question can be represented by a regular expression.

∎

Theorem 1.6 provides yet another way of characterizing regular languages: They are the languages accepted by deterministic finite automata, the languages accepted by nondeterministic finite automata, the languages generated by regular grammars, and the languages represented by regular expressions.

From this we can conclude that the expressive power of regular expressions is rather limited, but this does not imply that regular expressions are useless. To the contrary, these expressions give insights into the structure of regular languages that may not be apparent in the other characterizations. Regular expressions also provide a relatively concise way of expressing and communicating regular languages. For instance, to describe a regular language by means of a finite automaton requires a definition of the transition function, perhaps in the form of a transition diagram or a transition table; to describe a language using a grammar requires a list of rewrite rules; but, by using a regular expression a language can be described via a single line of type.

A prime example of where this concise notation is advantageous is found in many of today's text editors, which allow one to search a file for a particular pattern that is to be deleted or replaced with another string. In this setting a notation system is required for communicating the form of the target pattern. Although the syntax actually used might differ from that introduced here, the theme of expressing the pattern via the operations of union, concatenation, and Kleene star is fundamental in such applications. As a particular example, when using the UNIX editor *ed*, the command

$$s/xx*/z/$$

instructs the system to substitute the first occurrence of one or more xs with a single z. Here, the expression $xx*$ represents a single x concatenated with the Kleene star of x.

Finally, a consequence of theorems 1.3 and 1.6 is that pattern-matching systems that rely on only union, concatenation, and Kleene star for representing patterns are rather restrictive in the patterns that can be requested. On the other hand, as a testimonial to the scope of regular languages, many very useful systems have been designed with these limitations.

Exercises

1. Which of the languages described by the following regular expressions over the alphabet $\{x, y, z\}$ are infinite? Describe the contents of these infinite languages in a single sentence and exhaustively list the strings in the languages that are finite.

   a. $(x \circ (y \circ z^*))$ e. $(y \circ y)^*$

   b. $(x^* \circ (y \circ z))$ f. $(x^* \cup y^*)$

   c. $((z \cup y) \circ x)$ g. $((x \circ x) \cup z)$

   d. $(z \cup y)^*$ h. $((z \cup y) \cup x)$

2. Draw a transition diagram that accepts the Kleene star of the language accepted by the following diagram.

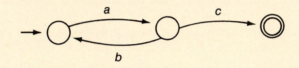

3. Draw a transition diagram that accepts the union of the languages accepted by the following diagrams.

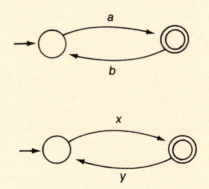

4. Draw a transition diagram that accepts the concatenation of the language accepted by

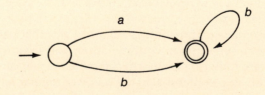

followed by the language accepted by

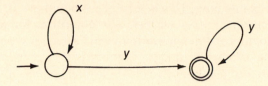

5. Construct a regular expression that describes the language accepted by the following transition diagram.

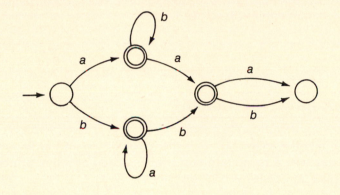

1.7 CLOSING COMMENTS

This chapter has introduced the class of regular languages and has shown how these languages can be characterized by means of finite automata, regular grammars, and regular expressions. In addition to being important on their own, many of the topics presented in this chapter also serve to introduce the topics in the remaining chapters. For example, we have introduced both deterministic and nondeterministic machines—a distinction that does not affect the computational power of finite automata. However, in the following chapter we will see that this distinction can have significant ramifications in other contexts. We have also seen how the lexical analysis tasks of a compiler can be reduced to a simple table lookup process. Although potentially useful in this context, such use of tables is more prominent today in the parsing routines of compilers, as we will see in the next chapter.

The concept of a grammar introduced in this chapter is important, as the syntax of most programming languages today is described by grammars, and it is on this grammatical structure that the compiling process is based. Much of our study in the next few chapters will involve the question of what languages can be generated by grammars whose rewrite rules conform to various restrictions. This is significant because as the rewrite rules of a grammar become more complex, the algorithm for recognizing the associated language becomes more involved. Thus, if we were given the task of designing a compiler for a programming language (or some form of processor for a natural language), we would like to base our design on the simplest grammar possible.

Our ultimate goal, however, is to discover the extent to which machines can be used to solve problems; the problem we have chosen for now is that of parsing languages. As we shall see in the coming chapters, this problem is complex enough that the pursuit of its solution will lead us to the apparent limits of computational processes.

Chapter Review Problems

1. Show that the collection of all strings of xs, ys, and zs that contain an odd number of xs, an odd number of ys, and an even number of zs is a regular language over the alphabet $\{x, y, z\}$.

2. Show that if L_1 and L_2 are regular languages, then $L_1 \cap L_2$ is regular.

3. Show that if L_1 and L_2 are regular languages, then $L_1 - L_2$ is regular.

4. a. If Σ is an alphabet, is the collection of palindromes in Σ^* a regular language? Why or why not?

    b. If L is a regular language, is the collection of palindromes in L a regular language? Why or why not?

5. Show that if L is a regular language over alphabet Σ, then the language consisting of all strings of the form wv, where $w \in L$ and $v \in \Sigma^* - L$, is regular.

6. Show that if L is a regular language, then the language obtained by writing the strings from L backward is also regular.

7. Show that if L is a regular language, then the collection of strings in L whose reversals are also in L is regular.

8. The string 527943001 is a listing of the digits that appear in the addition problem below as they would appear if we read down columns from right to left. (We have filled in the zeros that are assumed to be in the leftmost column.) Design a transition diagram for a finite automaton

that accepts those and only those strings of digits that can be obtained from addition problems in this fashion.

$$
\begin{array}{r}
95 \\
+42 \\
\hline
137
\end{array}
$$

9. A rewrite rule in a grammar that replaces a nonterminal with a terminal–nonterminal pair is said to be **left linear** or **right linear,** depending on whether the nonterminal is on the left or right (respectively) of the terminal. (The rule $N \rightarrow Mx$ would be left linear whereas the rule $N \rightarrow xM$ would be right linear.) Observe that our definition of regular grammars allowed right linear rules but not left linear rules. Show that regular languages are again generated if we change the definition to allow for left linear rules while excluding right linear ones.

    Explain how this problem relates to Problem 6.

10. Show that the language over $\{x, y\}$ that consists of those strings with the same number of xs as ys is not regular.

11. Show that the language over $\{x, y\}$ that consists of those strings that do not contain three consecutive xs is regular.

12. Show that any finite language is regular.

13. Design a transition diagram for a deterministic finite automaton that will accept the same strings as the nondeterministic finite automaton represented below.

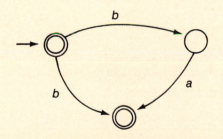

14. Suppose we allowed finite automata to shift from one state to another without reading a symbol from their input tapes. Such a transition is normally represented in a transition diagram as an arc labeled by λ rather than by a symbol from the alphabet, and is known as a **λ-transition.** Show that every transition diagram having λ-transitions can be modified so that it no longer contains such transitions but still accepts the same language as before. (The modified diagram may be nondeterministic.)

15. Describe the language represented by each of the following regular expressions.

 a. $((z \cup y)^* \circ x)$
 b. $((x \circ x^*) \circ (y \circ y^*))$
 c. $((x \circ x^*) \cup (y \circ y^*))$
 d. $((x^* \circ y^*) \circ z^*)$

16. Write regular expressions that describe the following languages.
 a. All strings consisting of an odd number of xs.
 b. All strings consisting of an odd number of xs and an even number of ys.
 c. All strings of xs and ys such that each y is immediately preceded by an x and immediately followed by an x.

17. Develop a grammar for generating those strings that constitute literals of type real in the Pascal programming language.

18. Suppose L is a regular language over alphabet $\Sigma = \{x, y\}$. Show that $\{w\colon w \in \Sigma^* \text{ and } xw \in L\}$ and $\{w\colon w \in \Sigma^* \text{ and } wx \in L\}$ are also regular languages over Σ.

19. Find a regular language (not containing λ) that cannot be the language accepted by any deterministic finite automaton having only one accept state.

20. Show that if a deterministic finite automaton M accepts a string containing more symbols than M has states, then M must accept an infinite number of strings.

21. Design an algorithm that converts transition diagrams for finite automata into equivalent regular expressions.

22. Show that the language $\{x^n\colon n \text{ is prime}\}$ is not regular.

23. Show that the language $\{x^n\colon n = m^2 \text{ for some } m \in \mathbb{N}\}$ is not regular.

24. Find a regular expression that represents the intersection of the languages represented by each of the following pairs of regular expressions.
 a. $(x \cup y^*)$ and $(x \cup y)^*$
 b. $(x \circ (x \cup y)^*)$ and $((x \cup y)^* \circ y)$
 c. $(((x \cup y) \circ y) \circ (x \cup y)^*)$ and $(y \circ (x \cup y)^*)$
 d. $((x \circ y)^* \circ (x \cup \varnothing))$ and $((x \cup y) \circ (x \circ y)^*)$

25. Show that if L is a regular language, then the set of strings in L of odd length is also a regular language.
 Is the same true for the set of strings of even length? Justify your answer.

26. Show that if L is a regular language that does not contain λ, then L can be accepted by a nondeterministic finite automaton with only one accept state.

27. We have shown that the union of two regular languages is regular. Is

the union of a collection of regular languages always regular? Justify your answer.

28. Find a transition diagram that accepts the language generated by the regular grammar below. (The start symbol is S.) Then, find a regular expression representing the same language.

$$S \rightarrow xN$$
$$S \rightarrow x$$
$$N \rightarrow yM$$
$$N \rightarrow y$$
$$M \rightarrow zN$$
$$M \rightarrow z$$

29. Show that a regular language that does not contain λ can be generated by a regular grammar that does not contain any λ-rules.

30. Show that if the language accepted by a finite automaton contains a nonempty string, then it must contain a nonempty string whose length is no greater than the number of states in the automaton.

31. Design a transition diagram for a finite automaton that accepts the language that consists of those strings over the alphabet $\{w, x, y, z\}$ in which the pattern xy is always followed by a w and the pattern yx is always followed by a z.

32. Is every regular language the language accepted by a deterministic finite automaton whose transition diagram can be drawn on a flat surface without requiring arcs to cross one another?

Programming Problems

1. Write a program that tests input strings to see if they conform to the patterns described by Figure 1.17.

2. Design and implement an algorithm for testing regular grammars to see if they generate at least one nonempty string. (You may want to start by translating Chapter Review Problem 30 into a statement about grammars.)

3. Develop a software package that automatically generates parsers for regular languages. First, write a program that accepts regular grammars as its input and generates corresponding transition tables as its output. Then, write a program that analyzes its input string according to the transition table generated by the previous program.

4. Develop a package that is the same as in Programming Problem 3 except that it accepts regular expressions rather than regular grammars.

CHAPTER 2

Pushdown Automata and Context-Free Languages

In the previous chapter we saw how lexical analyzers can be constructed using the principles of finite automata and investigated the regular languages that these automata are able to recognize. We also found that the simple techniques associated with finite automata are limited. In particular, we found that parsing systems based on such automata would not be able to handle many of the syntax structures that occur in general programming languages.

In this chapter we generalize the concepts of finite automata and regular grammars to obtain techniques for parsing a broader range of languages known as the context-free languages. This we do by adding an internal memory system (in the form of a stack) to the automata being studied. This enhancement significantly increases the language processing powers of the automata and provides a context in which several efficient parsing algorithms are formulated; we will close this chapter with a discussion of some of the parsing techniques found in modern compilers.

To classify the languages recognized by the enhanced automata, we will again use the concept of a grammar. By allowing more complexity in the structure of a grammar's rewrite rules, we will be able to identify the grammars that generate the languages recognized by our enhanced machines. This grammatical characterization will prove advantageous in numerous settings; it is by means of such grammars that the syntax of most modern programming languages is described.

2.1   PUSHDOWN AUTOMATA

Recall from Chapter 1 that there is no finite automaton that can recognize the language $\{x^n y^n : n \in \mathbb{N}\}$. In fact, it was this language (with x being a left parenthesis and y being a right parenthesis) that was our primary example of the limitations of finite automata. We hypothesized that this problem occurs because finite automata have no way of remembering how many xs were found in the first part of the string, and so they are unable to check whether the same number of ys follow. Consequently, we now speculate that the problem could be resolved by adding some form of memory to the conceptual machine being considered.

Definition of Pushdown Automata

Following this lead, we introduce the class of machines known as **pushdown automata.** Such a machine is represented in Figure 2.1. As with finite automata, a pushdown automaton has an input stream and a control mechanism that can be in any one of a finite number of states. One of these states is designated as the initial state and at least one state is designated as an accept state. The major difference between pushdown automata and finite automata is that the former are endowed with a stack on which they can store information for later recall. (A stack is sometimes called a pushdown store or a pushdown stack and hence the name pushdown automata.)

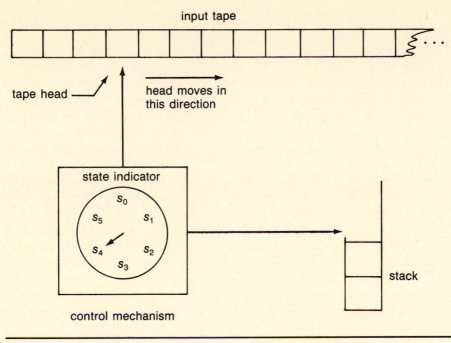

Figure 2.1 A pushdown automaton

The symbols that can be stored on this stack (known as the machine's **stack symbols**) constitute a finite set that may include some or all of the symbols in the machine's alphabet and perhaps some additional symbols for the machine to use as internal markers. For instance, a machine might wish to store special symbols on its stack to separate sections of the stack having different interpretations. More precisely, if a machine pushes a special symbol on the stack before performing any other calculations, then the presence of that symbol on top of the stack can be used as a "stack empty" indicator during later computations. We adopt the symbol # for this purpose in our examples.

Transitions executed by a pushdown automaton must be variations of the following basic sequence: read a symbol from the input, pop a symbol from the stack, push a symbol on the stack, and enter a new state. We represent this process with the notation $(p, x, s; q, y)$ where p, x, s, q, and y are the current state, the symbol in the alphabet that is read from the input, the symbol popped from the stack, the new state, and the symbol pushed on the stack, respectively. This notation is designed to indicate that the current state, input symbol, and top-of-stack symbol collectively help to determine the new state and the symbol to be pushed on the stack.

Variations of the basic transition process are obtained by allowing transitions to read, pop, or push the empty string. For example, a possible transition would be $(p, \lambda, \lambda; q, \lambda)$. That is, from state p the machine could decline to advance its tape head (which we think of as reading the empty string), decline to pop a symbol from its stack (pop the empty string), decline to push a symbol on the stack (push the empty string), and enter state q. Another example is the transition that merely transfers from state p to state q while popping the symbol s from the stack, as represented by $(p, \lambda, s; q, \lambda)$. Still other examples include such transitions as $(p, x, \lambda; q, z)$, $(p, \lambda, \lambda; q, z)$, etc.

To represent the collection of transitions available to a given pushdown automaton, it is convenient to use a transition diagram which resembles that of a finite automaton—states are represented as small circles and transitions as arcs between circles. However, in the case of pushdown automata, the labeling of arcs is more elaborate since there is more information to convey. An arc from state p to state q that represents the transition $(p, x, y; q, z)$ would be labeled $x, y; z$. For example, Figure 2.2 shows a transition diagram for a pushdown automaton in which the initial state is state 1 (as indicated by the pointer) and states 1 and 4 are accept states (indicated by double circles). From this diagram we can see that if the machine reads an x from the input while in state 2, it will push an x on the stack and return to state 2; if the machine reads a y from the input and is able to pop an x from the stack while in state 3, it will return to state 3; or if the symbol # is at the top of the stack when the machine is in state 3, the machine can pop this symbol and move to state 4.

As in the case of finite automata, pushdown automata can be implemented using a variety of technologies, and thus, we isolate the definitive properties of pushdown automata in the following formal definition.

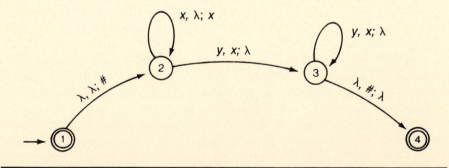

Figure 2.2   A transition diagram for a pushdown automaton

A pushdown automaton is a sextuple of the form $(S, \Sigma, \Gamma, T, \iota, F)$, where:

a. S is a finite collection of states.
b. Σ is the machine's alphabet.
c. Γ is the finite collection of stack symbols.
d. T is a finite collection of transitions.
e. ι (an element of S) is the initial state.
f. F (a subset of S) is the collection of accept states.

Pushdown Automata as Language Accepters

We can use pushdown automata to analyze strings in much the same way we used finite automata: We place the string to be analyzed on the machine's input tape with the machine's tape head over the leftmost cell of the tape. Then we start the machine from its initial state with an empty stack, and declare the string to be accepted if it is possible for the machine to reach an accept state after it has read the entire string. This does not mean the machine must find itself in an accept state immediately after it has read the last symbol from the input string, but it does mean the machine does not read any further down the tape. For instance, having read the last symbol from the input, a pushdown automaton may execute numerous transitions of the form $(p, \lambda, x; q, y)$ before it finally accepts the string.

We used "possible" in defining string acceptance by pushdown automata because the pushdown automata being considered here are nondeterministic; we have not made any restrictions as to the number of transitions that might be applicable at any given time. Hence, as in the case of nondeterministic finite automata, there may be several transition sequences that could be traversed from the machine's initial configuration, only one of which must lead to an accept state for us to declare the string accepted. (It is unfortunate that common terminology does not emphasize the nondeterministic nature of pushdown automata. Technically, they should be called nondeterministic pushdown automata.)

Again following the lead of finite automata, we refer to the collection of all strings accepted by a pushdown automaton M as the language accepted by the machine, denoted as $L(M)$. Once again we emphasize that the language $L(M)$ is not merely any collection of strings accepted by M, but *the* collection of *all* strings accepted by M.

An important class of machines is obtained by restricting the transitions available to pushdown automata to those of the form $(p, x, \lambda; q, \lambda)$. Steps of this form ignore the fact that the machine has a stack, and therefore the activities of the machine depend merely on the current state and the current input symbol. Thus, the class of machines constructed in this manner is the class of finite automata. Therefore, *the languages accepted by pushdown automata include the regular languages.*

Pushdown automata can also accept languages that finite automata cannot, one example being the language $\{x^n y^n : n \in \mathbb{N}\}$. In fact, Figure 2.2 is a transition diagram of such a machine. The first step is to mark the bottom of the stack with the symbol # and then push the xs on the stack as they are read from the input. Then the machine pops an x from the stack each time a y is read. Thus, when the symbol # reappears at the top of the stack, as many ys have been read as there were xs. Note that since the initial state is also an accept state, the machine is allowed to accept the string $x^0 y^0$, which is λ.

Before we close this section, some additional comments are in order. Recall that the acceptance criterion given earlier allows a pushdown automaton to declare a string to be accepted without first emptying its stack. For example, a pushdown automaton based on the diagram in Figure 2.3 would accept the language $\{x^m y^n : m, n \in \mathbb{N}^+ \text{ and } m \geq n\}$, but those strings with more xs than ys would be accepted with xs remaining on the stack. (Note that the automaton could not accept strings with more ys than xs because it would not be able to read all the symbols from such a string.)

One might conjecture that the application of a theory based on such automata could easily lead to program modules that return control to other modules, while leaving remnants of their computations on the stack where these remnants might confuse future computations. For this reason, we often prefer to consider only pushdown automata that empty their stacks before reaching an accept state. We can see from Theorem 2.1 that this restriction does not reduce the power of the machines being considered.

THEOREM 2.1

For each pushdown automaton that accepts strings without emptying its stack, there is a pushdown automaton that accepts the same language but empties its stack before reaching an accept state.

PROOF

Suppose that $M = (S, \Sigma, \Gamma, T, \iota, F)$ is a pushdown automaton that accepts strings without necessarily emptying its stack. We could modify M as follows:

1. Remove the "initial" designation from the initial state of M. Then, introduce a new initial state and a transition that allows M to move from the new initial state to the old one while pushing a special symbol # (that was not previously in Γ) on the stack.

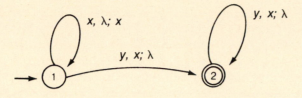

Figure 2.3   A pushdown automaton that can accept strings without an empty stack

2. Remove the accept status from each accept state of M. Then, introduce a state p along with transitions that allow the machine to move from each of the old accept states to p without reading, pushing, or popping any symbols.
3. For each x in Γ (not including #) introduce the transition $(p, \lambda, x; p, \lambda)$.
4. Introduce a new accept state q and the transition $(p, \lambda, \#; q, \lambda)$.

Note that the modified version of M merely marks the bottom of its stack before performing any computations, then simulates the computations of the original machine until that original machine would have declared the input to be accepted. At this point the modified machine shifts to state p, empties its stack, and then shifts to its accept state q while removing the bottom-of-stack marker. Thus, both the original and modified machines accept the same strings, except that the modified version reaches its accept state only when its stack is empty.

∎

Figure 2.4 shows the result of applying the technique in the preceding proof to the diagram in Figure 2.3. A pushdown automaton based on this new diagram will accept the same strings as the original, but cannot accept a string unless its stack is empty.

Finally, it is important to remind ourselves again that the pushdown automata being considered here are nondeterministic. The modification process described in the proof of Theorem 2.1 could introduce numerous points of nondeterminism via the transitions that lead from the old accept states of the machine to the new state p.

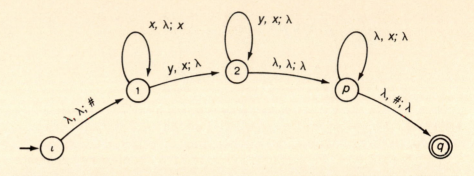

Figure 2.4   The diagram of Figure 2.3 after being modified to empty its stack before accepting a string

Exercises

1. Design a pushdown automaton M such that $L(M) = \{x^n y^m x^n : m, n \in \mathbb{N}\}$.

2. What language is accepted by the pushdown automaton whose transition diagram is shown below?

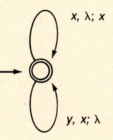

3. Modify the transition diagram in Exercise 2 so that the associated pushdown automaton will accept the same set of strings but will do so with its stack empty.

4. Show how two pushdown automata M_1 and M_2 can be combined to form a single pushdown automaton that would accept the language $L(M_1) \cup L(M_2)$.

2.2   CONTEXT-FREE GRAMMARS

Now that we have extended the machines under consideration from finite automata to pushdown automata, our investigation turns to the question of what languages these extended machines can recognize. We begin to look for an answer by returning to the concept of grammars.

Definition of Context-Free Grammars

To characterize the languages recognized by pushdown automata, we introduce the concept of a **context-free grammar.** In contrast to regular grammars, these grammars have no restrictions on the form of the right side of their rewrite rules, although the left side of each rule is still required to be a single nonterminal. The grammar in Figure 2.5 is a context-free grammar but not a regular grammar.

The term "context-free" reflects the fact that since the left side of each rewrite rule can contain only a single nonterminal, the rule can be applied regardless of the context in which that nonterminal is found. In contrast, consider a rewrite rule whose left side contains more than a nonterminal, such as $xNy \rightarrow xzy$. Such a rule says that the nonterminal N can be replaced by the terminal z only when it is surrounded by the terminals x and y. The ability to remove N by applying the rule would therefore depend on the context rather than being context-free.

Context-free grammars generate strings via derivations, just as regular grammars. However, in the case of context-free grammars, questions can arise as to which nonterminal to replace at a particular step in the derivation. For example, when generating a string with the grammar of Figure 2.5, the first step yields the string $zMNz$, providing the option of replacing either the nonterminal M or N in the next step. Consequently, to generate the string $zazabzbz$, one might produce the derivation

$$S \Rightarrow zMNz \Rightarrow zaMaNz \Rightarrow zazaNz \Rightarrow zazabNbz \Rightarrow zazabzbz$$

by following the rule of thumb of always applying a rewrite rule to the leftmost nonterminal in the current string (this is called a **leftmost derivation**). One might also produce the derivation

$$S \Rightarrow zMNz \Rightarrow zMbNbz \Rightarrow zMbzbz \Rightarrow zaMabzbz \Rightarrow zazabzbz$$

by always applying a rewrite rule to the rightmost nonterminal, which

$$S \rightarrow zMNz$$
$$M \rightarrow aMa$$
$$M \rightarrow z$$
$$N \rightarrow bNb$$
$$N \rightarrow z$$

Figure 2.5 A context-free grammar that generates strings of the form $za^nza^nb^mzb^mz$, where $m, n \in \mathbb{N}$

would result in a **rightmost derivation.** One could even follow other patterns and obtain other derivations of the same string.

The point is that the order in which the rewrite rules are applied has no effect when determining which strings can be generated from a given context-free grammar. This becomes clear by recognizing that *if a string can be generated by any derivation, it can be generated by a leftmost derivation.* To see this we first consider the parse tree associated with a derivation.

A **parse tree** is nothing more than a tree whose nodes represent terminals and nonterminals from the grammar, with the root node being the grammar's start symbol and the children of each nonterminal node being the symbols that replace that nonterminal in the derivation. (No terminal symbol can be an interior node of the tree, and no nonterminal symbol can be a leaf.) A parse tree for the string *zazabzbz* using the grammar of Figure 2.5 and either of the previous derivations is shown in Figure 2.6.

Now, to see that any string generated from a context-free grammar can be generated by a leftmost derivation, we observe that derivations that differ merely in the order in which rewrite rules are applied correspond to the same parse tree. The order in which the rules are applied simply reflects the order in which the branches of the parse tree are constructed. A leftmost derivation corresponds to constructing the parse tree in a left-branch-first fashion, whereas a rightmost derivation corresponds to a right-branch-first construction. However, the order in which the branches are constructed does not affect the structure of the final tree, as each branch is independent

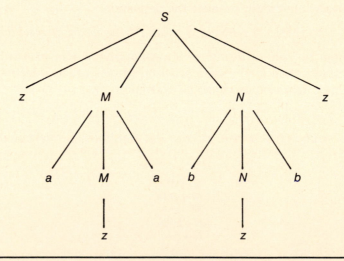

Figure 2.6 The parse tree for the string *zazabzbz* using the grammar of Figure 2.5

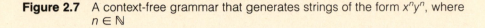

$$S \rightarrow xSy$$
$$S \rightarrow \lambda$$

Figure 2.7 A context-free grammar that generates strings of the form $x^n y^n$, where $n \in \mathbb{N}$

of the others. Thus, given a derivation that is not leftmost, one could construct the associated parse tree and then construct a leftmost derivation of the same string by a systematic "leftmost evaluation" of the tree.

Finally, we note that the flexibility allowed in context-free grammars provides for the construction of a grammar that generates the language $\{x^n y^n : n \in \mathbb{N}\}$ as shown in Figure 2.7. This example combined with the fact that any regular grammar is also a context-free grammar allows us to conclude that the context-free grammars generate a larger collection of languages than the regular grammars. We call the languages generated by context-free grammars the **context-free languages**.

Context-Free Grammars and Pushdown Automata

Before considering the relationship between context-free grammars and pushdown automata, we must clarify a point in notation. It will be convenient in the following discussions to consider single transitions that push more than one symbol on the stack such as $(p, a, s; q, xyz)$. In this case the symbols z, y, and x (in that order) are to be pushed on the stack. Hence, after executing the transition, x will be at the top of the stack (with y below it, and z on the bottom). Note that allowing transitions of this form is merely a matter of notational convenience and does not add any capabilities to the machine. Indeed, the multiple push transition $(p, a, s; q, xyz)$ could be simulated by the sequence of traditional transitions $(p, a, s; q_1, z)$, $(q_1, \lambda, \lambda; q_2, y)$, and $(q_2, \lambda, \lambda; q, x)$, where q_1 and q_2 are additional states that cannot be reached by any other sequence of transitions.

Now we must show that *the languages generated by context-free grammars are exactly the languages accepted by pushdown automata.* This we do in two stages. First, we show that for any context-free grammar G, there is a pushdown automaton M such that $L(M) = L(G)$ (Theorem 2.2). Then, we show that for any pushdown automaton M, there is a context-free grammar G such that $L(G) = L(M)$ (Theorem 2.3).

THEOREM 2.2
For each context-free grammar G, there is a pushdown automaton M such that $L(G) = L(M)$.

PROOF

Given a context-free grammar G we construct a pushdown automaton M as follows:

1. Designate the alphabet of M to be the terminal symbols of G, and the stack symbols of M to be the terminal and nonterminal symbols of G along with the special symbol #. (We may assume # is neither a terminal nor a nonterminal symbol in G.)
2. Designate the states of M to be ι, p, q, and f, ι being the initial state, and f being the only accept state.
3. Introduce the transition $(\iota, \lambda, \lambda; p, \#)$.
4. Introduce a transition $(p, \lambda, \lambda; q, S)$ where S is the start symbol in G.
5. Introduce a transition of the form $(q, \lambda, N; q, w)$ for each rewrite rule $N \rightarrow w$ in G. (Here we are using our new convention that allows a single transition to push more than one stack symbol. In particular, w may be a string of zero or more symbols including both terminals and nonterminals.)
6. Introduce a transition of the form $(q, x, x; q, \lambda)$ for each terminal x in G (i.e., for each symbol in the alphabet of M).
7. Introduce the transition $(q, \lambda, \#; f, \lambda)$.

A pushdown automaton constructed in this fashion will analyze an input string by first marking the bottom of the stack with the symbol #, then pushing the start symbol of the grammar on the stack and entering state q. From there until the symbol # returns to the top of the stack, the automaton will either pop a nonterminal from the top of the stack and replace it with the right side of an applicable rewrite rule, or it will pop a terminal from the top of the stack while reading the same terminal from the input. Once the symbol # returns to the top of the stack, the automaton will shift to its accept state f, indicating that the input consumed thus far is acceptable.

Note that the string of symbols making up the right side of a rewrite rule is pushed on the stack from right to left. Thus, the leftmost nonterminal in this string will be the first one to surface at the top of the stack; therefore, it will also be the first nonterminal on the stack to be replaced. Consequently, the automaton analyzes its input by performing a leftmost derivation according to the rules of the grammar on which it is based. But, as we have seen, the strings generated by a context-free grammar are exactly those that have a leftmost derivation. Thus, the automaton accepts exactly the same language as generated by the grammar.

■

The role of the various transitions constructed in the proof of Theorem 2.2 is probably best understood by means of an example. Let us consider the steps performed by the pushdown automaton described in the transition diagram of Figure 2.8, which was constructed from the context-free grammar in Figure 2.5. To evaluate the string *zazabzbz*, we start the machine from the configuration represented in Figure 2.9a. From this configuration the machine marks the bottom of the stack with the symbol # and shifts to state *q* while pushing the nonterminal *S* on the stack, to arrive at the configuration represented in Figure 2.9b. From this point on, the stack is used to hold a description of the structure that the machine hopes to find on the remaining part of its input stream. Thus, the *S* currently on the stack indicates that the machine hopes the remaining symbols on its input constitute a structure that can be generated from the nonterminal *S*.

However, since *S* is not a terminal the machine cannot expect to find the contents of its stack appearing on the input explicitly, and thus the nonterminal must be replaced before the machine tries to compare its stack directly to the input stream. This, in fact, is a general rule followed by the

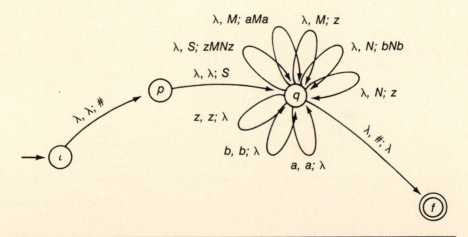

Figure 2.8   The transition diagram for a pushdown automaton constructed from the grammar of Figure 2.5 using the techniques presented in the proof of Theorem 2.2

a.

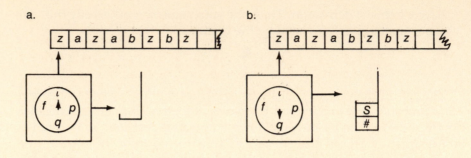

b.

c.

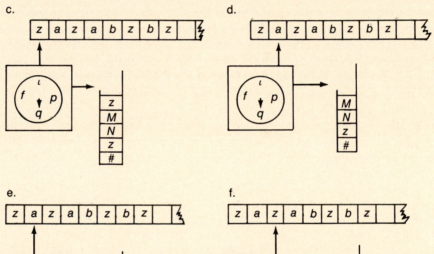

d.

e.

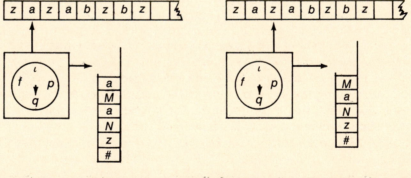

f.

Figure 2.9 A pushdown automaton at work

machine: Any time the top of the stack contains a nonterminal, that nonterminal must be replaced with an equivalent yet more detailed description of the structure. This is the purpose of the transitions introduced by rule 5 in the proof of Theorem 2.2. Their execution replaces a nonterminal on top of the stack with a more detailed description of the structure according to some rewrite rule in the original grammar. Thus, the machine in our example proceeds by executing the transition $(q, \lambda, S; q, zMNz)$ to arrive at the configuration represented in Figure 2.9c.

Now the top of the machine's stack contains the terminal z, and thus the top of the stack can be compared to the input string via the transition $(q, z, z; q, \lambda)$. After this transition is executed the machine's stack contains *MNz* and the remaining symbols in the input string are *azabzbz*, as depicted in Figure 2.9d.

Again, the top of the stack contains a nonterminal that the machine must replace. However, in contrast to the previous replacement of the nonterminal S, there are two rewrite rules that can be applied to replace the nonterminal M. The pushdown automaton could execute the transition $(q, \lambda, M; q, z)$, which would cause the machine to fail on this attempt to accept the string, or it could execute $(q, \lambda, M; q, aMa)$, which in this case would be the correct choice. (This pushdown automaton is nondeterministic.) Let us assume the correct option since our goal is to observe how the machine could accept the input string in question. (Recall that a string is in the language of a nondeterministic machine if it is *possible* for the machine to accept the string.) After executing $(q, \lambda, M; q, aMa)$ the machine appears as shown in Figure 2.9e, with the terminal a on top of the stack. This terminal is then compared to the input string via the transition $(q, a, a; q, \lambda)$, leaving the stack containing *MaNz* with the symbols *zabzbz* yet to be read from the input string, as shown in Figure 2.9f.

The remaining activities of the machine are summarized in Figure 2.10. Observe that reading the last symbol from the input uncovers the marker # on the stack. Then, the transition $(q, \lambda, \#; f, \lambda)$ transfers the machine to the accept state f where the input is declared accepted.

Let us now prepare ourselves for Theorem 2.3. Suppose we are given a pushdown automaton that accepts strings only with its stack empty. Then, from the automaton's point of view, its task is to try to move from its initial state to an accept state in such a way that its stack is in the same condition as when the computation started. How it accomplishes that goal depends on the transitions available. If, for example, ι is the machine's initial state and $(\iota, \lambda, \lambda; p, \#)$ is an available transition, then the automaton may try to accomplish its goal by first executing this transition. This would result in the machine finding itself in state p with the symbol # on its stack, and thus the goal of the machine would then be to move from state p to an accept state while removing the symbol # from its stack.

Contents of stack	Remaining input	Transition executed
λ	zazabzbz	$(\iota, \lambda, \lambda; p, \#)$
#	zazabzbz	$(p, \lambda, \lambda; q, S)$
S#	zazabzbz	$(q, \lambda, S; q, zMNz)$
zMNz#	zazabzbz	$(q, z, z; q, \lambda)$
MNz#	azabzbz	$(q, \lambda, M; q, aMa)$
aMaNz#	azabzbz	$(q, a, a; q, \lambda)$
MaNz#	zabzbz	$(q, \lambda, M; q, z)$
zaNz#	zabzbz	$(q, z, z; q, \lambda)$
aNz#	abzbz	$(q, a, a; q, \lambda)$
Nz#	bzbz	$(q, \lambda, N; q, bNb)$
bNbz#	bzbz	$(q, b, b; q, \lambda)$
Nbz#	zbz	$(q, \lambda, N; q, z)$
zbz#	zbz	$(q, z, z; q, \lambda)$
bz#	bz	$(q, b, b; q, \lambda)$
z#	z	$(q, z, z; q, \lambda)$
#	λ	$(q, \lambda, \#; f, \lambda)$

Figure 2.10   The complete analysis of the string *zazabzbz* by the pushdown automaton described in Figure 2.8

In general, we represent such a goal by $<p, x, q>$, where p and q are states and x is a stack symbol of the machine. That is, $<p, x, q>$ represents the desire to move from state p to state q in such a way that the symbol x is removed from the top of the stack. A somewhat special case is denoted by $<p, \lambda, q>$, representing the goal of moving from state p to state q in a manner that leaves the stack essentially undisturbed. That is, upon reaching state q, the stack is to be the same as it was when in state p. An example of this is the original goal of moving from the initial state to an accept state as discussed above. Indeed, for each accept state f the automaton has a major goal represented by $<\iota, \lambda, f>$, where ι is the machine's initial state.

We are now in position to show that the languages accepted by pushdown automata are context-free.

THEOREM 2.3
For each pushdown automaton M, there is a context-free grammar G such that $L(M) = L(G)$.

PROOF
Given a pushdown automaton M, our task is to produce a context-free grammar G that generates the language $L(M)$. As a result of Theorem 2.1, we can assume that the pushdown automaton M accepts strings only with its stack empty. Having made this observation,

we construct G in such a way that its nonterminals represent the goals of M, as introduced above, and its rewrite rules represent refinements of large goals in terms of smaller ones.

More precisely, we specify that the nonterminals of G consist of the start symbol S together with all the goals of M, i.e., all syntactic structures of the form $<p, x, q>$ where p and q are states in M and x is either λ or a stack symbol in M. (Thus, even if M is a small automaton, G could have a large number of nonterminals.) The terminals of G are the symbols in the alphabet of M.

We are now prepared to introduce the first collection of rewrite rules of G. These rules are obtained as follows:

1. For each accept state f of M form the rewrite rule $S \rightarrow <\iota, \lambda, f>$, where ι is the initial state of M.

Rewrite rules obtained by #1 guarantee that any derivation using this grammar will start by replacing the grammar's start symbol with a major goal of the automaton.

Another collection of rewrite rules is obtained by

2. For each state p in M form the rewrite rule $<p, \lambda, p> \rightarrow \lambda$.

Rules obtained by #2 reflect the fact that a goal of moving from a state to itself without modifying the stack can be dropped from consideration.

Each of the remaining rewrite rules in G is constructed from a transition in M by either process #3 or #4 below.

3. For each transition $(p, x, y; q, z)$ in M (where y is not λ), generate a rewrite rule $<p, y, r> \rightarrow x<q, z, r>$ for each state r in M.

Rules generated by #3 reflect the fact that the goal of moving from state p to state r while removing y from the stack may be accomplished by first moving to state q while reading x from the input and exchanging z for y on the stack (using the transition $(p, x, y; q, z)$), and then trying to move from state q to state r while removing z from the stack.

4. For each transition of the form $(p, x, \lambda; q, z)$, generate all rewrite rules of the form $<p, w, r> \rightarrow x<q, z, k><k, w, r>$, where w is either a stack symbol or λ, while k and r (possibly equal) are states of M.

Rewrite rules constructed from #4 reflect the fact that the goal of moving from state p to state r while removing w from the stack may be accomplished by first moving to state q while reading x from the input and pushing z on the stack (using the transition $(p, x, \lambda;$ $q, z)$), and then trying to move from state q to state r through some state k while removing z and w from the stack.

Observe that the rewrite rules constructed by #1 through #4 above form a context-free grammar. It remains to show that this grammar generates the same language that the automaton accepts: We must show that any string generated by the grammar can be accepted by the automaton, and that any string accepted by the automaton can be generated by the grammar. Both of these statements will follow if we prove the following claim.

A nonterminal of the form <p, α, q> *(where α is either λ or a stack symbol) can be rewritten as a string of terminals* w *by applying rules of the grammar if and only if the automaton can move from state* p *to state* q *along a path whose traversal results in α being removed from the stack and the string* w *being read from the machine's tape.*

Let us proceed by proving the "only if" portion of this claim, using induction on the number of steps required to rewrite $<p, \alpha, q>$ into w. If just one step is required, then the nonterminal $<p, \alpha, q>$ must actually be $<p, \lambda, p>$ since this is the only form of nonterminal that can be rewritten as a terminal string in a single step. This in turn means that w must be λ. Thus, our claim holds for this base case since the automaton can always move from some state p to p while removing nothing from the stack and reading nothing from its tape.

Now, let us assume that the desired path in the automaton is present for any case in which a nonterminal representing some goal can be rewritten as a string of terminals in n or fewer steps, and suppose that $<p, \alpha, q>$ can be rewritten as the string w of terminals in $n + 1$ steps. Note that the first step of this process must be the application of a rewrite rule from either #3 or #4 above. Let us suppose it is obtained from #3 by the transition $(p, w_1, \alpha; r, \beta)$. (The case of #4 is only a slight generalization of this case.) The first step of the rewriting process appears as $<p, \alpha, q> \Rightarrow w_1<r, \beta, q>$. This means that the rest of the rewriting process converts $<r, \beta, q>$ into a string w_2, such that $w = w_1w_2$, in only n steps. Thus, by our induction hypothesis, the automaton can move from state r to state q with the net effect of reading w_2 while removing β from its stack. By preceding this computation with the transition $(p, w_1, \alpha; r, \beta)$, we obtain a computation that starts in state p and moves to state q while reading the string w from the tape and removing α from the stack. Hence, we can conclude that the "only if" portion of our claim must hold.

Let us now consider the "if" portion of the claim. Again we apply induction, but this time on the length of the path from p to q. If this path has length zero, the path requires no transitions and q must be equal to p. Hence, the single rewrite rule $<p, \lambda, p> \to \lambda$ suffices.

Next we assume that if the automaton can move from any state r to some state s, along a path consisting of no more than n transitions and whose traversal results in the string v being read from the tape and α (where α is λ or a stack symbol) being removed from the stack, then there are rewrite rules in the grammar that allow $<p, \alpha, q>$ to be rewritten as w. Consider a path of $n + 1$ steps from state p to q whose traversal results in the string w being read from the tape and α (where α is λ or a stack symbol) being removed from the stack. Let us suppose that the first step along this path is the execution of the transition $(p, w_1, \alpha; t, z)$, where $\alpha \neq \lambda$. (The other possible first steps are handled similarly.) Then, the remaining portion of the path must move from state t to state q in only n transitions and result in removing nothing from the stack while reading the string w_2, where $w = w_1 w_2$, from the tape. By our induction hypothesis, however, this means there must be rewrite rules in the grammar that allow $<t, \lambda, q>$ to be rewritten as w_2. Moreover, the existence of the transition $(p, w_1, \alpha; t, z)$ implies the existence of the rule $<p, \alpha, q> \to w_1 <t, \lambda, q>$. Thus, the nonterminal $<p, \alpha, q>$ can be rewritten as w by first applying this rule and then proceeding to rewrite $<t, \lambda, q>$ as w_2.

We conclude that both the "if" and "only if" portions of our claim must hold, and hence the context-free grammar constructed from #1, #2, #3, and #4 must generate the same language that is accepted by the pushdown automaton M.

■

Again, an example should help clarify many of the points in the preceding proof. Consider the task of building a context-free grammar that accepts the language $\{cb^n c : n \in \mathbb{N}^+\}$ from the pushdown automaton of Figure 2.11. Our first observation is that there are numerous nonterminals in the resulting grammar, including the start symbol S plus one nonterminal of the form $<p, x, q>$ for each triple (p, x, q), where x is either λ or c (since c is the only stack symbol), and p and q (possibly equal) are states in the machine. Moreover, there are numerous rewrite rules that can be formed as shown in Figure 2.12, where the rules are listed together with their associated transition where appropriate. Finally, a derivation of the string

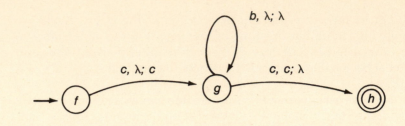

Figure 2.11   A transition diagram for a pushdown automaton that accepts $\{cb^nc: n \in \mathbb{N}^+\}$

cbbc is shown in Figure 2.13. Here we see that the rewrite rules associated with transitions that read symbols from the machine's input introduce these same symbols into the string being derived. Thus, once the derivation process has removed all the nonterminals, the symbols found in the remaining string are exactly those that would have been read by the corresponding computation of the pushdown automata.

In summary, we now have two characterizations for the context-free languages. They are the languages accepted by pushdown automata as well as the languages generated by context-free grammars.

Chomsky Normal Form

One benefit of classifying languages in terms of grammars is that such classifications provide insights into the string structures that may appear in the corresponding languages. At first glance, however, the flexibility allowed in context-free grammars appears to place little restriction on the potential string structures that might be found in context-free languages. Hence, you may be surprised to learn that context-free languages do in fact have grammars whose rewrite rules conform to extremely rigid formats. Let us, then, investigate more thoroughly the structure of the rewrite rules found in context-free grammars.

We start our investigation by considering the necessity of λ-rules in a context-free grammar. If the language generated by the grammar contains the empty string, then at least one λ-rule must appear in the grammar; otherwise, there would be no way of deriving the empty string from the grammar's start symbol. However, we might ask to what extent λ-rules are required if the language to be generated does not contain the empty string.

To answer this question, we first note that the existence of a λ-rule may allow more nonterminals than just the nonterminal appearing in the rule to be rewritten as the empty string. For instance, if a grammar contained the rules $N \rightarrow \lambda$ and $M \rightarrow N$, then both M and N could be rewritten as λ

From rule 1

$S \rightarrow <f, \lambda, h>$

From rule 2

$<f, \lambda, f> \rightarrow \lambda$
$<g, \lambda, g> \rightarrow \lambda$
$<h, \lambda, h> \rightarrow \lambda$

From rule 3, transition $(g, c, c; h, \lambda)$

$<g, c, f> \rightarrow c <h, \lambda, f>$
$<g, c, g> \rightarrow c <h, \lambda, g>$
$<g, c, h> \rightarrow c <h, \lambda, h>$

From rule 4, transition $(f, c, \lambda; g, c)$

$<f, \lambda, f> \rightarrow c <g, c, f> <f, \lambda, f>$	$<f, c, f> \rightarrow c <g, c, f> <f, c, f>$
$<f, \lambda, f> \rightarrow c <g, c, g> <g, \lambda, f>$	$<f, c, f> \rightarrow c <g, c, g> <g, c, f>$
$<f, \lambda, f> \rightarrow c <g, c, h> <h, \lambda, f>$	$<f, c, f> \rightarrow c <g, c, h> <h, c, f>$
$<f, \lambda, g> \rightarrow c <g, c, f> <f, \lambda, g>$	$<f, c, g> \rightarrow c <g, c, f> <f, c, g>$
$<f, \lambda, g> \rightarrow c <g, c, g> <g, \lambda, g>$	$<f, c, g> \rightarrow c <g, c, g> <g, c, g>$
$<f, \lambda, g> \rightarrow c <g, c, h> <h, \lambda, g>$	$<f, c, g> \rightarrow c <g, c, h> <h, c, g>$
$<f, \lambda, h> \rightarrow c <g, c, f> <f, \lambda, h>$	$<f, c, h> \rightarrow c <g, c, f> <f, c, h>$
$<f, \lambda, h> \rightarrow c <g, c, g> <g, \lambda, h>$	$<f, c, h> \rightarrow c <g, c, g> <g, c, h>$
$<f, \lambda, h> \rightarrow c <g, c, h> <h, \lambda, h>$	$<f, c, h> \rightarrow c <g, c, h> <h, c, h>$

From rule 4, transition $(g, b, \lambda; g, \lambda)$

$<g, \lambda, f> \rightarrow b <g, \lambda, f> <f, \lambda, f>$	$<g, c, f> \rightarrow b <g, \lambda, f> <f, c, f>$
$<g, \lambda, f> \rightarrow b <g, \lambda, g> <g, \lambda, f>$	$<g, c, f> \rightarrow b <g, \lambda, g> <g, c, f>$
$<g, \lambda, f> \rightarrow b <g, \lambda, h> <h, \lambda, f>$	$<g, c, f> \rightarrow b <g, \lambda, h> <h, c, f>$
$<g, \lambda, g> \rightarrow b <g, \lambda, f> <f, \lambda, g>$	$<g, c, g> \rightarrow b <g, \lambda, f> <f, c, g>$
$<g, \lambda, g> \rightarrow b <g, \lambda, g> <g, \lambda, g>$	$<g, c, g> \rightarrow b <g, \lambda, g> <g, c, g>$
$<g, \lambda, g> \rightarrow b <g, \lambda, h> <h, \lambda, g>$	$<g, c, g> \rightarrow b <g, \lambda, h> <h, c, g>$
$<g, \lambda, h> \rightarrow b <g, \lambda, f> <f, \lambda, h>$	$<g, c, h> \rightarrow b <g, \lambda, f> <f, c, h>$
$<g, \lambda, h> \rightarrow b <g, \lambda, g> <g, \lambda, h>$	$<g, c, h> \rightarrow b <g, \lambda, g> <g, c, h>$
$<g, \lambda, h> \rightarrow b <g, \lambda, h> <h, \lambda, h>$	$<g, c, h> \rightarrow b <g, \lambda, h> <h, c, h>$

Figure 2.12   The rewrite rules obtained from the pushdown automaton in Figure 2.11

$$S \Rightarrow <f, \lambda, h>$$
$$\Rightarrow c<g, c, h> <h, \lambda, h>$$
$$\Rightarrow cb<g, \lambda, g> <g, c, h> <h, \lambda, h>$$
$$\Rightarrow cb<g, c, h> <h, \lambda, h>$$
$$\Rightarrow cbb<g, \lambda, g> <g, c, h> <h, \lambda, h>$$
$$\Rightarrow cbb<g, c, h> <h, \lambda, h>$$
$$\Rightarrow cbbc<h, \lambda, h> <h, \lambda, h>$$
$$\Rightarrow cbbc<h, \lambda, h>$$
$$\Rightarrow cbbc$$

Figure 2.13 The derivation of *cbbc* using rewrite rules in Figure 2.12

even though the rule $M \rightarrow \lambda$ may not be in the grammar. To identify the effect of the λ-rules in a context-free grammar, we must isolate all the nonterminals that can be rewritten as the empty string. To this end we define a λ-chain of length n to be a sequence of rules of the form $N_n \rightarrow N_{n-1}$, $N_{n-1} \rightarrow N_{n-2}, \cdots, N_0 \rightarrow \lambda$, and define the nonterminal N_n to be the origin of the chain.

Now, if G is a context-free grammar that does not generate the empty string, we define U_0 to be the set of nonterminals appearing as the origin of λ-chains of length zero, that is, the nonterminals that appear on the left side of λ-rules. To this set we add the origins of all λ-chains of length one to form another set, U_1. Then to U_1 we add the origins of all λ-chains of length two to obtain a set called U_2, etc. (If G were the grammar in Figure 2.14a, then U_0 would be $\{Q\}$ and U_1 would be $\{P, Q\}$.)

Because there are only a finite number of nonterminals in a grammar, there must be a point at which this process of constructing sets ceases to introduce additional nonterminals. At this point we would have collected all the nonterminals in G that can be rewritten as the empty string. We denote this set by U. (Note that since G does not generate the empty string, U cannot contain the start symbol of G.)

Now for each rewrite rule of the form $N \rightarrow w$, where w is a string of terminals and nonterminals, we add to G all rules of the form $N \rightarrow w'$, where w' is any *nonempty* string obtained by removing one or more occurrences of nonterminals in U from w. (Again, referring to Figure 2.14a, the set U would be $\{P, Q\}$ so we would add the following rules to the grammar.

$$\left.\begin{array}{l} S \rightarrow zPzz \\ S \rightarrow zzQz \\ S \rightarrow zzz \end{array}\right\} \text{from } S \rightarrow zPzQz$$

$$P \rightarrow xx \qquad \text{from } P \rightarrow xPx$$
$$Q \rightarrow yy \qquad \text{from } Q \rightarrow yPy$$

a.　$S \rightarrow zPzQz$　　　　b.　$S \rightarrow zPzQz$
　　$P \rightarrow xPx$　　　　　　　$S \rightarrow zzQz$
　　$P \rightarrow Q$　　　　　　　　$S \rightarrow zPzz$
　　$Q \rightarrow yPy$　　　　　　　$S \rightarrow zzz$
　　$Q \rightarrow \lambda$　　　　　　　$P \rightarrow xPx$
　　　　　　　　　　　　　$P \rightarrow xx$
　　　　　　　　　　　　　$P \rightarrow Q$
　　　　　　　　　　　　　$Q \rightarrow yPy$
　　　　　　　　　　　　　$Q \rightarrow yy$

Figure 2.14　A context-free grammar (that does not generate the empty string) and another grammar that generates the same language without using λ-rules

Note that we do not add the rule $P \rightarrow \lambda$ that would be obtained from the rule $P \rightarrow Q$. See Figure 2.14b.)

Having added these new rules to the grammar, we no longer need the λ-rules. Indeed, suppose a derivation of a string using the original grammar required the application of some λ-rule, and let N be the origin of the longest λ-chain appearing in the derivation that terminates with this λ-rule. Then, this occurrence of N must be introduced in the derivation by the application of some rule of the form $M \rightarrow w_1 N w_2$ where w_1 and w_2 are strings of terminals and nonterminals, one of which must be nonempty. (N was chosen as the origin of the λ-chain which terminates with the λ-rule. Moreover, N is not the start symbol since $N \in U$ and $S \notin U$.) This means that the rule $M \rightarrow w_1 w_2$ is one of the rules that we added to the grammar. Hence, we can eliminate the use of the λ-rule in the derivation by using the rule $M \rightarrow w_1 w_2$ rather than $M \rightarrow w_1 N w_2$. In this manner, we can eliminate any use of λ-rules in any derivation. In turn, we can remove all the λ-rules from the grammar without reducing its generative powers.

As an example, consider the derivation in Figure 2.15a based on the grammar of Figure 2.14a. The last step of this derivation uses the λ-rule $Q \rightarrow \lambda$. The origin of the λ-chain that led to the use of this rule is the nonterminal Q introduced in the first step of the derivation. Thus, we change this step using the new rule $S \rightarrow zPzz$ to obtain the derivation in Figure 2.15b. This derivation uses the λ-rule $Q \rightarrow \lambda$ in its last step. The origin of the λ-chain leading to this rule is the nonterminal P introduced in the second step. Thus, we alter this step to take advantage of the new rule $P \rightarrow xx$, thereby obtaining the derivation in Figure 2.15c that uses only rules from the modified grammar in Figure 2.14b.

Finally, we note that the grammar resulting from this λ-rule removal

a. $S \Rightarrow$ zPzQz
      $\Rightarrow$ zxPxzQz
      $\Rightarrow$ zxQxzQz
      $\Rightarrow$ zxxzQz
      $\Rightarrow$ zxxzz

b. $S \Rightarrow$ zPzz
      $\Rightarrow$ zxPxzz
      $\Rightarrow$ zxQxzz
      $\Rightarrow$ zxxzz

c. $S \Rightarrow$ zPzz
      $\Rightarrow$ zxxzz

Figure 2.15   Modifying a derivation based on the grammar of Figure 2.14a to obtain a derivation based on the grammar of Figure 2.14b

process cannot generate strings that were not generated by the original grammar. After all, any of the rules that were added can be simulated by short sequences of rules from the original grammar. Hence, we conclude that *any context-free language that does not contain the empty string can be generated by a context-free grammar having no λ-rules.*

Using this conclusion as a springboard, we can prove the following theorem.

THEOREM 2.4

If L is a context-free language that does not contain the empty string, then there is a context-free grammar G such that $L(G) = L$ and the right side of any rewrite rule in G consists of either a single terminal or exactly two nonterminals.

PROOF

Let L be a context-free language that does not contain the empty string. We already know that L can be generated by a context-free grammar G that does not contain any λ-rules. Our approach is to modify this grammar so that it conforms to the restrictions of the theorem.

For each terminal x in G, we introduce a new, unique nonterminal X and the rewrite rule $X \to x$, and then replace all occurrences of the terminal x in the other rules of G with X. This produces a context-free grammar G' in which the right side of each rewrite rule is a single terminal or a string of nonterminals. Moreover, $L(G') = L(G)$.

We now replace each rule in G' of the form

$$N \rightarrow N_1 N_2 \cdots N_n$$

where $n > 2$, with the collection of rules

$$N \rightarrow N_1 R_1$$
$$R_1 \rightarrow N_2 R_2$$

$$\cdot$$
$$\cdot$$
$$\cdot$$

$$R_{n-1} \rightarrow N_{n-1} N_n$$

where each R_k is a unique nonterminal that appears nowhere else in the grammar. Clearly, this modification does not change the language generated by the grammar.

At this stage we have a context-free grammar G' that generates L and for which the right side of each rewrite rule is a single terminal, two nonterminals, or a single nonterminal. Hence, our remaining task is to remove the rules of the latter form. To do this we consider each sequence of rewrite rules of the form $N_n \rightarrow N_{n-1}$, $N_{n-1} \rightarrow N_{n-2}, \cdots, N_2 \rightarrow N_1$, introduce the rule $N_n \rightarrow x$ if $N_1 \rightarrow x$ is a rule in G', and introduce the rule $N_n \rightarrow AB$ if $N_1 \rightarrow AB$ is in G'. With these rules added, we can remove all the rules whose right sides contain a single nonterminal without reducing the generative powers of the grammar. After all, any derivation that took advantage of rules of the form $M \rightarrow N$ could be modified to use the rules just introduced instead. Thus, the resulting grammar generates L and satisfies the restrictions of the theorem.

■

To clarify the steps of the preceding proof, consider how they would affect the grammar in Figure 2.16a, with start symbol S. The first step would introduce the new nonterminals X, Y, and Z and convert the grammar to the grammar G' shown in Figure 2.16b. Next, the rule $S \rightarrow ZMZ$ would be replaced by the pair of rules $S \rightarrow ZR_1$ and $R_1 \rightarrow MZ$, and $M \rightarrow YMY$ would be replaced by $M \rightarrow YP_1$ and $P_1 \rightarrow MY$, to obtain the grammar in Figure 2.16c. Finally, the sequence $N \rightarrow X$ and the sequence $M \rightarrow N$ and $N \rightarrow X$ would give rise to the rules $N \rightarrow x$ and $M \rightarrow x$, producing the grammar in Figure 2.16d.

a. $S \to zMz$
    $M \to N$
    $M \to yMy$
    $N \to x$

b. $S \to ZMZ$
    $M \to N$
    $M \to YMY$
    $N \to X$
    $X \to x$
    $Y \to y$
    $Z \to z$

c. $S \to ZR_1$
    $R_1 \to MZ$
    $M \to N$
    $M \to YP_1$
    $P_1 \to MY$
    $N \to X$
    $X \to x$
    $Y \to y$
    $Z \to z$

d. $S \to ZR_1$
    $R_1 \to MZ$
    $M \to x$
    $M \to YP_1$
    $P_1 \to MY$
    $N \to x$
    $X \to x$
    $Y \to y$
    $Z \to z$

Figure 2.16 Applying the process described in the proof of Theorem 2.4

A grammar whose rewrite rules conform to the restrictions of Theorem 2.4 is said to be in **Chomsky normal form** (named for N. Chomsky). For example, the grammar

$$S \to XM$$
$$M \to SY$$
$$X \to x$$
$$Y \to y$$

whose start symbol is S is in Chomsky normal form, whereas

$$S \to xSy$$
$$S \to xy$$

which generates the same language, is not in Chomsky normal form.

In short, then, Theorem 2.4 says that any context-free language that does not contain the empty string can be generated by a context-free grammar in Chomsky normal form. Although it is limited to a subset of the context-free languages, this characterization is still quite general. For example, most languages in applied settings, such as programming languages, do not contain the empty string; even for those languages which do contain the empty string the characterization still has merit. Indeed, if a context-free language L contains λ, we can find a context-free grammar that is "almost" in Chomsky normal form but still generates L. To do this we first find a context-free grammar G in Chomsky normal form that generates

Grammar for $L-\{\lambda\}$ with start symbol S	Grammar for L with start symbol S'
	$S' \to \lambda$ $\quad$ $S' \to MN$ $\quad$ } New rules
$S \to MN$	$S \to MN$
$N \to MS$	$N \to MS$
$N \to x$	$N \to x$
$M \to x$	$M \to x$

Figure 2.17 Modifying a Chomsky normal form grammar that generates $L - \{\lambda\}$ to obtain a new grammar that generates L

$L - \{\lambda\}$. Then, we modify G by adding a new nonterminal S' that becomes the modified grammar's start symbol; next we add the rule $S' \to \lambda$ (so that the modified grammar will generate λ); and finally for each rule in G whose left side consists of the old start symbol of G, we add a new rule in which the new nonterminal S' has been substituted on the left side in place of the old start symbol (see Figure 2.17). Clearly this modified grammar will generate those strings and only those strings in the language L. (Introducing the new start symbol S' eliminates the possibility of the λ-rule interacting with other rules in the grammar.) Consequently, even context-free languages that contain the empty string can be generated by grammars that are almost in Chomsky normal form.

Exercises

1. Show that each string derived from a context-free grammar by a leftmost derivation can also be derived by a rightmost derivation.

2. A grammar that allows more than one parse tree for a single string is said to be ambiguous (see Appendix C, Section C.1). Show that the grammar below is ambiguous by showing that the string *ictictses* has derivations that produce different parse trees.

$$S \to ictS$$
$$S \to ictSeS$$
$$S \to s$$

(You will recognize this problem as one you have probably encountered before if you associate the following words with the terminal symbols in the above grammar: $i = $ if, $c = $ condition, $t = $ then, $e = $ else, and $s = $ statement.)

3. Use the procedure described in Theorem 2.3 to construct a context-free grammar that generates the language accepted by the pushdown automaton whose transition diagram is shown below.

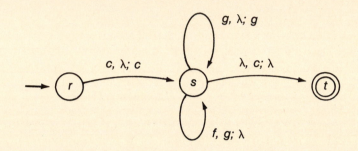

4. Show that the union of two context-free languages is context-free by showing how two context-free grammars for the original languages can be combined to form a context-free grammar that generates the union.

5. Convert the following grammar, with start symbol S, into a grammar in Chomsky normal form that generates the same language.

$$S \rightarrow xSy$$
$$S \rightarrow wNz$$
$$N \rightarrow S$$
$$N \rightarrow \lambda$$

2.3   THE LIMITS OF PUSHDOWN AUTOMATA

At this point we have characterized the context-free languages both as those languages that are generated by context-free grammars and as those languages accepted by pushdown automata. However, we have not yet considered the scope of these languages: We have not asked whether or not there are languages that are not context-free. Moreover, the pushdown automata we have considered thus far have been nondeterministic, and since our plan is to develop compiler design tools based on the properties of pushdown automata, it behooves us to understand the role of determinism within pushdown automata. These are the concerns addressed in this section.

The Scope of Context-Free Languages

We first present a language that is not context-free. For this we use the following theorem, which is known as a **pumping lemma** because it shows how strings in some context-free languages can be produced by "pumping up" portions of other strings.

THEOREM 2.5

If L is a context-free language containing infinitely many strings, then there must be a string in L of the form $svuwt$, where s, v, u, w, and t are substrings, at least one of v and w is nonempty, and sv^nuw^nt is in L for each $n \in \mathbb{N}^+$.

PROOF

Let L be a context-free language containing infinitely many strings, and let G be a context-free grammar such that $L(G) = L$. Let m be the maximum number of symbols (terminals and nonterminals) found on the right side of any rewrite rule in G, i.e., m is the length of the longest right side among the rewrite rules in G. Then each node in a parse tree based on G can have at most m children. In turn, any parse tree of depth d can produce a string of length at most m^d (where the depth of a tree is the number of edges in the longest path from the root to a leaf).

Now let j be the number of nonterminal symbols in G, and pick a string in L of length greater than m^j. Then, any parse tree T for that string must have depth greater than j. This implies that there is a path in T from the root to a leaf containing more than j nonterminals. Consequently, some nonterminal N must appear at least twice on the path. Let us consider the subtree of T whose root node is the highest occurrence of N on this path, and in which the next occurrence of N is a leaf (as indicated by the shaded region in Figure 2.18). In other words, we consider the subtree of T whose root is the highest occurrence of N and then throw away everything below the next occurrence of N.

This subtree indicates that the pattern vNw is derived from the first occurrence of N, where v and w are the concatenations of the leaves of the subtree to the left and right of the second N, respectively (again see Figure 2.18). We can assume that either v or w must be nonempty, for otherwise we could remove the shaded region of Figure 2.18 to obtain the tree in Figure 2.19a, thereby shortening the path we have chosen. But if all paths of length greater than j could be shortened in this manner, we could produce a parse tree for the chosen string of depth less than j—a contradiction.

Observe that other parse trees can be constructed by repeating copies of the selected subtree an arbitrary number of times as shown in Figure 2.19b, and each such parse tree represents a string that

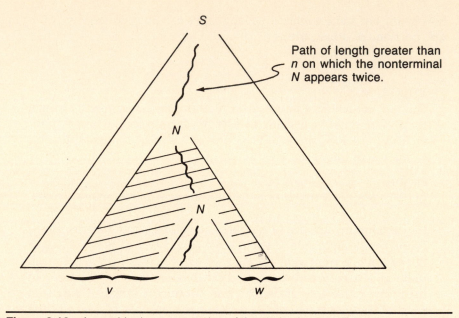

Path of length greater than *n* on which the nonterminal *N* appears twice.

Figure 2.18   A graphical representation of the derivation tree *T*

can be generated by the grammar G. Thus, G generates strings that contain structures of the form $v^i N w^i$ for each positive integer i. In turn, there must be a string in L of the form $svuwt$ where $sv^n uw^n t$ is in L for each $n \in \mathbb{N}^+$, as claimed in the theorem.

■

A consequence of Theorem 2.5 is that the language $\{x^n y^n z^n : n \in \mathbb{N}^+\}$ is not context-free. Indeed, this language contains infinitely many strings, but there is no string in the language that contains segments that can be repeated as dictated by the theorem and still produce strings in the language. (If each of the two repeated segments consist of only xs, only ys, or only zs, then the result will no longer contain the same number of each symbol. Furthermore, if we repeat a segment with more than one type of symbol, then the result will either have ys occurring before xs or zs before ys.)

The fact that the language $\{x^n y^n z^n : n \in \mathbb{N}^+\}$ is not context-free might seem insignificant, so let us consider an example where such patterns occur. Within a typical word processor, words to be underlined when printed are sometimes stored as a string of symbols—the word—followed by the same number of back spaces, followed by the same number of underlines. Such underlined words therefore constitute strings that conform to the pattern

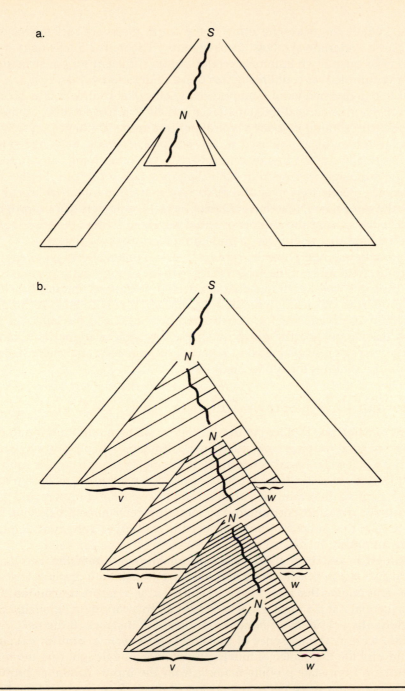

Figure 2.19 Parse trees that can be constructed by modifying the tree in Figure 2.17

$x^n y^n z^n$, where the xs are the letters in the word, the ys are back spaces, and the zs are underline symbols. Consequently, Theorem 2.5 tells us that the powers of pushdown automata would not be sufficient for constructing a parsing routine that could recognize these underlined words.

If this underlined-word example seems somewhat contrived, it is because the collection of context-free languages comes very close to encompassing the structures found in today's typical programming languages. In fact, the popular syntax diagrams used to express programming language syntax are essentially context-free rewrite rules. On the other hand, there are still several language features that such diagrams fail to capture. Syntax diagrams are unable to convey the restriction that different variables cannot have the same name, that the number of formal parameters of a subprogram must be the same as the number of actual parameters when the subprogram is called, and that references to undefined identifiers are illegal.

Nonetheless, the power of context-free grammars allows us to capture a significant number of the syntax rules of today's programming languages, and thus it is well worth our time to develop parsing techniques based on the properties of pushdown automata. In fact, it is with such techniques that many compilers are now constructed. In these cases the language features that lie outside the grasp of context-free grammars are handled as special cases or else evaluated as a part of the semantic analysis instead of within the routines for syntax analysis.

Deterministic Pushdown Automata

There remains one problem to resolve before we turn our attention to producing parsing routines from pushdown automata. The pushdown automata discussed so far have been nondeterministic, and our compiler routines must be deterministic. If we are to use pushdown automata as design tools for developing deterministic parsing routines, we should understand what limitations, if any, are encountered by requiring deterministic behavior. Our first step in this direction is to introduce the concept of deterministic pushdown automata.

Roughly speaking, a **deterministic pushdown automaton** is a pushdown automaton in which one and only one transition is applicable at any time. This implies that if $(p, x, y; q, z)$ and $(p, x, y; r, w)$ are transitions, then q must equal r and z must equal w. However, this condition alone does not preclude the possibility of nondeterminism. For instance, if the next input symbol were x, the presence of transitions $(p, \lambda, y; q, z)$ and $(p, x, y; q, z)$ would provide the choice of moving from state p while ignoring the input or moving from state p while reading from the input. A similar problem would occur if a machine with y on top of its stack were given the choice between $(p, \lambda, \lambda; q, z)$ and $(p, x, y; q, z)$. Should the machine move from state p while ignoring the stack or move from state p while popping a symbol from the stack?

Based on these observations, we define a deterministic pushdown automaton to be a pushdown automaton $(S, \Sigma, \Gamma, T, \iota, F)$ such that for each triple (p, x, y) in $S \times \Sigma \times \Gamma$, there is one and only one transition in T of the form $(p, u, v; q, z)$, where (u, v) is in $\{(x, y), (x, \lambda), (\lambda, y), (\lambda, \lambda)\}$, q is in S, and z is in Γ. For example, this restriction would rule out the presence of both $(p, \lambda, y; q, z)$ and $(p, x, \lambda; r, s)$, since both (x, λ) and (λ, y) are in $\{(x, y), (x, \lambda), (\lambda, y), (\lambda, \lambda)\}$.

To emphasize the subtleties involved in the development of a deterministic pushdown automaton, suppose we wanted to design a portion of such a machine so that when in state p the transition $(p, x, y; q, \lambda)$ will be executed if a y is on top of the stack, whereas the transition $(p, x, \lambda; q, \lambda)$ will be executed otherwise. There is no uncertainty involved here, but the simple approach shown in Figure 2.20a introduces some nonetheless. In particular, the diagram would allow the machine a choice if the top of the stack contained a y; both $(p, x, y; q, \lambda)$ and $(p, x, \lambda; q, \lambda)$ would be applicable. To resolve this problem we turn to the approach shown in Figure 2.20b, where we have assumed that the stack symbols of the machine are x, y, and #. There we have introduced explicit options for the machine to take in case the symbol on top of the stack is not a y. In such cases the machine is told to pop a symbol from the stack and then push it back on again. Of course, this approach requires that the stack be nonempty when

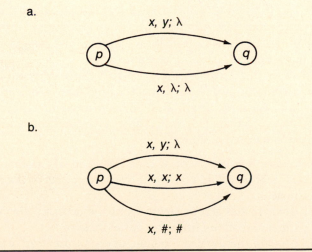

Figure 2.20 A portion of a transition diagram for a pushdown automaton that introduces nondeterminism and its deterministic counterpart

the machine is in state p for otherwise none of the transitions would be applicable. This is why we have introduced the stack symbol # that is assumed to be placed on the bottom of the stack at the beginning of any computation and kept there until the end.

As in the previous chapter, our use of the term deterministic implies that the system is fully defined. However, the claims we are about to make regarding deterministic pushdown automata are valid regardless of whether or not the automata involved are fully defined. Moreover, requiring that the automata be fully defined results in rather cluttered diagrams. As we saw in the case of finite automata, including arcs for all possible cases can become an exercise in patience rather than content (compare Figure 1.5 to Figure 1.11). Thus, when drawing diagrams for deterministic pushdown automata, we will often represent only those transitions that are pertinent to the task at hand, with the understanding that the resulting skeletal diagrams could be completed if necessary.

Our next task is to decide whether or not requiring deterministic behavior reduces the power of the pushdown automata. To our dismay, it does as shown by the following theorem.

THEOREM 2.6
There is a context-free language that is not the language accepted by any deterministic pushdown automaton.

PROOF
We prove this theorem by showing that the language $L = \{x^n y^n: n \in \mathbb{N}^+\} \cup \{x^n y^{2n}: n \in \mathbb{N}^+\}$ is context-free but cannot be the language accepted by any deterministic pushdown automaton. First, observe that Figure 2.21 shows a transition diagram for a pushdown automaton that accepts L. Thus, L is context-free.

To show that L cannot be accepted by any deterministic pushdown automaton, we show that assuming otherwise leads to a contradiction. Assume, then, that M is a deterministic pushdown automaton such that $L(M) = L$. Using M we construct another pushdown automaton as follows:

1. Create two copies of M called M_1 and M_2. States in M_1 and M_2 will be called cousins if they are copies of the same state in M.
2. Remove the accept status from the accept states of M_1 and the initial status from the initial state of M_2.
3. Change the destination state of each transition originating at an old accept state in M_1 to the destination's cousin in M_2. (These altered transitions form links between M_1 and M_2 in

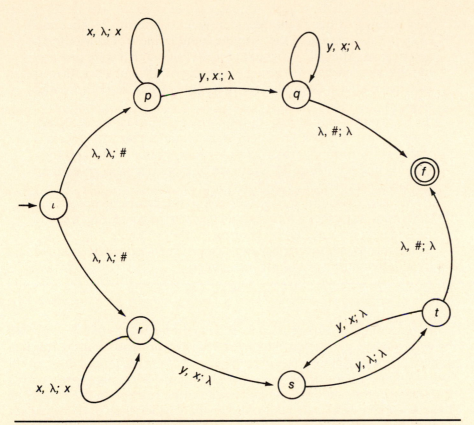

Figure 2.21   A transition diagram for a pushdown automaton M for which $L(M) = \{x^n y^n : n \in \mathbb{N}^+\} \cup \{x^n y^{2n} : n \in \mathbb{N}^+\}$

such a way that the two machines become a single pushdown automaton.)

4. Modify all those transitions that read a y from the input and have their destination states in M_2 (possibly including those transitions altered in step 3 above), so that they read the symbol z instead.

We claim that the language accepted by the pushdown automaton so constructed from M_1 and M_2 would be $\{x^n y^n z^n : n \in \mathbb{N}\}$. Indeed, if this machine were given an input string of the form $x^n y^n z^n$, it would have to reach one of the old accept states of M_1 after reading the xs and ys but before reading any zs. (The original M_1 would have accepted $x^n y^n$, and since it is deterministic, it must reach the same state after reading $x^n y^n$ regardless of what symbols may follow.) At this point execution would shift into M_2 (because of step 3 above), where the zs in the input string would lead to an accept state. After all, M_2 would proceed as though it were processing the latter portion of a string of the form $x^n y^{2n}$, but since its read instructions have been altered, it would actually read zs instead of ys.

To see that only strings of the form $x^n y^n z^n$ could be accepted, observe that to reach an accept state requires that M_1 process a string of the form $x^n y^n$ in order to transfer control to M_2, and then that M_2 find n zs, since M_2 proceeds as though it were processing the latter part of $x^n y^{2n}$.

We see, then, that our assumption that L can be accepted by a deterministic pushdown automaton leads to the conclusion that the language $\{x^n y^n z^n : n \in \mathbb{N}\}$ is context-free. But we know this is false. Consequently, our assumption must be in error: L cannot be accepted by a deterministic pushdown automaton.

■

In recognition of Theorem 2.6 we refer to the languages that are accepted by deterministic pushdown automata as the **deterministic context-free languages.** The fact that this class of languages does not include all the context-free languages indicates that our goal of building deterministic parsing routines based on pushdown automata will not be reached in the case of all the context-free languages, but only for the smaller class of deterministic context-free languages.

In fact, the picture is even bleaker. The deterministic pushdown automata we are considering accept strings without necessarily emptying their stacks, and as mentioned earlier, such a model is likely to lead to program segments that clutter a computer's memory with remnants of previous calculations. Unfortunately, this problem is more serious for deterministic pushdown automata than it is for ordinary pushdown automata, since we cannot modify every deterministic pushdown automaton so that it empties its stack before reaching an accept state.

To convince ourselves of this, consider the language L obtained by forming the union of $\{x^n : n \in \mathbb{N}\}$ and $\{x^n y^n : n \in \mathbb{N}\}$, which is accepted by the deterministic pushdown automaton represented by the skeletal diagram in Figure 2.22, and is therefore a deterministic context-free language. We claim that L cannot be accepted by a deterministic pushdown automaton that is required to empty its stack before reaching an accept state. Indeed, if M were such a machine and was given an input of the form $x^n y^n$, it would have to reach an accept state with an empty stack after reading each x. (Since the machine is deterministic, it must follow the same execution path

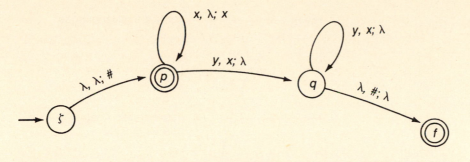

Figure 2.22 A skeletal diagram for a deterministic pushdown automaton M for which $L(M) = \{x^n: n \in \mathbb{N}^+\} \cup \{x^n y^n: n \in \mathbb{N}^+\}$

while processing the xs in $x^n y^n$ that it would follow when processing any string of xs, and since any string of xs is itself an acceptable string, the machine must empty its stack and move to an accept state after reading each x.) Now if we pick n to be greater than the number of states in M, we can conclude that at some point when processing the xs in the string $x^n y^n$ the machine must be in some state p with its stack empty at least twice. If m is the number of xs read between these visits to p, M must accept the string $x^{n+m} y^n$, which contradicts the definition of M.

In summary, we have found a hierarchy of languages associated with pushdown automata, as illustrated in Figure 2.23. The largest class is the collection of context-free languages that are accepted by general pushdown automata. Properly contained within this class are the deterministic context-free languages that are accepted by deterministic pushdown automata (those that are not required to empty their stacks). Then, properly contained within the class of deterministic context-free languages are the languages that can be accepted by deterministic pushdown automata that empty their stacks before accepting an input string.

The Lookahead Principle

At this point our hope of developing useable program segments for parsing a broad class of languages may begin to fade. It appears that any technique developed will be restricted to the smallest class of languages in Figure 2.23. Fortunately, the situation improves if we reconsider the manner in which the automata accept input strings. Recall from Section 2.1 that to accept a string a pushdown automaton must satisfy its accept criterion after reading the string but without moving its tape head any farther down the tape. This means that a pushdown automaton must reach an accept state without actually reading an end-of-string marker. The result is what we

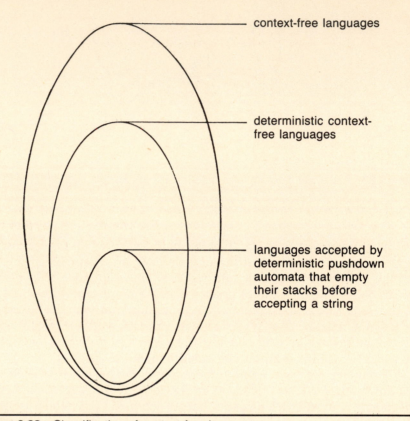

Figure 2.23 Classification of context-free languages

might consider a passive acceptance process in that the machine must "stumble" into an accept configuration without being told to do so by an end-of-string marker. In contrast, if we imagine a system by which the machine could peek at the next symbol on its tape (without actually advancing its tape head), it could detect an oncoming end-of-string marker and perform special "wrap-up" activities that it would not have executed otherwise.

We will refer to the technique of peeking at future symbols without actually reading them as the **lookahead principle.** Its application is exemplified by the while loop structure as displayed by the program segment in Figure 2.24. This segment essentially peeks at the next symbol and uses the information obtained to decide whether or not to process the symbol within the while structure. It is within the various case options that the routine finally decides whether to consume the symbol and prepare to process another one. Thus, the variable symbol is actually a holding place, or buffer, for the next input symbol. A symbol held there can be considered when

```
read (symbol);
while (symbol not end-of-string marker)
      case symbol of
            x: push (y) and read (symbol)
            y: exit to error routine
            z: push (#) and read (symbol)
      end case
end while
```

Figure 2.24   A typical *while* loop

making decisions but need not be consumed (or officially read) until the decision is made to process it. In particular, the end-of-string marker will not be consumed by this routine but will remain in the buffer after the while structure has terminated, where it will be available as input to the next routine. After all, in an actual compiler the end-of-string marker might well be the first symbol of the next structure to be analyzed.

   We see, then, that applying the lookahead principle is a common programming technique. We are also about to see that by applying this principle when converting pushdown automata into program segments, we can construct programs that overcome the nondeterminism found in some pushdown automata. Thus, the theory of pushdown automata provides a foundation from which parsing routines for a wide range of context-free languages can be developed. How this is done is the subject of the next two sections.

Exercises

1. Apply Theorem 2.5 to prove that the language $\{x^m y^n x^m y^n x^m y^n: m, n \in \mathbb{N}^+\}$ is not context-free.

2. Give examples of each of the following:
   a. A language that is not context-free.
   b. A language that is context-free but not deterministic context-free.
   c. A language that is deterministic context-free but is not accepted by a deterministic pushdown automaton that is required to empty its stack.
   d. A language that is accepted by a deterministic pushdown automaton that is required to empty its stack but is not regular.

3. Draw the pertinent portion of a transition diagram for a deterministic pushdown automaton that from state p will move to state q while reading an x, popping a y, and pushing a z if the top of the stack contains a y, or will move to state q while reading an x, popping nothing, and pushing a z if the top of the stack is not a y.

4. Identify the situations that would produce uncertainties in the execution of a pushdown automaton containing the transitions $(p, \lambda, y; q, z)$ and $(p, x, \lambda; r, w)$.

2.4   *LL(k)* PARSERS

It is time now to consider how parsing routines can be developed from pushdown automata. Traditionally this problem is encountered when a language is first described in terms of grammatical rewrite rules. Then, parsing routines are developed for the language using the theory of pushdown automata as a design tool. This is the context in which we frame our discussion.

The *LL* Parsing Process

One technique for translating context-free grammars into pushdown automata is to follow the process described in the proof of Theorem 2.2. This construction produces a pushdown automaton that analyzes its input string by first marking the bottom of the stack and pushing the grammar's start symbol on the stack. Then, it repeatedly executes the following three steps as applicable.

1. If the top of the stack contains a nonterminal from the grammar, replace that nonterminal according to one of the grammar's rewrite rules.
2. If the top of the stack contains a terminal, remove that terminal from the stack while reading the same terminal from the input. If the symbol on the input does not match the symbol on the stack, the input is declared to be an illegal string.
3. If the bottom-of-stack marker surfaces on the stack, remove it and declare the portion of the input string processed so far to be acceptable.

Recall that this process parses the input string by producing a leftmost derivation while reading the string from left to right. Consequently, a program segment obtained by translating the automaton directly into program statements will proceed in the same fashion. Parsers developed in this fashion are known as **LL parsers.** The first *L* denotes that the parser reads its input from *Left* to right; the second *L* denotes that the goal of the parser is to produce a *Leftmost* derivation.

Figure 2.25b shows a transition diagram constructed from the grammar in Figure 2.25a using the process presented in the proof of Theorem 2.2. (This is the context-free grammar we met in Figure 2.7 that generates strings of the form $x^n y^n$ for nonnegative integers n.) To produce a parsing routine from this grammar, we might convert the transitions of the machine directly into program statements to obtain the routine in Figure 2.26, where we have used the traditional while structure to simulate the activities available to the machine when in state q. (While the symbol on top of the stack is not the bottom-of-stack marker, the machine remains in state q.)

a. $S \rightarrow xSy$
     $S \rightarrow \lambda$

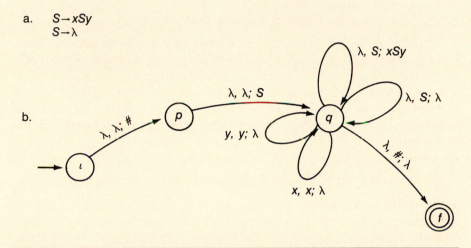

b.

Figure 2.25   A context-free grammar and an associated transition diagram for a pushdown automaton

```
State : = ι ;
push (#);
State : = p;
push (S);
State : = q;
while top-of-stack ≠ # do
        case top-of-stack do
            S: either pop (S) and push (xSy)
                or pop (S);
            x: pop (x), read an x from the input;
            y: pop (y), read a y from the input;
        end case
end while;
pop (#);
State : = f
```

Figure 2.26   A "program" segment obtained by translating the diagram in Figure 2.25 into statements

Obviously, the segment in Figure 2.26 is not a finished product. For one thing, we have not allowed for errors caused by invalid inputs. For instance, if an x surfaces on the stack within the while loop, our routine assumes that the next symbol on the input is an x and executes the statement "read an x from the input string." In reality the next symbol may not be an x, so our routine should account for this possibility. Hence, we should expand the instruction "read an x from the input string" into the following pair of instructions:

> read(symbol);
> if symbol not x then exit to error routine;

Another minor problem with the routine in Figure 2.26 is that it may arrive at state f with an empty stack without having read the entire input string. For example, the string xyx is not in the language described by the original grammar, but our routine will never realize this. Instead, it will read only as far into the input as xy, where it will stop with the assumption that its input string was valid. This problem can be corrected by adding the statements

> read(symbol);
> if symbol not end-of-string marker then exit to error routine;

to the end of the routine.

There is, however, one problem in our routine that is more severe than the preceding ones: In some cases the directions present unresolved options. Indeed, if the current state is q and the symbol on top of the stack is S, the routine provides the choice of either replacing that S with xSy or merely removing the S from the stack. This problem is fundamentally different from the issues just discussed, in that it involves the selection of instructions rather than the mere clarification or refinement of an instruction's details.

Applying the Lookahead Principle

Fortunately, the nondeterminism in our routine can be resolved by employing the lookahead principle introduced in the previous section. If we find an x by peeking at the next symbol in the input, then we should replace S with the string xSy; otherwise we should replace it with the empty string. (Pushing xSy on the stack knowing that the next symbol in the input string is not an x would be admitting defeat. Once we push a terminal symbol on the stack, we must be able to match that symbol with an input symbol before it can be removed from the stack. If we pushed xSy on the stack while facing a symbol other than x on the input, the input symbol would not match the terminal x on top of the stack, and we would never be able to empty the stack and move to the accept state.)

```
State := ι;
push (#);
State := p;
push (S);
State := q;
read (Symbol);
while top-of-stack ≠ # do
    case top-of-stack of
        S: if Symbol ≠ x then pop (S)
                else pop (S), push (xSy);
        x: if Symbol not x then exit to error routine
                else pop (x), read (Symbol);
        y: if Symbol not y then exit to error routine
                else pop (y), read (Symbol);
    end case
end while;
pop (#)
if Symbol not end-of-string marker then exit to error routine;
State := f
```

Figure 2.27   A parsing routine based on the grammar of Figure 2.25

Following this lead, we can convert the nondeterministic diagram in Figure 2.25 into the deterministic program segment shown in Figure 2.27. Here we have used the variable symbol as a buffer in which to store the next symbol in the input. From this buffer the symbol can be interrogated when necessary to make decisions, but not processed until its time has come. In particular, note that the end-of-string marker, although detected, is not consumed by the routine. It is left in the buffer where it can be used as the first symbol in the next structure to be analyzed by the parsing system.

The problem encountered in the preceding example is a common phenomenon in *LL* parsers because it originated when the grammar proposed more than one way of rewriting the same nonterminal. Such multiple options are essential to grammars that must generate languages containing more than a single string. (A context-free grammar that provides only one way of rewriting each nonterminal is capable of generating only one string.) Thus, the underlying activity of *LL* parsers is that of predicting which of several rewrite rules should be used to process the remaining input symbols. Consequently, these parsers are called **predictive parsers**.

Many of the uncertainties faced by predictive parsers can be resolved by applying the lookahead principle. However, even in cases where the lookahead principle is the right technique its application may not be as straightforward as in our example. If we were to build a parser from the grammar in Figure 2.28, we would find that the decision regarding the

$$S \rightarrow xSz$$
$$S \rightarrow xyTyz$$
$$T \rightarrow \lambda$$

Figure 2.28   A context-free grammar that requires an $LL(2)$ parser

---

rewriting of S cannot be resolved merely by peeking at the next input symbol. (Knowing that the next symbol is x does not tell us to apply $S \rightarrow xSy$ as opposed to $S \rightarrow xyTyz$.) Rather, the decision depends on the next two symbols. Thus, to develop a deterministic parsing routine we must provide buffer space for two input symbols.

As a result, there is a hierarchy of LL parsers whose distinguishing feature is the number of input symbols involved in their lookahead systems. These parsers are called **LL(k) parsers,** where k is an integer indicating the number of lookahead symbols employed by the parser. The example in Figure 2.27 is an $LL(1)$ parser, whereas a parser based on the grammar in Figure 2.28 would be an $LL(2)$ parser.

You may guess (correctly) that the burden of prediction placed on $LL(k)$ parsers ultimately restricts the languages such parsers can handle. In truth, there are languages well within the bounds of pushdown parsers that cannot be recognized by any $LL(k)$ parser, regardless of the size of k. The language $\{x^n: n \in \mathbb{N}\} \cup \{x^n y^n: n \in \mathbb{N}\}$, which we have already seen is deterministic context-free, is an example. Intuitively, any context-free grammar that generates this language must allow some nonterminal to be rewritten with either a string containing only xs or a string containing a balanced combination of xs and ys. This means there will be at least two rules for rewriting this nonterminal. In turn, any $LL(k)$ parser will be faced with the problem of deciding which of these rules to apply when that nonterminal surfaces at the top of the stack. Unfortunately, regardless of the size of k, there are strings in the language in which the presence or absence of trailing ys cannot be detected without peeking beyond more than k xs. Thus, any particular $LL(k)$ parser would be unable to handle the decisions required to parse this language.

The existence of a deterministic context-free language that cannot be parsed by any $LL(k)$ parser suggests that there may be parsers based on the theory of pushdown automata that are more powerful than these predictive parsers—an hypothesis that leads us to the next section. However, with additional power comes additional complexity, and thus the simplicity of $LL(k)$ parsers makes them a popular choice when they are capable of handling the language under investigation. For now, then, we forgo our quest for power and consider how $LL(k)$ parsers can be simplified through the use of parse tables.

LL Parse Tables

A parse table for an *LL*(1) parser is a two-dimensional array. The rows are labeled by the nonterminals in the grammar on which the parser is based. The columns are labeled by the terminals in the grammar plus one additional column labeled EOS (representing the end-of-string marker). The $(m, n)^{th}$ entry in the table indicates what action should be performed when the nonterminal m appears on top of the stack and the lookahead symbol is n. If, in this setting, the nonterminal m should be replaced according to some rewrite rule, the right side of that rule appears as the $(m, n)^{th}$ entry. Otherwise, the entry contains an error indicator. For example, Figure 2.29 presents a parse table for the grammar of Figure 2.5.

Once a parse table has been constructed, the task of writing a program segment to parse the language is quite simple. All the segment must do is push the grammar's start symbol on the stack and then, until the stack becomes empty, either match terminals on top of the stack with those in the input or replace nonterminals on top of the stack as directed by the parse table. For example, the routine in Figure 2.30 is an *LL*(1) parser using the table in Figure 2.29.

	a	*b*	*z*	EOS
S	error	error	*zMNz*	error
M	*aMa*	error	*z*	error
N	error	*bNb*	*z*	error

Figure 2.29 An *LL*(1) parse table for the grammar in Figure 2.5

```
push (S);
read (Symbol);
while stack not empty do
    case top-of-stack of
        terminal: if top-of-stack = Symbol
            then pop stack and read (Symbol)
            else exit to error routine;
        nonterminal: if table [top-of-stack, Symbol] ≠ error
            then replace top-of-stack with table [top-of-stack, Symbol]
            else exit to error routine;
    end case
end while
if Symbol not end-of-string marker then exit to error routine
```

Figure 2.30 A generic *LL*(1) parsing routine

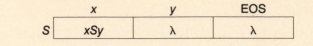

	x	y	EOS
S	xSy	λ	λ

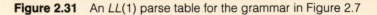

Figure 2.31   An $LL(1)$ parse table for the grammar in Figure 2.7

Another advantage of using parse tables is that they allow the actual parsing algorithm to be standardized. The same algorithm can be used for any $LL(1)$ parser; to obtain a parser for another language, we merely substitute a new parse table in place of the old one. To emphasize this point, we close by observing that combining the program segment in Figure 2.30 with the parse table in Figure 2.31 produces a parser for the language generated by the grammar in Figure 2.7.

Exercises

1. Rewrite the program segment in Figure 2.30 using a repeat $\cdots$ until structure instead of a while structure.

2. Translate the transition diagram below directly into a program segment for parsing the language involved. What uncertainties must be resolved to obtain a deterministic routine?

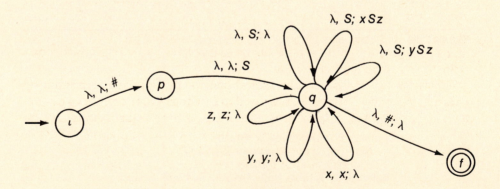

3. Design an $LL(1)$ parse table for the following grammar.

$$S \rightarrow xSz$$
$$S \rightarrow ySz$$
$$S \rightarrow \lambda$$

4. How many symbols of lookahead would be required by an *LL* parser when parsing strings based on the following grammar? Design a corresponding parse table.

$$S \rightarrow xSy$$
$$S \rightarrow xy$$

2.5   *LR(k)* PARSERS

In the previous section we argued that the predictive nature of *LL(k)* parsers restricts the class of languages that these parsers are able to handle. In this section we introduce a class of parsers that avoid many of the problems associated with their predictive counterparts. These parsers are known as **LR(k) parsers,** as they read their input from *L*eft to right while constructing a *R*ightmost derivation of their input strings using a lookahead system involving *k* symbols.

The *LR* Parsing Process

Roughly speaking, an *LR(k)* parser transfers symbols from its input to a stack until the uppermost stack symbols match the right side of some rewrite rule in the grammar on which the parser is based. At this point the parser can replace these symbols with the single nonterminal found on the left side of the rewrite rule before additional symbols are transferred from the input to the stack. In this manner the stack accumulates strings of terminals and nonterminals that are in turn replaced by nonterminals "higher" in the grammar. Ultimately, the entire contents of the stack collapses to the grammar's start symbol, indicating that the symbols read to that point form a string that can be derived by the grammar.

Based on this overall scheme, *LR(k)* parsers are classified as **bottom-up parsers** since their activities correspond to constructing occurrences of nonterminals from their components until the grammar's start symbol is generated. In contrast, *LL(k)* parsers are known as **top-down parsers** since they begin with the start symbol on the stack and repeatedly break the nonterminals on the stack into their components until a string of symbols matching the input string has been generated.

Let us back up now and develop the specifics of *LR(k)* parsers. Recall that an *LL(k)* parser is based on a pushdown automaton constructed from a context-free grammar; this construction is based on the process outlined in the proof of Theorem 2.2. In a similar manner, an *LR(k)* parser is based on a pushdown automaton constructed from a context-free grammar, except that the automaton is constructed as described by the following five steps.

1. Establish four states: an initial state called ι, an accept state called f, and two other states called p and q.
2. Introduce the transitions $(\iota, \lambda, \lambda; p, \#)$ and $(q, \lambda, \#; f, \lambda)$, where we assume $\#$ is a symbol that does not occur in the grammar.
3. For each terminal symbol x in the grammar, introduce the transition $(p, x, \lambda; p, x)$. These transitions allow the automaton to transfer the input symbols to the stack while remaining in state p. The execution of such a transition is called a **shift operation** since its effect is to shift a symbol from the input string to the stack.
4. For each rewrite rule $N \rightarrow w$ (where w represents a string of one or more symbols) in the grammar, introduce the transition $(p, \lambda, w; p, N)$. (Here we allow a transition to remove more than one symbol from the stack. More precisely, the transition $(p, \lambda, xy; p, z)$ is a short form for the transition $(p, \lambda, y; p_1, \lambda)$ followed by $(p_1, \lambda, x; p, z)$, where p_1 is a state that cannot be reached by any other transition. Thus, to execute the transition $(p, \lambda, xy; p, z)$, an automaton must have a y on top of its stack with an x below it.) The presence of these transitions means that if the symbols on the uppermost portion of the stack agree with the right side of a rewrite rule, then those symbols can be replaced with the single nonterminal found on the left side of that rule. The execution of such a transition is called a **reduce operation** since its effect is to reduce the contents of the stack to a simpler form.
5. Introduce the transition $(p, \lambda, S; q, \lambda)$, where S is the start symbol in the grammar. The presence of this transition means that if the symbols on the stack have been reduced to S, the automaton can move to state q while popping S from the stack.

As an example of this construction, consider the diagram in Figure 2.32 that was constructed from the grammar in Figure 2.5. A pushdown automaton based on this transition diagram would analyze the string *zazabzbz* as summarized in Figure 2.33. It would begin by marking the bottom of its stack with the symbol $\#$ and moving to state p with the string *zazabzbz* on its input as indicated by the first row in the figure. From this configuration the automaton would shift the first z from the input to its stack via the transition $(p, z, \lambda; p, z)$, and assume the configuration represented in the second row of Figure 2.33. At this stage the automaton would have the choice of executing $(p, \lambda, z; p, M)$, $(p, \lambda, z; p, N)$, or $(p, a, \lambda; p, a)$. (This automaton is nondeterministic.) In our example, the first two options represent incorrect choices. They should be taken if the z on the top of the stack should be analyzed as being a refinement of either the nonterminal M or N, respectively. The third option represents the correct move in our case since more of the string should be read before a reduce operation is executed.

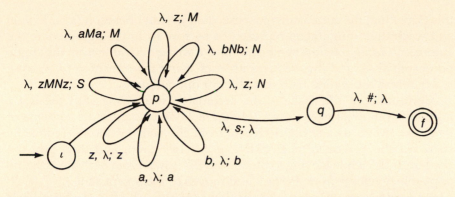

Figure 2.32 Another transition diagram for a pushdown automaton based on the grammar of Figure 2.5

	Current state	Contents of stack	Remaining input
1	p	#	zazabzbz
2	p	#z	azabzbz
3	p	#za	zabzbz
4	p	#zaz	abzbz
5	p	#zaM	abzbz
6	p	#zaMa	bzbz
7	p	#zM	bzbz
8	p	#zMb	zbz
9	p	#zMbz	bz
10	p	#zMbN	bz
11	p	#zMbNb	z
12	p	#zMN	z
13	p	#zMNz	
14	p	#S	
15	q	#	
16	f	empty	

(Row numbers)

Figure 2.33 The complete analysis of the string *zazabzbz* by the pushdown automaton in Figure 2.32

Since our goal here is to show how the automaton can accept the string *zazabzbz*, we pursue this latter option. In fact, the automaton should continue to execute shift operations until it arrives at the configuration represented by row four of Figure 2.33. At this stage the correct action is to execute the transition $(p, \lambda, z; p, M)$ in recognition of the fact that the z on top of the stack is derived from an occurrence of the nonterminal M. After this transition, the automaton must execute the shift operation $(p, a, \lambda; p, a)$ and reach the configuration represented by row six in the figure. Here the automaton recognizes the symbols aMa as a string derivable from the single nonterminal M, and thus reduces its stack using the transition $(p, \lambda, aMa; p, M)$ before continuing with further shift operations.

Continuing in this fashion, the automaton will finally shift the last z from its input to its stack (row 13 of Figure 2.33), recognize the contents of its stack, $zMNz$, as a string derivable from the start symbol S, reduce its stack via the transition $(p, \lambda, zMNz; p, S)$ (14th row), and then pop the nonterminal S while moving to the state q (15th row). From here the machine pops the symbol # from its stack and moves to the accept state f.

As a side issue, we are now in position to justify the R in the term $LR(k)$ parser, which we claimed indicated that these parsers analyze their inputs by constructing rightmost derivations. Recall that a derivation is a sequence of rewrite rules that transforms the start symbol into the derived string. However, the bottom-up process summarized in Figure 2.33 does this in reverse: It generates the start symbol from the derived string. Consequently, the derivation involved appears in reverse order. To find it, we read the "contents of stack" column in Figure 2.33 from bottom to top while recording the rewrite rules that were applied by the automaton. In our example this reveals the derivation

$$S \Rightarrow zMNz \Rightarrow zMbNbz \Rightarrow zMbzbz \Rightarrow zaMabzbz \Rightarrow zazabzbz$$

which is a rightmost derivation as promised.

The Implementation of $LR(k)$ Parsers

Two major problems are encountered when trying to convert pushdown automata such as the one in Figure 2.32 into a more traditional program format. The first is one of nondeterminism similar to that occurring in the case of LL parsers: When given a choice, how do we know whether to shift or reduce? Moreover, if our choice is to reduce, there could be more than one possible reduction. (If z is on top of the stack, do we reduce with $(p, \lambda, z; p, M)$ or $(p, \lambda, z; p, N)$?) As you may guess, these issues are resolved by applying the lookahead principle.

The second major problem deals with the technicalities of interrogating the stack. For example, before we can decide to execute the transition $(p, \lambda, aMa; p, M)$, we must be able to deduce that the top three stack symbols are a, M, and a. However, only the topmost symbol of a stack is available for observation at any one time. It may seem that this problem can be solved by implementing the stack as a hybrid structure that allows observation of symbols below the top, but this modification ignores the real underlying problem—the need for repeated stack searches. Indeed, it would appear that any implementation of an *LR* parsing routine would incorporate a significant pattern-recognition component for comparing the stack contents to the right sides of the rewrite rules.

Perhaps the most fascinating result in the field of compiler construction is that this stack interrogation problem can be resolved without expensive searches or even the need to resort to hybrid stack structures. In fact, in the case of deterministic context-free languages, the information needed to solve this stack interrogation problem, as well as the problem of resolving choices, can be built into a single parse table.

An example table for an *LR*(1) parser is shown in Figure 2.34. It is based on the grammar in Figure 2.5. The columns of this table are labeled by the symbols in the grammar (including both terminals and nonterminals) along with an end-of-string marker (represented by EOS). The rows are labeled by numbers that represent special tokens. (We will see that these tokens are used to represent patterns that may appear on the stack.)

To describe the entries in the table, let us consider the process in which the table is used. The parsing of any string begins by assigning a token

	a	b	z	EOS	S	M	N
1			shift 2		14		
2	shift 3		shift 7			4	
3	shift 3		shift 7			8	
4		shift 5	shift 9				6
5		shift 5	shift 9				10
6			shift 11				
7	M→z	M→z	M→z				
8	shift 12						
9		N→z	N→z				
10		shift 13					
11				S→zMNz			
12	M→aMa	M→aMa	M→aMa				
13		N→bNb	N→bNb				
14				accept			

Figure 2.34　An *LR*(1) parse table based on the grammar of Figure 2.5

variable the value one and pushing this value on the otherwise empty stack. (From this point on, pushing a symbol onto the stack will be followed by pushing the current value of the token variable on top of it. This means that the stack will alternately contain symbols and tokens, with each token representing the pattern that lies below it. Therefore, we can investigate the internal structure of the stack by looking at the single token on the top.)

Once the current token has been established and saved on the stack, we refer to the parse table. The row of interest is determined by the current token and the column by the lookahead symbol. The simplest cases occur when the corresponding table entry is either empty or contains the word accept. In the former case, the input string is judged to be invalid and an appropriate error routine should be executed. The latter case indicates that the string read from the input has been found to be acceptable and the parsing process should be terminated.

Another possibility is for the table entry to be a shift entry, indicating that a shift operation should be performed. In this case the next input symbol (the lookahead symbol) should be read from the input and placed on the stack; the token variable should be assigned the value given in the shift entry and this new token value should be pushed on the stack; and finally the lookahead symbol should be updated.

The final possibility is for the table entry to contain a rewrite rule from the grammar, indicating that a reduce operation is required. The process required here involves replacing a string of stack symbols (the right side of the rewrite rule) with a single nonterminal (the left side of the rewrite rule). However, to handle the token values that are also stored on the stack requires a bit more detail. First, two symbols should be removed from the stack for each symbol on the right side of the rewrite rule. This removes each symbol in the right side of the rule as well as the token value stored above it. At this point the top of the stack will be the token value that was placed there after the lower (remaining) portion of the stack was created. This value must be remembered as the "temporary token," and the nonterminal from the left side of the rewrite rule should be pushed on top of it. Next, this nonterminal is used to identify a column in the parse table, while the temporary token determines a row. The entry found in this location of the parse table should be assigned to the token variable as well as pushed on the stack.

Thus, when using a parse table, an *LR* parser simply refers to the table in a cyclic fashion until a blank or an accept entry is found. An *LR*(1) parsing algorithm using the parse table in Figure 2.34 is given in Figure 2.35. Figure 2.36 summarizes the parser's activities when processing the string *zazabzbz*. Note that this figure is essentially the same as Figure 2.33 except for the additional token values on the stack.

```
Token : = 1;
push (Token);
read (Symbol);
TableEntry : = Table [Token,Symbol];
while TableEntry is not "accept" do
    if TableEntry is a shift
        then begin
                push (Symbol); Token : = TableEntry.State;
                push (Token); read (Symbol)
                end
    else if TableEntry is a reduction
        then begin
                pop (right side of TableEntry.RewriteRule);
                Token : = top-of-stack; (*This is not a pop*)
                push (left side of TableEntry.RewriteRule);
                Token : = Table [Token, left side of TableEntry.RewriteRule];
                push (Token)
                end
    else if TableEntry is blank then exit to error routine;
    TableEntry : = Table [Token,Symbol];
end while;
if Symbol not EOS then exit to error routine;
empty stack
```

Figure 2.35 An *LR*(1) parse algorithm

LR Parse Tables

Although the construction of an *LR* parse table is more within the subject of compiler construction than the subject of formal language theory, we should not ignore the issue altogether. Indeed, the construction of these tables is an important application of finite automata theory. The table for an *LR*(1) parser is based on the existence of a finite automaton that accepts exactly those strings of grammar symbols (terminals and nonterminals) that lead to reduce operations. We present a short example of this here; more detail is given in Appendix A.

The diagram in Figure 2.37 is the transition diagram of the finite automaton from which the parse table in Figure 2.34 was constructed. Note that it accepts such strings as *zaMa*, *zMbNb*, and *zMNz*, which when found on the parser's stack, should be reduced to *zM*, *zMN*, and *S*, respectively. In terms of this diagram, the goal of the *LR* parser is to reach state 14 by traversing the arc labeled *S*. To accomplish this it performs what might appear to be a trial and error process in which the parser repeatedly follows some path to an accept state, backtracks to a previous state along that path, and from there sets out in a new direction.

Contents of stack	Remaining input
empty	*zazabzbz*
①	*zazabzbz*
① *z* ②	*azabzbz*
① *z* ② *a* ③	*zabzbz*
① *z* ② *a* ③ *z* ⑦	*abzbz*
① *z* ② *a* ③ *M* ⑧	*abzbz*
① *z* ② *a* ③ *M* ⑧ *a* ⑫	*bzbz*
① *z* ② *M* ④	*bzbz*
① *z* ② *M* ④ *b* ⑤	*zbz*
① *z* ② *M* ④ *b* ⑤ *z* ⑨	*bz*
① *z* ② *M* ④ *b* ⑤ *N* ⑩	*bz*
① *z* ② *M* ④ *b* ⑤ *N* ⑩ *b* ⑬	*z*
① *z* ② *M* ④ *N* ⑥	*z*
① *z* ② *M* ④ *N* ⑥ *z* ⑪	
① *S* ⑭	
empty	

Figure 2.36 Parsing the string *zazabzbz* with the algorithm of Figure 2.35 and the table in Figure 2.34

This process, however, is not one of trial and error, but rather a well-defined sequence of events ultimately guided by the symbols found in the string being parsed. The idea is to begin the parsing process by following the path determined by the input string until an accept state is reached. At this point the path traversed by the finite automaton corresponds to the symbol pattern that has been shifted onto the stack by the parser. The parsing process then backs up along this path across those symbols that are to be removed from the parser's stack during the reduce operation. From this point, the parser traverses the arc in the finite automaton's transition diagram that is labeled by the nonterminal placed on the stack by the corresponding reduce operation. Thus, once the reduce operation has been completed, the symbols on the parser's stack will again correspond to the symbols along the path being traversed by the finite automaton.

To see this process at work, let us again consider the task of parsing the string *zazabzbz*. As the parser reads the symbols *zaz*, the finite automaton moves through the sequence of states 1, 2, 3, 7. At this point a reduce operation based on the rule $M \rightarrow z$ is required. Thus the finite automaton

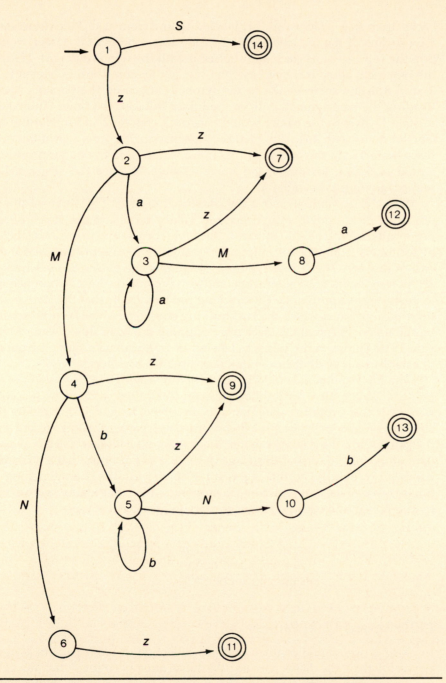

Figure 2.37 The finite automaton from which the table in Figure 2.34 was constructed

backs up to state 3 (across the arc labeled z), and from state 3 moves to state 8 by means of the arc labeled M. At the same time the LR parser would pop the top z from its stack and replace it with the nonterminal M. Hence, the new path being traversed by the finite automaton (through states 1, 2, 3, and 8) again corresponds to the symbol pattern on the parser's stack. Reading the next symbol, a, from the input will lead the finite automaton to state 12, where the parser would backtrack to state 2 and follow the arc labeled M to state 4. In this manner, the parsing process will ultimately reach state 11 via the arcs z, M, N, and z. From here the parsing process would backtrack to state 1 and move to state 14 since the string $zMNz$ reduces to the start symbol S.

With this scenario in mind the construction of an $LR(1)$ parse table is not difficult to understand. The token values represent the states of the finite automaton. The shift entries in the table correspond to the arcs labeled by terminals, while the token found in that entry represents the state at the end of that arc. The reduce entries indicate that the parser has reached an accept state in the finite automaton, and also provide the information needed to perform the appropriate backtracking process. (Note that the state in the finite automaton at which the backtracking should stop will be represented by the token on top of the stack after popping the right side of the rewrite rule.) The entries in the columns labeled by nonterminals allow the parser to establish a new direction in the diagram after backtracking.

One final comment should be made before leaving our discussion of LR parsers. To complete a compiler, a parser must be combined with a code generator that produces statements in the object language that reflect the structures found by the parser. When using an LR parser, this linkage between the parser and the code generator occurs in connection with each reduce operation. Indeed, it is at this stage in the parsing process that a structure has been recognized so this is a natural time to ask the code generator to build the code for that structure. In summary, the computation performed by the parser and code generator follows the basic pattern of

```
repeat
     parse until a reduction is performed
     generate some code
until parsing is complete
```

$LR(k)$ Versus $LL(k)$ Parsers

In closing, we should confirm that the collection of $LR(k)$ parsers is more powerful than the $LL(k)$ parsers. We have already argued that no $LL(k)$ parser can handle the language $\{x^n: n \in \mathbb{N}\} \cup \{x^n y^n: n \in \mathbb{N}\}$. However, a grammar for this language and its related $LR(1)$ parse table is given in Figure 2.38. Combining this table with the algorithm in Figure 2.35 produces an

$$S \to X$$
$$S \to Y$$
$$S \to \lambda$$
$$X \to xX$$
$$X \to x$$
$$Y \to xYy$$
$$Y \to xy$$

	x	y	EOS	S	X	Y
1	shift 2		$S \to \lambda$	9	8	7
2	shift 2	shift 6	$X \to x$		3	4
3			$X \to xX$			
4		shift 5				
5		$Y \to xYy$	$Y \to xYy$			
6		$Y \to xy$	$Y \to xy$			
7			$S \to Y$			
8			$S \to X$			
9			accept			

Figure 2.38   A context-free grammar and its *LR*(1) parse table

LR(1) parser that recognizes the language. (This it does by shifting the *x*s from its input to its stack until either a *y* or an end-of-string marker is reached. At this point the parser is able to apply the appropriate rewrite rules to analyze the string correctly.)

There are, however, context-free languages that cannot be recognized by any *LR(k)* parser. In fact, the class of languages that can be parsed by *LR(k)* parsers is exactly the class of deterministic context-free languages. Although we will not prove this, we should at least point out that this bound on the powers of *LR(k)* parsers conforms to intuition: An *LR(k)* parser must be deterministic and since its structure is based on some pushdown automaton, it should follow that only those languages that can be accepted by deterministic pushdown automata can be parsed by an *LR(k)* parser.

An example of a context-free language that cannot be parsed by any *LR(k)* parser is the language

$$\{x^n y^n : n \in \mathbb{N}^+\} \cup \{x^n y^{2n} : n \in \mathbb{N}^+\}$$

Intuitively, the problem here is that once the first y is reached in the input, the parser must decide which rewrite rule to apply while knowing only the next k symbols in the string. If n is larger than k, knowing only the next k symbols does not allow the parser to detect whether the input will contain n ys or $2n$ ys, and therefore the parser is unable to select the correct rewrite rule.

Exercises

1. Using the alternative process for constructing a pushdown automaton from a context-free grammar as described in this section, construct a transition diagram for a pushdown automaton from the grammar below.

$$S \rightarrow xSz$$
$$S \rightarrow ySz$$
$$S \rightarrow \lambda$$

2. Identify the derivation obtained by the pushdown automaton constructed in Exercise 1 when analyzing the input string $yxyzzz$.

3. Construct an $LR(1)$ parse table for the grammar below. (There are algorithmic processes for doing this that we have not discussed [for more information see Appendix A], but this grammar is simple enough that a table can be developed based merely on an understanding of how an $LR(1)$ parse table is used.)

$$S \rightarrow xSy$$
$$S \rightarrow \lambda$$

2.6   CLOSING COMMENTS

We should first clarify the relationship between the hierarchy associated with context-free languages and the class of regular languages presented in the previous chapter. We have already observed that regular languages are context-free, but the classification can be more precise. The regular languages are properly contained in the class of languages accepted by deterministic pushdown automata that empty their stacks before accepting a string. This can be seen by observing that any regular language can be accepted by some deterministic finite automaton, which is essentially a deterministic pushdown automaton whose transitions never use the stack, and since the stack is never used, it must be empty when an accept state is reached. Moreover, the containment is proper since the language $\{x^ny^n : n \in$

$\mathbb{N}\}$ is not regular but can be accepted by a deterministic pushdown automaton that empties its stack before accepting a string (Figure 2.2).

Thus, we can summarize our study of languages to this point with the diagram in Figure 2.39, which is an extension of Figure 2.23.

Finally, as a means of introducing some of the issues in the remaining chapters, note that the context-free languages are not closed under intersection. For example, the languages $\{x^n y^n z^m : m, n \in \mathbb{N}\}$ and $\{x^m y^n z^n : m, n \in \mathbb{N}\}$ are each context-free (the first is generated by $S \rightarrow TZ$, $T \rightarrow \lambda$, $T \rightarrow xTy$,

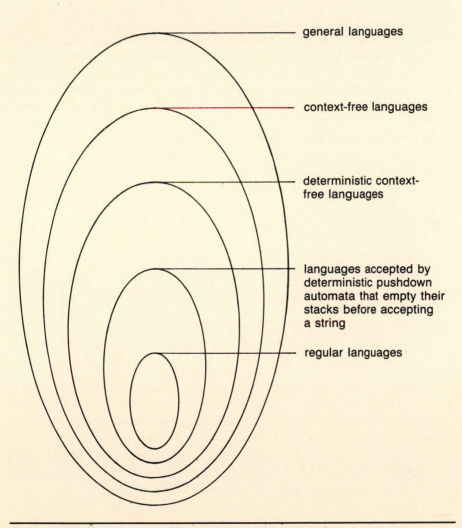

general languages

context-free languages

deterministic context-free languages

languages accepted by deterministic pushdown automata that empty their stacks before accepting a string

regular languages

Figure 2.39   The hierarchy of languages introduced thus far

$Z \to \lambda$, $Z \to zZ$, and the second is similar), but their intersection is the language $\{x^n y^n z^n : n \in \mathbb{N}\}$, which we have shown is not context-free. Combining this with the fact that the context-free languages are closed under finite union, and applying DeMorgan's laws, reveals that the context-free languages are not closed under complementation. That is, there are subsets of Σ^* that are context free but whose complements in Σ^* are not context-free.

This means that the ability of a pushdown automaton to accept the strings in a language is not symmetric with the ability to reject the strings that are not in the language. (The ability to reject the strings not in the language would be equivalent to the ability to accept the language's complement.) Thus, there is an important distinction between the ability to answer yes when a string is in a language and the ability to answer yes or no when the string is or is not in the language. (In the former case, if the input is not in the language, the machine may become trapped in a loop and never reply. In the latter case, the machine must ultimately answer correctly regardless of whether the answer is yes or no.) This lack of symmetry will be significant in future discussions.

Chapter Review Problems

1. For each level in the hierarchy of Figure 2.39, give an example of a language that is at that level but not in the next lower level.

2. Show that the language $\{x^r y^s z^t : s = r + t\}$ is context-free.

3. Show that:
   a. The language $\{x^m y^n : m, n \in \mathbb{N}^+\}$ is regular.
   b. The language $\{x^m y^n x^m : m, n \in \mathbb{N}^+\}$ is context-free but not regular.
   c. The language $\{x^m y^n x^m y^n : m, n \in \mathbb{N}^+\}$ is not context-free.

4. Show that the language over the alphabet $\{x, y\}$ that consists of those strings with the same number of xs and ys is deterministic context-free.

5. Show that if L is a context-free language, then the language consisting of the strings in L written backward is also context-free.

6. Based on the grammar in Figure 2.5, draw the parse tree for the string *zzbbzbbz*. How many different derivations of this string are possible? Demonstrate the leftmost and rightmost derivations.

7. Construct a pushdown automaton M for which $L(M) = \{w^r x^s y^t z^u : r, s, t, \text{ and } u \text{ are nonnegative integers such that } r + t = s + u\}$.

8. Describe the language accepted by the pushdown automaton whose transition diagram is shown below.

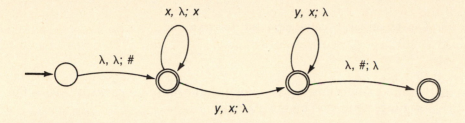

9. Describe the language accepted by the pushdown automaton whose transition diagram is shown below. Describe the strings that are accepted with the machine's stack not empty. Modify the diagram so that it accepts the same strings as before but only after emptying its stack.

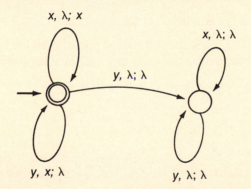

10. Find a context-free grammar for the language $\{x^n y^m : m$ and n are positive integers such that $m = n$ or $m = 2n\}$.

11. Develop a context-free grammar that describes the structure of a Pascal-like programming language that only allows variables of type integer or real, contains no procedures or functions, and whose only procedural statements are assignment and while statements.

12. Design an $LL(1)$ parse table for the grammar

$$S \rightarrow xSz$$
$$S \rightarrow y$$

13. Design an $LL(1)$ parse table for the grammar

$$S \rightarrow xSy$$
$$S \rightarrow y$$

14. Design an $LR(1)$ parse table for the grammar

$$S \rightarrow xSz$$
$$S \rightarrow y$$

15. Design an $LR(1)$ parse table for the grammar

$$S \rightarrow xSy$$
$$S \rightarrow y$$

16. Design a deterministic pushdown automaton M for which $L(M)$ is the language generated by the grammar

$$S \rightarrow xSx$$
$$S \rightarrow y$$

17. Design a deterministic pushdown automaton M for which $L(M)$ is the language generated by the grammar

$$S \rightarrow xSy$$
$$S \rightarrow y$$

18. Design a deterministic pushdown automaton M for which $L(M)$ is the language generated by the grammar below, with start symbol S.

$$S \rightarrow xyN$$
$$N \rightarrow zS$$
$$N \rightarrow z$$
$$N \rightarrow \lambda$$

19. Let $\Sigma = \{x, y, \circ, \cup, *,), (, \emptyset\}$. Design a pushdown automaton M such that $L(M)$ is the set of all strings that are regular expressions over the alphabet $\{x, y\}$.

20. Construct a context-free grammar G such that $L(G)$ is the set of all strings formed by concatenating a string in $\{x, y\}^*$ with the same string written backward.

21. Show that the language consisting of the palindromes in $\{x, y\}^*$ is context-free. (A palindrome is a string that is identical to itself written backward.)

22. a. Design a context-free grammar that generates the language $\{x^m y^n$: m and n are nonnegative integers with $n < m\}$.
    b. Design a context-free grammar that generates the language $\{x^m y^n$: m and n are nonnegative integers with $n > m\}$.

23. a. Design a pushdown automaton M such that $L(M) = \{x^m y^n$: m and n are nonnegative integers and $m \leqslant n \leqslant 2m\}$.

b. Design a pushdown automaton M such that $L(M) = \{x^m y^n: m$ and n are nonnegative integers and $n < m$ or $2m < n\}$.

24. Show that the language $\{x^n: n$ is a prime positive integer$\}$ is not context-free.

25. Show that the language $\{x^n: n = m^2$ for some $m \in \mathbb{N}\}$ is not context-free.

26. Show that the language $\{x^n y^n z x^n y^n: n \in \mathbb{N}\}$ is not context-free.

27. Is the language $\{x^m y^n: m, n \in \mathbb{N}$ and $m \leq n \leq 2m\}$ context-free? Support your answer.

28. Is the union of a collection of context-free languages always context-free? Justify your answer.

29. Using a cardinality argument, show that there must be languages that are not context-free.

30. Apply the technique used in the proof of Theorem 2.3 to construct a context-free grammar that generates the language accepted by the pushdown automaton described below.

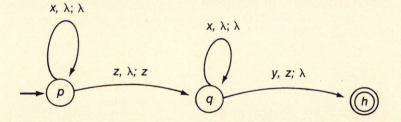

31. Apply the technique used in the proof of Theorem 2.3 to construct a context-free grammar that generates the language accepted by the pushdown automaton described by Figure 2.2.

32. Convert the following grammar, with start symbol S, to Chomsky normal form.

$$S \rightarrow MzN$$
$$M \rightarrow xM$$
$$M \rightarrow \lambda$$
$$N \rightarrow yN$$
$$N \rightarrow \lambda$$

33. Find a context-free grammar in Chomsky normal form that generates the same language as generated by the grammar in Figure 2.5.

34. Why would the collection of rewrite rules

$$X \to xY$$
$$Y \to yZ$$
$$Z \to z$$
$$Z \to \lambda$$

be preferred over

$$X \to xyz$$
$$X \to x$$

when constructing a parser?

35. Show that if L is a context-free language that does not contain the empty string, then there is a context-free grammar G in which the right side of each rewrite rule consists of a single terminal followed by zero or more nonterminals. (Grammars of this form are said to be in Griebach normal form.)

36. Show that the intersection of a regular language and a context-free language is always context-free.

37. Find a context-free grammar for the language over $\{x, y\}$ consisting of those strings in which the ratio of the number of xs to the number of ys is three to two.

Programming Problems

1. Implement the $LL(1)$ parsing algorithm shown in Figure 2.30. Apply the results to the parse tables in figures 2.29 and 2.31 as well as to your answer to Chapter Review Problem 13.

2. Implement the $LR(1)$ parsing algorithm shown in Figure 2.35. Apply the results to the parse tables in figures 2.34 and 2.38 as well as to your answer to Chapter Review Problem 15.

3. Write a program to convert context-free grammars that do not generate the empty string into grammars in Chomsky normal form.

CHAPTER 3

Turing Machines and Phrase-Structure Languages

To this point we have introduced the classes of finite and pushdown automata. In each case our goal has been to understand the language recognition powers of these theoretical machines. In this chapter we introduce yet another, and still more general, class of automata known as Turing machines and study the computational power of these machines in the context of solving language recognition problems.

A major result will be that Turing machines are able to accept exactly those languages that can be generated by unrestricted phrase-structure grammars. Thus, the language processing power of this class of machines is limited by the same bounds that limit the generative power of grammars. The importance of this equivalence is amplified by the fact that no one has yet been able to define a class of computational machines that is more powerful than the class of Turing machines. In fact, we will learn that the conjecture that the power of any computational process is captured within the class of Turing machines is generally accepted by computer scientists today. (This conjecture is known as Turing's thesis.) Thus, the correspondence between the language recognition powers of Turing machines and the generative power of the grammars that we will study in this chapter is believed to define the ultimate limits of any computational language recognition system.

In short, then, the introduction of Turing machines in this chapter will serve to culminate our study of grammars, languages, and parsing algorithms. However, this does not mean that our overall study will be finished; rather, the apparent limitations to computational powers discovered in this chapter will merely launch our study of computability.

3.1   TURING MACHINES

The class of automata now known as **Turing machines** was proposed by Alan M. Turing in 1936. (The fundamental idea of Turing was to study algorithmic processes by means of a computational model. A similar approach was also introduced by Emil L. Post in the same year. Both approaches have since been shown to be equivalent in computational power.) For our purpose it is convenient to consider Turing machines as generalized versions of the automata introduced in previous chapters. Turing machines are similar to finite automata in that they consist of a control mechanism and an input stream that we envision as a tape. The distinction is that Turing machines can move their tape heads both forward and backward and can write on as well as read from their tapes. We will see that these features add significantly to the capabilities of the machines.

Basic Properties of Turing Machines

Just as the other machines we have studied, a Turing machine contains a control mechanism that can be in one of a finite number of states at any given time. One of these states is called the initial state and represents the state in which the machine starts a computation. Another state is designated as the machine's **halt state.** Once the machine reaches this state, all computation ceases. Thus, the halt state of a Turing machine differs from the accept states of finite and pushdown automata in that these latter automata can continue computation after reaching an accept state, whereas a Turing machine must stop as soon as its halt state is reached. (Note: As defined above a Turing machine's initial state cannot also be the machine's halt state. Thus, every Turing machine must have at least two states.)

A more significant distinction between a Turing machine and the automata in the previous chapters is that a Turing machine can both read from and write on its input medium. More precisely, a Turing machine is equipped with a tape head that can be used both to read and write symbols on the machine's tape. (As with the other automata, this tape has a left end but extends indefinitely to the right.) Thus, a Turing machine can use its tape for auxiliary storage in much the same way as a pushdown automaton uses its stack. However, a Turing machine is not limited to push and pop operations when accessing this storage. Rather, a Turing machine can scan over the data on its tape, modifying those cells it wants to modify while leaving the other cells unchanged.

When using its tape for auxiliary storage purposes, it is convenient for a Turing machine to use special markers to distinguish between various portions of the tape. For this purpose, we allow a Turing machine to read and write symbols that may not appear in any input data. That is, we distinguish between the (finite) set of symbols, called the machine's alphabet, in which any initial input data must be coded and the possibly larger (finite) set of symbols, called the machine's **tape symbols,** that the machine is capable of reading and writing. (This distinction is similar to the distinction between a pushdown automaton's alphabet and its stack symbols.) Thus, the tape symbols of a Turing machine may include special markers that are not symbols in the machine's alphabet.

One symbol that falls in this category is the blank. This is the symbol that is assumed to be recorded in any tape cell that is not otherwise occupied. For instance, if a Turing machine should read beyond the input symbols on its tape, it will encounter and read the blank cells found there. Moreover, a Turing machine might need to erase a cell by writing a blank in it. Thus, the blank symbol is often considered to be a member of a Turing machine's set of tape symbols, but we do not consider the blank to be a member of a machine's alphabet.

On the printed page the blank symbol can easily lead to confusion and misunderstandings. For communication purposes we adopt the symbol $\triangle$ to represent the blank symbol. This convention eliminates the ambiguity between the strings $x\,y$ and $x\ \ y$ since the former can be expressed as $x\triangle y$ and the latter as $x\triangle\triangle y$.

The individual actions that can be performed by a Turing machine consist of write operations and move operations. A write operation consists of replacing a symbol on the tape with another symbol and then shifting to a new state (which may be the same as the old state). A move operation consists of moving the tape head one cell to the right or one cell to the left and then shifting to a new state (which again may be the same as the old state). Which action will be performed at a particular time depends on the symbol (the current symbol) in the cell currently visible to the tape head (the current cell) as well as the current state of the machine's control mechanism.

If we represent the set of tape symbols of a Turing machine by Γ, the set of states by S, and the set of nonhalt states by S', then the transitions of the machine can be represented by a function, called the machine's **transition function,** of the form $\delta{:}(S' \times \Gamma) \to S \times (\Gamma \cup \{L, R\})$, where we assume the symbols L and R are not symbols in Γ.

The semantics of this functional representation are as follows:
a. $\delta(p, x) = (q, y)$ means "If the current state is p and the current symbol is x, replace the x with the symbol y and shift to state q."
b. $\delta(p, x) = (q, L)$ means "If the current state is p and the current symbol is x, move the tape head one cell to the left and shift to state q."
c. $\delta(p, x) = (q, R)$ means "If the current state is p and the current symbol is x, move the tape head one cell to the right and shift to state q."

Note that since a Turing machine's transitions are described by a function, the machine is deterministic. More precisely, there is one and only one transition associated with any state/symbol pair in which the state is not the halt state.

During normal operation, a Turing machine proceeds by repeatedly executing transitions until the halt state is reached. (This means that under certain conditions a Turing machine's computation may never cease since its internal program may get caught in a nonterminating loop.) There is, however, one anomaly that may occur during this process—the machine's tape head may "fall off" the left end of the tape. In this case the machine will abort the computation, and we say that the machine's execution suffered an **abnormal termination.**

As with other automata, it is helpful to picture a Turing machine as shown in Figure 3.1. There the machine's control mechanism is represented by a rectangle with a type of clock face that indicates the machine's current state. Above this rectangle is the machine's tape. The position of the machine's tape head is represented with a pointer in the same manner as that of finite and pushdown automata.

Again as with other automata, the collection of transitions provided in a Turing machine can be conveniently represented by a transition diagram

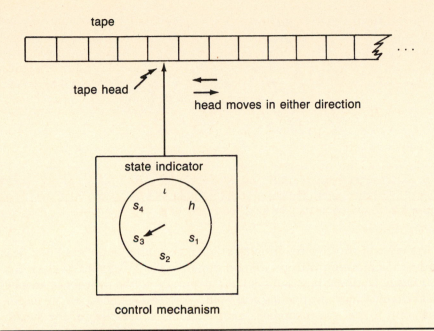

Figure 3.1 A representation of a Turing machine

in which the states of the machine are depicted as small circles (with the initial and halt states identified by a pointer and double circle, respectively) connected by arcs representing the possible transitions. Each arc in a transition diagram for a Turing machine is labeled with a pair of symbols separated by a slash. The first symbol of the pair represents the tape symbol that must be in the current cell for the transition to be applicable. The second symbol is the symbol to be written in the current cell (if the transition is a write operation) or else one of the symbols L or R (if the transition is a move operation). Thus, the transition $\delta(p, x) = (q, y)$ would be represented in the transition diagram as an arc from circle p to circle q labeled x/y; or $\delta(p, x) = (q, L)$ would appear as an arc from p to q labeled x/L. As an example, Figure 3.2 is a complete transition diagram for a Turing machine with tape symbols $\{a, b, \triangle\}$ that moves its tape head to the right until a blank is found.

Based on our experience with other automata, you should not be surprised to find that a complete transition diagram for a Turing machine is often rather cumbersome and hard to understand. Thus, we sometimes draw skeletal diagrams containing only those arcs that are pertinent to the discussion with the understanding that the other arcs could be added if required.

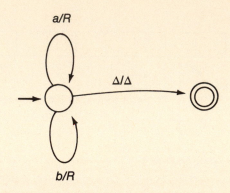

Figure 3.2   A transition diagram for a Turing machine

As we will shortly see, Turing's original computational "machine" was a human computing with pencil and paper. With the advent of electronic computing equipment, this model has given way to the concept of an electromechanical machine reading and writing on a magnetic tape. The important point is that the theoretical computational capabilities of the system remain the same regardless of the technology in which its components are implemented. Indeed, the concept of a Turing machine, as with the other automata we have studied, is independent of its implementation. Thus, let us isolate the definitive features of a Turing machine in the following formal definition.

A Turing machine is a sextuple of the form $(S, \Sigma, \Gamma, \delta, \iota, h)$, where:
a. S is a finite collection of states.
b. Σ is a finite set of nonblank symbols called the machine's alphabet.
c. Γ is a finite set of symbols, including those in Σ, called the machine's tape symbols.
d. δ is the machine's transition function.
e. ι is a member of S called the initial state.
f. h is a member of S called the halt state.

At times it is convenient to have a concise notation that represents the configuration of a Turing machine's tape, including the contents of its cells and the position of the tape head. In such cases we will list the contents of the tape cells, with the position of the tape head underlined. Thus, $\triangle x y \underline{z} \triangle \triangle \cdots$ will represent a tape containing a blank, followed by the symbols x, y, and z, followed by blanks, with the tape head over the cell containing the z.

The Origins of Turing Machines

The purpose for which Turing machines were developed differs somewhat from the other automata we have studied in that Turing machines were designed to capture the full power of computational processes. That is, Turing's intention was to develop a system in which one could model any process that might be considered a computation.

Keep in mind that this was well before today's computing machinery was developed. Turing envisioned a computation being performed by a human with paper and pencil. In this setting, Turing reasoned that the human could concentrate on only a restricted portion of the paper at any given time and, in turn, the collection of marks found on this portion of the paper could be considered collectively as a single symbol. Hence, Turing considered the paper to be divided into sections, each section being the amount of paper required to record a single symbol. Turing also concluded that any computational process could involve only a finite number of symbols. Indeed, since each symbol must be recordable in a fixed amount of space, the existence of an increasingly large number of symbols would dictate that different symbols must have arbitrarily small distinguishing features. At some point, then, the human's ability to distinguish between different symbols would begin to fail, which would result in a limited number of effective symbols.

Turing argued that when considering a particular section of the paper, the human could either alter that section or choose to move to another section. Which action would be taken and the details of that action would depend on the symbol currently in that section and the human's state of mind. As with the number of symbols, Turing reasoned that the human was capable of only a finite number of distinguishable states of mind. Turing considered the human to be in a special initial state when the computation started and in a state designated as the halt state when the computation was completed.

To keep the availability of paper from restricting the power of the model, Turing proposed that the amount of paper available for the computation be unlimited.

It is significant that no one has been able to produce a widely accepted model of computation that is more powerful than that of Turing. Turing's model is actually more general than today's computers since a Turing machine is never restricted by the lack of more storage space whereas an actual machine must ultimately exhaust its storage potential. Thus, **Turing's thesis** that *the computational power of Turing machines is as great as any possible computational system* is generally accepted by computer scientists. Moreover, this thesis and the results supporting it have important implications regarding questions of computability today. To solve a problem with a computer requires the development of a computational process (or an algorithm) for solving the problem. Thus, answers to questions posed in Turing's day, such as, "What can be done via a computational process?" help answer current questions such as, "What can be done by a modern computer?"

In Chapter 4 we will return to the role of Turing machines in the study of computational processes as well as investigate the relationship between these abstract notions and the issues of programming language design. In this chapter, however, we continue by introducing a useful technique for constructing Turing machines and then pursue the relationship between Turing machines, grammars, and languages.

Exercises

1. With what tape configuration will the Turing machine represented below halt if it is started with its tape configured as $\underline{x}xx\triangle\triangle\triangle\cdots$?

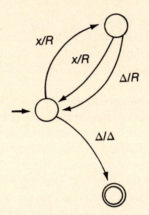

2. Design a Turing machine with tape symbols x, y, and $\triangle$ that will search its tape for the pattern $xyxy$ and halt if and only if that pattern is found.

3. Design a Turing machine that, when started with its tape head over the leftmost tape cell, will suffer an abnormal termination if and only if an x is recorded somewhere on its tape. If you applied your machine to a tape that did not contain an x, would the machine ever detect that fact?

4. Show that allowing Turing machines to have more than one halt state would not increase their computational abilities since any such machine could be simulated by a Turing machine with only one halt state.

3.2   MODULAR CONSTRUCTION OF TURING MACHINES

Although the major purpose of this chapter is the study of the language acceptance capabilities of Turing machines, an important side effect is the introduction of Turing machine fundamentals, since these machines will prove to be important tools in the chapters to follow. We therefore investigate Turing machines more carefully before proceeding with our study of languages. Our goal for this section is to develop techniques by which complex Turing machines can be constructed from elementary building blocks. Such an approach will make the machines encountered later in our study easier to construct as well as easier to understand.

Combining Turing Machines

Although we will speak in terms of combining Turing machines to form larger Turing machines, our approach will actually be to combine Turing machine programs in much the same way that program modules are combined to develop large software systems. For this, it is helpful to represent Turing machine programs as transition diagrams and combine them in ways reminiscent of the way we formed the union and concatenation of finite automata.

Suppose that we have two Turing machines M_1 and M_2 having transition diagrams T_1 and T_2, respectively, and tape symbols from the set Γ. If we wanted to develop a transition diagram for another machine that simulates the activities of M_1 followed by the activities of M_2, we could simply remove the halt designation from the halt state of T_1 and the initial designation from the initial state of T_2, and then for each x in Γ, draw an arc labeled x/x from the old halt state of T_1 to the old initial state of T_2.

Clearly the result would behave as desired, but this simple approach has various drawbacks. For instance, it has the potential of introducing a large number of transitions that merely rewrite the contents of the current cell. (This inefficiency would introduce difficulties in our discussion of complexity in Chapter 5.) Furthermore, suppose we wanted the composite machine to halt after simulating M_1 unless the current symbol, upon reaching the halt state, is z, in which case we would like the new machine to simulate the actions of M_2; or suppose we needed to combine three diagrams with control to pass from one to another depending on the value of the current symbol each time an old halt state is reached. In these cases a slightly more complex linkage is required.

Suppose then that we need to combine the transition diagrams of several Turing machines to obtain a machine that simulates some combination of the original machines. We proceed as follows:

1. Remove the initial designation from the initial states of all but the one machine in which the new composite machine is to start.
2. Remove the halt designation from the halt states of all the machines and introduce a new halt state that is not in any of the diagrams being combined.
3. For each old halt state p and each x in Γ, draw an arc as follows:
    a. If the composite machine should halt upon reaching p with cur-

rent symbol x, draw an arc labeled x/x from p to the new halt state.

b. If upon reaching p with current symbol x, the composite machine should transfer control to the machine $M = (S, \Sigma, \Gamma, \delta, \iota, h)$, then draw an arc labeled x/z from p to state q of M, where $\delta(\iota, x) = (q, z)$.

Figure 3.3 provides an example of this construction. Here we have started with the transition diagrams for three separate machines, each having tape symbols x, y, and $\triangle$. One moves its tape head one cell to the right, another finds the first x to the right of the current cell, and the third finds the first y to the right of the current cell. Using the above composition process and these machines as building blocks, we have constructed a composite machine that finds the second occurrence of the nonblank symbol to the right of its initial head position.

Just as when dealing with large software systems, we will find it convenient to avoid the details interior to the building blocks from which we construct more complex Turing machines. If we know what task each of the smaller machines performs, then our concern will be with the proper linkage of these machines and not with how each performs its individual task. Thus, we will avoid the use of detailed transition diagrams as shown in Figure 3.3 and instead use composite diagrams. These are diagrams in which each building block used is represented as a single node with arrows between nodes to indicate the transitions between the blocks. These arrows are labeled according to the value that must appear in the current cell in order to traverse the arrow. That is, if an arrow from node A to node B is labeled x, then if A should arrive at its old halt state with an x in the current cell, execution will be transferred to the machine B. Following the lead of transition diagrams, the node in a composite diagram in which execution should begin is marked with a pointer. For example, the composite machine shown in Figure 3.3 could be summarized by the composite diagram

where node A represents the machine that moves its tape head one cell to the right, B the machine that searches for an x, and C the machine that searches for a y.

As a matter of convenience, there are several notational shortcuts that are customary when drawing composite diagrams for Turing machines. One of these is to replace several arrows that have the same source and destination with a single arrow labeled by a list of symbols, or perhaps by $\neg x$ (read "not x") if the arrow should be traversed for all current symbol values other than x. Another shortcut is to use an unlabeled arrow to represent a

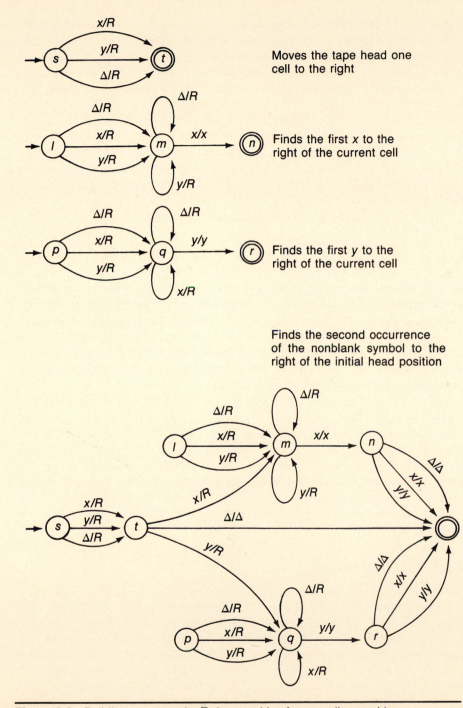

Moves the tape head one cell to the right

Finds the first x to the right of the current cell

Finds the first y to the right of the current cell

Finds the second occurrence of the nonblank symbol to the right of the initial head position

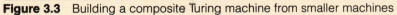

Figure 3.3   Building a composite Turing machine from smaller machines

transition to be traversed regardless of the value in the current cell. This particular situation is often further abbreviated by removing the arrow entirely and merely listing the nodes side-by-side. For instance, the sequence $\rightarrow A \rightarrow B \rightarrow C$ could be simplified to $\rightarrow ABC$.

As examples, Figure 3.4a shows a composite diagram of a machine constructed from M_1 and M_2. The composite machine simulates the actions of M_1 until it would normally halt and then simulates the actions of M_2. Figure 3.4b represents a machine that simulates M_1 and then transfers to M_2 only if the current cell contains an x; otherwise, it halts upon completing the actions of M_1. Finally, Figure 3.4c represents the composite machine that starts by simulating M_1 and then simulates M_2 or M_3 depending on whether the current symbol is or is not x.

Another shortcut we will use is to apply the notation

$$\xrightarrow{x,\ y,\ z} \left.\right\} \xrightarrow{\omega}$$

to indicate that when the current symbol is x, y, or z, the machine should proceed in this direction with ω representing the symbol that is actually present. This notation allows us to avoid cluttering the diagram with similar yet separate routines for each of the symbols x, y, and z. Instead, we are able to present a single generic routine dealing with the symbol ω in a manner similar to that in which a subprogram presents a generic routine in terms of formal parameters. Thus, if the machine

$$\rightarrow M_1 \xrightarrow{x,\ y} \left.\right\} \xrightarrow{\omega} M_2 \xrightarrow{\omega}$$

were to reach the old halt state of M_1 with current symbol x or y, it would continue by executing M_2, and if this should lead to the old halt state of M_2 with the same current symbol as when M_2 was entered, then execution would return to M_1.

Basic Building Blocks

With this notational system established, we now consider the elementary Turing machines that we will use as building blocks in later discussions. We get a clue as to what these blocks should be by recalling that the only activities available to any Turing machine are to move the tape head one cell to the right, to move the head one cell to the left, and to write a symbol in the current cell. Consequently, if we construct individual machines that perform these simple tasks, then any other Turing machine must be a composite of these blocks.

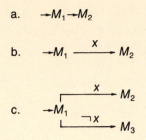

a. $\rightarrow M_1 \rightarrow M_2$

b. $\rightarrow M_1 \xrightarrow{\quad x \quad} M_2$

c. $\rightarrow M_1$ with branches $\xrightarrow{\quad x \quad} M_2$ and $\xrightarrow{\quad \neg x \quad} M_3$

Figure 3.4   Examples of composite Turing machines

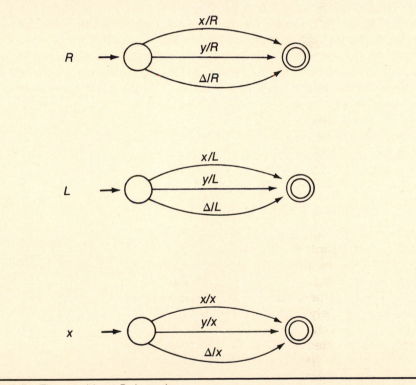

Figure 3.5   The machines R, L, and x

   Figure 3.5 shows transition diagrams for Turing machines that perform each of these rudimentary activities, assuming that the tape symbols are x, y, and $\triangle$. (Machines for other tape symbols are simple generalizations of these machines.) We represent the machine that moves its head one cell to the right by R, the machine that moves its head one cell to the left by L, and the machine that writes a particular symbol in the current cell by the symbol involved. Thus, a Turing machine that moves one cell to the right, writes the symbol y, moves one cell back to the left, and then halts could be represented by the composite diagram

$$\rightarrow R \rightarrow y \rightarrow L$$

or, in condensed form, as

$$\rightarrow RyL$$

Our next step is to establish a repertoire of slightly more complex machines. One group of these machines, shown in Figure 3.6, performs simple searches. More precisely, for any symbol x, the machine represented by R_x searches its tape to the right of the initial position for a cell containing the symbol x. If that symbol is found, the machine halts with that cell being the current cell; otherwise, the machine will continue to search forever. In a similar fashion, the machine $R_{\neg x}$ searches to the right of the initial position for any symbol other than x. These same searches are performed to the left of the initial position by the machines L_x and $L_{\neg x}$. (Note that in contrast to search-

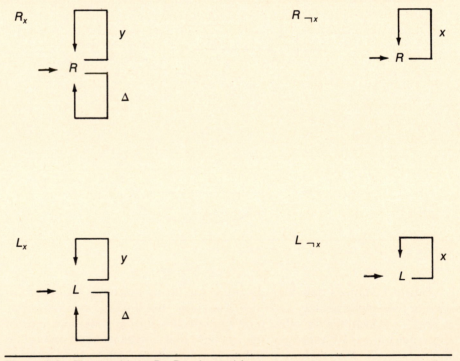

Figure 3.6   The machines R_x, $R_{\neg x}$, L_x, and $L_{\neg x}$

ing to the right of the initial position, a search to the left has the potential of causing an abnormal termination due to reaching the left end of the tape without finding the target of the search.) Of special use to us will be the machines R_Δ, $R_{\neg\Delta}$, L_Δ, and $L_{\neg\Delta}$ that can be used in the construction of composite machines that must search for either blank or nonblank cells.

Another useful collection of machines performs shift operations. Two such machines are described in Figure 3.7. The machine S_R shifts the string of nonblank symbols found at the left of the current cell one cell to the right. Thus, if the tape of S_R had the initial configuration $\triangle x y \underline{y} x x \triangle \triangle \triangle \cdots$, then S_R would halt with its tape configured as $\triangle \triangle x y y x \triangle \triangle \cdots$; or when applied to $\triangle y x y \underline{\triangle} \triangle x x y \triangle \triangle \cdots$, S_R would produce $\triangle \triangle y x \underline{y} \triangle x x y \triangle \triangle \cdots$. As a somewhat special case, if the cell at the left of the current cell contains a blank, S_R will merely erase the current cell. Hence, S_R would convert the tape configuration $x y \triangle \underline{y} x \triangle \triangle \cdots$ into $x y \triangle \underline{\triangle} x \triangle \triangle \cdots$.

In a similar manner, S_L performs a shift to the left. If the tape of S_L had the initial configuration $\triangle \underline{x} y y x x \triangle \triangle \triangle \cdots$, then S_L would halt with its tape

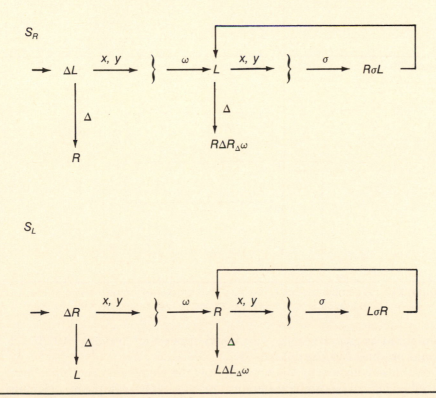

Figure 3.7 The machines S_R and S_L

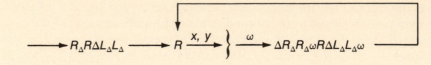

Figure 3.8 A copying machine that transforms a pattern of the form $\triangle w \triangle$ into $\triangle w \underline{\triangle} w \triangle$

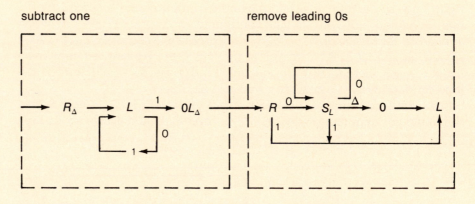

Figure 3.9 A Turing machine to decrement a binary representation by one

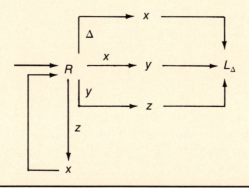

Figure 3.10 A composite Turing machine that produces the next string in the sequence λ, x, y, z, xx, yx, zx, xy, yy, zy, xz, yz, zz, xxx, yxx, $\cdots$

configured as $\triangle \underline{y}yxx\triangle\triangle\triangle\cdots$; or when applied to $\triangle yxy\triangle\underline{\triangle}xxy\triangle\triangle\cdots$, S_L would produce $\underline{\triangle}yxy\triangle\underline{x}xy\triangle\triangle\triangle\cdots$.

We close with several examples of how the elementary machines introduced so far can be combined to form more complex composite machines. Figure 3.8 defines a copying machine that transforms a pattern on its tape of the form $\triangle w \triangle$ into the form $\triangle w \triangle w \triangle$, where w is any string (possibly having length zero) of nonblank symbols. The machine shown in Figure 3.9 assumes its input represents a positive integer in binary notation and decrements the value represented by one. Finally, the machine in Figure 3.10 modifies strings over the alphabet $\{x, y, z\}$. More precisely, if we start the machine with its tape configured as $\triangle w_1 \triangle \triangle \triangle \cdots$, where w_1 is a string in $\{x, y, z\}^*$, then the machine will halt with its tape configured as $\triangle w_2 \triangle \triangle \triangle \cdots$, where w_2 is the string following w_1 in the sequence $\triangle$, x, y, z, xx, yx, zx, xy, yy, zy, xz, yz, zz, xxx, yxx, $\cdots$. This machine will prove to be a useful building block in later discussions.

Exercises

1. Combine the transition diagrams of the machines M_1 and M_2 shown below to form the transition diagram of the composite machine
   $$\rightarrow M_1 \overset{x}{\rightarrow} M_2.$$
   What does the composite machine do?

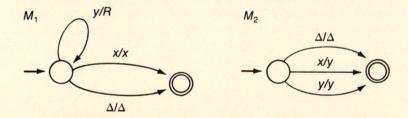

2. Using the building blocks introduced in this section, build a Turing machine that will replace the string of 0s and 1s immediately to the right of its tape head with that string's complement and then return the tape head to its original position. Assume that the right end of the string is marked with a blank. (The complement of a string of 0s and 1s is the string formed by replacing the original 0s with 1s and the original 1s with 0s.)

3. Under what circumstance would execution of the machine S_R result in an abnormal termination?

4. Describe the computation performed by the following Turing machine.

$$\rightarrow * \rightarrow R \overset{\neg \triangle}{\longrightarrow} \triangle \quad\quad \overset{\triangle}{\longrightarrow} L_* \triangle$$

3.3   TURING MACHINES AS LANGUAGE ACCEPTERS

The automata introduced in the previous chapters were presented as language accepters. We used them as a means of testing strings to determine their membership in a particular language. It is natural, then, to study Turing machines in the same light. In this section we discuss the issues of string acceptance by Turing machines; we begin by considering the context in which a Turing machine accepts an input string.

String Testing Procedures

To test a string over some alphabet Σ with a Turing machine, we record the string on the machine's otherwise blank tape starting at the second cell. (If we were testing the string $xxyy$, the tape would appear as $\triangle xxyy \triangle \triangle \cdots$.) Then, we place the machine's tape head at the leftmost cell of the tape and start the machine from its initial state. (See Figure 3.11.) We say that the machine accepts the string if, from this initial configuration, the machine finds its way to its halt state.

As an example, a composite diagram for a machine that accepts exactly the strings of the form $x^n y^n z^n$, where $n \in \mathbb{N}$, is shown in Figure 3.12. It interrogates its input by repeatedly reducing the length of a nonempty string of the form $x^n y^n z^n$ through the sequence $x^{n-1} y^n z^n$, $x^{n-1} y^{n-1} z^n$, and

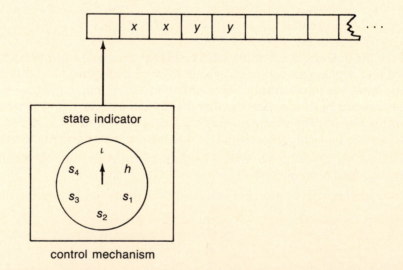

Figure 3.11   The initial configuration of a Turing machine when testing the string *xxyy*

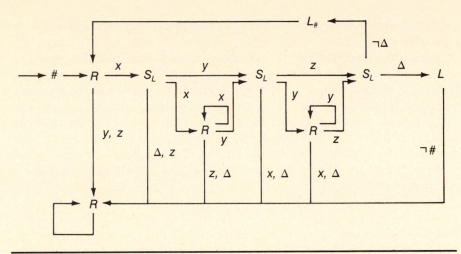

Figure 3.12   A Turing machine M for which $L(M) = \{x^n y^n z^n: n \in \mathbb{N}\}$

$x^{n-1} y^{n-1} z^{n-1}$. The machine halts if and only if this reduction process produces an empty string as a result of removing the same number of xs, ys, and zs. (The symbol # is used as a tape symbol to assist in finding the left end of the tape after each reduction sequence is completed.)

As with other automata, the collection of strings accepted by a Turing machine M is called the language accepted by the machine and is denoted by $L(M)$. A language L is said to be a **Turing-acceptable language** if there is a Turing machine M such that $L = L(M)$.

For our purposes Figure 3.12 is of special significance since it shows that Turing machines are able to accept languages that pushdown automata cannot. (Recall that $\{x^n y^n z^n: n \in \mathbb{N}\}$ is not a context-free language.) In fact, we will find that the class of Turing-acceptable languages properly contains all the context-free languages, but there is a bit of background work to do before we will be in position to prove this.

We have defined string acceptance by Turing machines in a manner that conforms with other automata. However, it is sometimes convenient to require that a Turing machine write an acceptance message on its tape before halting. For instance, we might want a Turing machine to accept a string only by halting with its tape in the configuration $\triangle Y \triangle \triangle \cdots$, where the symbol Y is used to represent the reply yes. (Under this convention, halting with any other tape configuration would not constitute acceptance.)

Fortunately, this additional acceptance criterion does not affect the class of languages that can be accepted by Turing machines. Given a Turing machine M that accepts strings by merely halting, there is another Turing machine M' that accepts the same strings by halting with its tape configured as $\triangle Y \triangle \triangle \cdots$, and vice versa. To justify this claim, we first consider a Turing machine M that accepts strings by merely halting and show that we can modify it so that it accepts the same strings by halting with its tape configured as $\triangle Y \triangle \triangle \cdots$.

Basically, all we must do is modify M so that it keeps track of the portion of the tape that is soiled during its computation. Then, having completed its normal computation, it will be able to erase that portion of the tape and write the appropriate message on the otherwise blank tape before halting. To keep track of the soiled portion of the tape we will use the special tape symbols $\#$ and $*$. The symbol $\#$ will be used to mark the left end of the tape, and the symbol $*$ will be used to mark the right end of the soiled portion of the tape. Thus, the modified machine should begin any computation with

$$\rightarrow R_\triangle S_R R* L_\triangle L \# R$$

That is, it should move to the right end of the input string and shift the string one cell to the right. Then it should mark the first cell to the right of the input with the symbol $*$, return to the leftmost tape cell, write the symbol $\#$, and position its tape head over the remaining blank at the left end of the input string. In short, given the initial tape configuration $\triangle w \triangle \triangle \cdots$, where w is the input string, the machine produces the tape configuration $\# \triangle w * \triangle \triangle \cdots$.

From this configuration our modified machine should continue by simulating the actions of M. However, when performing this simulation, the machine must watch for the occurrence of two special circumstances. The first occurs if the symbol $\#$ should become the current symbol. Note that since the entire input has been shifted one cell to the right, the cell containing the symbol $\#$ will not be read during the simulation unless the process being simulated has suffered an abnormal termination. Thus, if the current symbol should be $\#$, our modified machine should move its tape head another cell to the left so that it too will suffer an abnormal termination.

The other special circumstance is the occurrence of the symbol $*$ as the current symbol. This situation indicates that the computation being simulated has moved its tape head to the right over a previously unsoiled tape cell. In this case our modified machine should bump the marker $*$ one cell to the right by executing $\rightarrow R*L\triangle$ before continuing the simulation.

Having simulated the computation of M to the point where M has reached its halt state, our modified machine should erase its tape and write the message Y before halting. This is accomplished by attaching the block

$$\rightarrow R_* \rightarrow \triangle L \begin{array}{c} \downarrow \\ \neg \# \end{array}$$
$$\downarrow \#$$
$$\triangle RYL$$

at the end of our modified machine.

In summary the finished machine is

$$\rightarrow R_\triangle S_R R*L_\triangle L\#R \rightarrow M_0 \rightarrow R_* \rightarrow \triangle L \xrightarrow{\neg\#}$$
$$\downarrow\#$$
$$\triangle RYL$$

where M_0 is the machine that simulates M, except for the two special circumstances in which the symbol # or * surface as the current symbol.

Conversely, suppose we start with a Turing machine M' that accepts strings by halting with its tape configured as $\triangle Y\triangle\triangle\cdots$. We could then alter that machine to obtain a machine that never halts under any other conditions. All that is required is to insist that the machine check its tape for the configuration $\triangle Y\triangle\triangle\cdots$ before actually halting. To this end, we construct another machine that marks the left and right ends of its tape as described earlier, simulates the actions of M' while adjusting for the occurrence of # or * as the current symbol, and finally, if the simulation should find its way to the original halt state, confirms that the portion of its tape bounded by the markers # and * was configured as $\#\underline{\triangle}Y\triangle\triangle\cdots\triangle\triangle*$ before actually halting. This last step could be accomplished by a routine such as

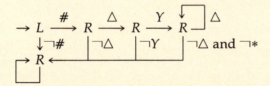

We conclude that there are a variety of ways we may require Turing machines to declare acceptance of their input strings: We can allow them to merely halt or insist that they respond with an acceptance message. Both approaches have assets and liabilities, but since they are equivalent in power, we are free to select the method most convenient for the application. We will, however, assume that a Turing machine accepts strings merely by halting unless stated otherwise.

Multiple-Tape Turing Machines

We now consider Turing machines that have more than one tape. (We call such a machine a k-tape Turing machine, where k represents a positive integer, in those cases where the number of tapes is significant.) Each of these tapes has a left end, extends indefinitely to the right, and is accessed by a separate read/write head. The transition to be executed at any time depends on the collection of symbols visible by these heads together with the current state of the machine. The action of a single transition affects only one of the machine's tapes. This action may be to write on the current cell of that tape, move that tape's head one cell to the left, or move the head one cell to the right.

To test a symbol string for acceptance using a multiple-tape Turing machine, we start the machine from its initial state with the input string recorded on its first tape (in the same format as on the single tape of a conventional machine), its other tapes blank, and all tape heads at the leftmost cells of their tapes. The string is accepted if, from this initial configuration, the machine halts.

One might expect that multiple-tape Turing machines would possess greater language processing power than their single-tape counterparts; however, the following theorem shows that this is not true. Although using a multiple-tape machine may be convenient at times, no more languages can be accepted by these machines than can be accepted by conventional Turing machines.

THEOREM 3.1
For each multiple-tape Turing machine M there is a traditional (one-tape) Turing machine M' such that $L(M) = L(M')$.

PROOF
Suppose M is a k-tape Turing machine that accepts the language L. Our approach is to show that the contents of the k tapes can be represented on a single tape in such a way that the actions of M can be simulated by a single-tape machine M'. We envision the tapes of M being placed parallel to each other with their left ends aligned as shown in Figure 3.13a, where the position of each tape's head is indicated by a pointer below the tape. Based on this arrangement, the contents of all k tapes together with the positions of their tape heads can be represented in a table containing $2k$ rows and an unlimited number of columns extending to the right as shown in Figure 3.13b. The odd-numbered rows of this table represent the tapes themselves. Each even-numbered row is used to indicate the position of the tape head associated with the tape of the preceding row. This is done by placing a 1 in the column associated with the current cell of the row above and leaving all the other cells blank.

Note that each column of the table just described is essentially a $2k$-tuple, whose odd-numbered components are tape symbols from M, and whose even-numbered components are elements of $\{\triangle, 1\}$. Hence, there are only a finite number of different symbol combinations that can appear in the columns. This means we can assign a unique new tape symbol to each of the possible $2k$-tuples, and then represent the entire table as an infinite string of these new

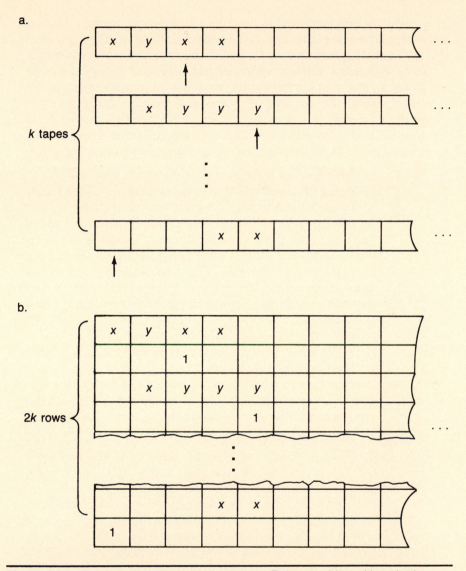

Figure 3.13 Representing the tapes in a k-tape Turing machine with a single array

symbols. In this manner, we can store on a single tape all the information stored on the tapes of the k-tape machine. Although each cell on the single tape contains only one symbol, that symbol represents a $2k$-tuple. It is, therefore, convenient to speak as if the cell contained the tuple directly rather than a symbol representing the tuple. We will adopt this informality.

We are now prepared to describe a single-tape machine M' that accepts the same language as the k-tape machine M. The alphabets of M and M' are the same. However, the collection of tape symbols of M' consists of the tape symbols of M, a symbol for each possible $2k$-tuple, and a # symbol for use as a special marking symbol. To test a string, the machine M' starts with its tape being an exact duplicate of tape 1 in the k-tape machine M. The first task of M' is to translate the contents of its tape into a format that represents all k tapes of M. To accomplish this, M' performs the following steps:

A1. Shift the tape contents one cell to the right using $\rightarrow R_\triangle S_R L_\triangle$. (The tape head will be left over the second cell on the tape.)

A2. Move the head one cell to the left (i.e., to the leftmost cell on the tape), write the special marker #, and then move one cell to the right. (The symbol # is assumed not to be a tape symbol of M. It is used here to mark the end of the tape. If it is read while simulating M, we know that M has gone off the end of its tape.)

A3. Repeat the following steps until the symbol replaced in step b is a blank.
   a. Move the tape head one cell to the right.
   b. Replace the current symbol, say x, with the tape symbol representing the tuple $(x, \triangle, \triangle, \triangle, \cdots, \triangle, \triangle)$.

A4. Execute $L_\triangle$ which will move the tape head back to the second cell on the tape. Replace the blank in this cell with the tape symbol representing the tuple $(\triangle, 1, \triangle, 1, \cdots, \triangle, 1)$.

Having performed these steps, M' will have translated its tape into a multiple-tape format, marked the left end of the tape with the symbol #, and returned its tape head to the tuple representing the leftmost cells of the k tapes of M (see Figure 3.14).

The task of M' would now be to simulate the actions of M until M halts or abnormally terminates. Of course, to simulate a single transition of M requires a sequence of several steps in M'. We design M' so that each such sequence begins from a special state, called a compound state, that reflects the current state of M as well as the collection of k symbols found in the current tape cells of M. Thus, each compound state is conceptually a $k+1$–tuple, where the first component is a state from M and the remaining components are symbols from the alphabet of M.

We construct M' such that being in the compound state $(p, x_1, x_2, \cdots, x_k)$ corresponds to M being in state p with current symbols $x_1, x_2, \cdots, x_k$. From each such state, M' will perform a sequence of steps designed to simulate the transition that M would

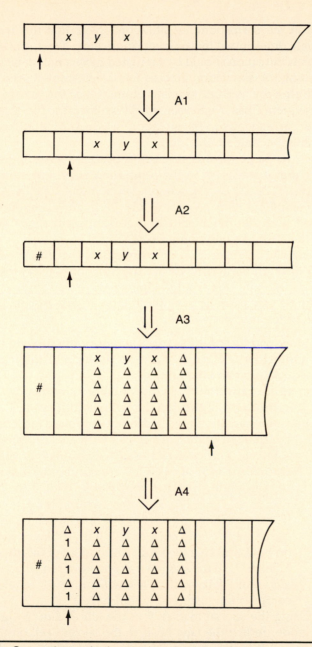

Figure 3.14 Converting a single tape into three-tape format

perform in the corresponding situation. (Note that this transition is uniquely determined by the compound state. Thus, the decision as to which transition should be simulated next is not made dynamically during the simulation process but is determined prior to execution during the machine's construction.) Once the transition simulation sequence has been executed, M' will shift to the compound state that corresponds to the situation in which M would be upon completing the single transition.

To set the stage for this simulation process, we refine step A4 above so that it leaves M' in the compound state representing the $k+1$–tuple $(\iota, \triangle, \triangle, \cdots, \triangle)$, where ι is the initial state of M. Thus, having completed step A4, M' would be in the compound state associated with the initial state and current symbols of M at the start of the string-recognition process.

To simulate the execution of a transition τ of M, M' executes steps B1 through B3, where we use the notation j_τ to represent the number of the tape that would be affected by transition τ. (Recall that a single transition of a multiple-tape Turing machine affects only one of the machine's tapes.)

B1. Move right until the $2j_\tau$ component of the tuple in the current cell is 1. (That is, find the position of the tape head associated with tape j_τ.)

B2. a. If the transition τ is a write operation, modify the $2j_\tau - 1$ component of the current cell accordingly.

b. If the transition τ is a right move, replace the 1 in the $2j_\tau$ component of the current cell with a blank, move right one cell, and change the $2j_\tau$ component of this tuple from blank to 1. (If a blank is encountered when moving to the right, replace the blank with the $2k$-tuple $(\triangle, \triangle, \triangle, \triangle, \cdots, \triangle, \triangle)$ before writing the 1.)

c. If the transition τ is a left move, replace the 1 in the $2j_\tau$ component of the current cell with a blank, move left one cell, and change the $2j_\tau$ component of this tuple from blank to 1. (If the symbol # is encountered when moving left, move left again. This will cause M' to abort the computation just as M would have.)

B3. Using the special marker # at the left end of the tape as a guide, return the tape head to the second cell on the tape and shift to the compound state in M' that reflects the configuration of M after executing the transition τ.

As an example, Figure 3.15 demonstrates the simulation of a three-tape machine moving its second tape head one cell to the right.

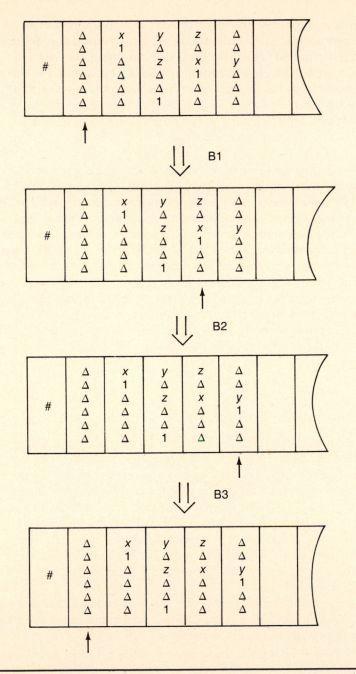

Figure 3.15   A single-tape simulation of a three-tape Turing machine performing a right move operation on its second tape

If execution of B1 through B3 leads to a compound state whose first component is the halt state of M, the computation being simulated has halted. Thus, we design M' so that it also halts.

Constructed in this manner, M' merely simulates the activities of M and therefore accepts a string if and only if M would have done likewise. Consequently, the single-tape machine M' accepts exactly the same language as the multiple-tape machine M.

∎

Among other things, Theorem 3.1 builds our confidence in Turing's thesis. Having extended the power of finite automata by adding additional memory to obtain the class of pushdown automata, we may be tempted to extend Turing machines in a similar manner. However, Theorem 3.1 indicates that this would not produce a more powerful language accepter. Any memory device we might add to a Turing machine could be modeled with additional tapes, and by Theorem 3.1, these additional tapes would not improve the language recognition power of the machine. Thus, we cannot contradict Turing's thesis by adding memory to Turing machines.

Another phenomenon that supports Turing's thesis is that no additional language recognition power is obtained by introducing nondeterminism when dealing with Turing machines. Our first step toward supporting this claim is to introduce the concept of a nondeterministic Turing machine.

Nondeterministic Turing Machines

A **nondeterministic Turing machine** is similar to a traditional Turing machine, the distinction being that a nondeterministic machine may not be fully defined or (more importantly) may provide more than one applicable transition for some current state/symbol pair. If a nondeterministic Turing machine should arrive at a current state/symbol pair from which no transition is applicable, the machine aborts the computation. If a nondeterministic Turing machine should arrive at a current state/symbol pair from which more than one transition is applicable, the machine makes a nondeterministic choice and proceeds with the computation by executing one of the applicable options.

In short, a nondeterministic Turing machine can be defined as a sextuple $(S, \Sigma, \Gamma, \rho, \iota, h)$ just like a deterministic Turing machine, except that the fourth component is merely a subset of $((S - \{h\}) \times \Gamma) \times (S \times (\Gamma \cup \{L, R\}))$ rather than a function from $(S - \{h\}) \times \Gamma$ into $S \times (\Gamma \cup \{L, R\})$. In this context, it is clear that the nondeterministic Turing machines form a class of machines that properly contains the traditional (deterministic) Turing machines discussed so far.

We say a string w is accepted by a nondeterministic Turing machine M if it is possible for M to reach its halt state after starting its computation with input w. We say *possible* in recognition of the fact that in the case of a nondeterministic machine, failure to reach the halt state on a particular attempt could be the result of a wrong decision by the machine rather than an improper input string. We define the collection of all strings accepted by the nondeterministic Turing machine M to be the language $L(M)$. Thus, a string w is in $L(M)$ if and only if there are choices available to M that would result in M reaching its halt state when given input w.

Since a nondeterministic Turing machine is a generalization of a traditional Turing machine, each language that is accepted by a traditional Turing machine can be accepted by a nondeterministic Turing machine. The more interesting fact is that, as shown in the following theorem, nondeterministic Turing machines are unable to accept more languages than the deterministic ones. Thus, as in the case of finite automata, the introduction of nondeterminism does not increase the language recognition power of Turing machines.

THEOREM 3.2
For each nondeterministic Turing machine M there is a deterministic Turing machine D such that $L(M) = L(D)$.

PROOF
Suppose M is a nondeterministic Turing machine that accepts the language $L(M)$. We must demonstrate the existence of a deterministic Turing machine that accepts the same language. This we do indirectly by showing that there is a deterministic three-tape Turing machine M' such that $L(M) = L(M')$, and thus, by Theorem 3.1, there must also be a traditional (deterministic, one-tape) Turing machine that accepts $L(M)$.

We design M' so that it tries all the options available to the nondeterministic machine M in a systematic manner, which it does in hopes of finding a combination that leads to the acceptance of the input string. The three tapes of M' are used as follows: the first tape holds the input string being tested; the second tape is used as a "work tape" on which M' repeatedly copies a fresh version of the input string and then, using this copy, simulates a sequence of transitions of M; the third tape is used to keep track of the transition sequence (of M) being applied as well as the sequences that have already been simulated.

The process of copying the input string from tape 1 to tape 2 involves two subtle but important points. First, M' must shift the string one cell to the right during the copy process. That is, the contents of cell one on tape 1 should be placed in cell two on tape 2, cell two on tape 1 goes to cell three on tape 2, etc. This allows M' to place a special symbol in the leftmost cell of its second tape, which in turn allows M' to detect an abnormal termination of M without aborting its own computation. If the transition sequence being simulated causes M to go off the end of its tape, M' will detect the special marker, realize that the current sequence is not productive, and begin the process of trying another sequence.

The second point involved in the copy process is that M' should place a special marker at the right end of the string on its second tape. If this marker is encountered while simulating transitions from M, it is bumped to the right. Thus, when M' needs to erase this tape before starting another simulation, it needs merely to erase as far as this special marker.

Finally, we should indicate how M' keeps track of the transition sequences of M being simulated. The idea here is quite simple. First, label each arc in a transition diagram of M by a unique symbol. If there were only five arcs in the diagram, the digits 1, 2, 3, 4, and 5 could be used. Next, construct a component within M' that generates all strings of these symbols in a systematic manner using tape 3 (as a model, see Figure 3.10). Each of these strings represents a sequence of transitions and each possible transition sequence will ultimately be represented.

Using this internal sequence generator, the activities of M' proceed as follows:

1. Copy the input string from tape 1 to tape 2 as described above.
2. Generate the next transition sequence on tape 3.
3. Simulate this sequence using tape 2.
4. If this simulation leads to a halt state in M, halt. Otherwise, erase tape 2 and return to step 1.

■

In summary, we are not able to extend the language recognition powers of Turing machines by adding tapes or by introducing nondeterministic behavior, an observation that supports Turing's thesis. This might lead us to the conjecture that the class of Turing-acceptable languages represents the end of our hierarchy of machine-recognizable languages and will therefore be important to our study. Hence, in the following sections we shall concentrate on learning more about this class of languages.

Exercises

1. a. Design a Turing machine that accepts the language Σ^*, where $\Sigma = \{x, y\}$.
    b. Design a Turing machine that accepts the language $\varnothing$.

2. Show that a Turing machine can be modified so that it avoids abnormal termination yet still accepts the same strings as before.

3. Show that allowing individual transitions of a multiple-tape Turing machine to affect more than one tape does not increase the power of the machine. In other words, show that any transition that operates on more than one tape can be simulated by a sequence of transitions each operating on a single tape.

4. Show that any computation by a "Turing machine" whose tape extends without bound to the left as well as to the right can be simulated by a two-tape Turing machine and thus by a traditional Turing machine.

3.4   TURING-ACCEPTABLE LANGUAGES

In the previous section we discussed the rudiments of Turing machines as language accepters and named the class of languages accepted by these machines the Turing-acceptable languages. In this section we describe this class of languages more thoroughly.

Turing-Acceptable Versus Phrase-Structure Languages

We introduced phrase-structure grammars in Chapter 1 and discussed how such a grammar defines a language that consists of those strings of terminals generated by the grammar. By restricting the forms of allowable rewrite rules we have been able to identify classes of grammars that generate the regular and context-free languages. We now wish to consider phrase-structure grammars with no restrictions on the structure of their rewrite rules. Thus, the left and right sides of a rewrite rule can consist of any finite string of terminals and nonterminals, as long as there is at least one nonterminal in the string on the left.

The languages generated by such grammars are known as **phrase-structure languages.** These are the languages that can be defined "grammatically," in the sense that their string structures can be analyzed using a hierarchy of phrase structures. Since regular grammars and context-free grammars are special cases of unrestricted grammars, the languages they

$$S \to xyNSz$$
$$S \to \lambda$$
$$yNx \to xyN$$
$$yNz \to yz$$
$$yNy \to yyN$$

Figure 3.16   A grammar that generates the language $\{x^n y^n z^n : n \in \mathbb{N}\}$

generate are contained in the class of phrase-structure languages. Moreover, Figure 3.16 shows an unrestricted grammar that generates the language $\{x^n y^n z^n : n \in \mathbb{N}\}$, which we know is not context-free. Thus, the phrase-structure languages constitute a larger class of languages than the context-free languages.

Our goal in this section is to characterize the phrase-structure languages as those languages that can be accepted by Turing machines. That is, *the phrase-structure languages are exactly the Turing-acceptable languages.* We prove this in two stages. First, in Theorem 3.3 we show that every Turing-acceptable language is a phrase-structure language. Then, in Theorem 3.4 we show that every phrase-structure language is Turing-acceptable.

The proof we will give for Theorem 3.3 hinges on the construction of a grammar that generates the same language as the one accepted by a given Turing machine. This construction requires a notational system for representing the entire configuration of a Turing machine at any stage of its computation. When using this system, the contents of the machine's tape are represented as a string of tape symbols enclosed in brackets. We represent the left end of the tape by [, then display the string of symbols found on the tape starting with the leftmost cell and including at least one blank following the last nonblank symbol, and finally close the representation with]. Thus, a tape containing $\triangle xxyx \triangle \triangle \cdots$ could be represented as $[\triangle xxyx\triangle]$ or perhaps $[\triangle xxyx\triangle\triangle\triangle\triangle\triangle]$, and a tape containing $\triangle\triangle\triangle xx\triangle yx\triangle x\triangle\triangle \cdots$ could be represented as $[\triangle\triangle\triangle xx\triangle yx\triangle x\triangle\triangle]$.

To complete the representation of the machine's configuration, we insert the current state immediately to the left of the current symbol in our representation of the tape. Thus, if p were a state in the machine, then $[\triangle xpxyxx\triangle]$ would represent the configuration in which the current state is p and the tape configuration is $\triangle x\underline{x}yxx\triangle\triangle\triangle \cdots$. Likewise, $[p\triangle xy\triangle]$ would represent the machine being in state p with its tape configured as $\underline{\triangle}xy\triangle\triangle \cdots$. (We can assume that the symbols used to represent the states of the machine are distinct from the machine's tape symbols.)

The significance of this notation for us is that it provides a means by which a Turing machine's computation can be expressed as a sequence of symbol strings, with each string representing the machine's configuration at a particular instant during the computation. Thus, if the machine is one

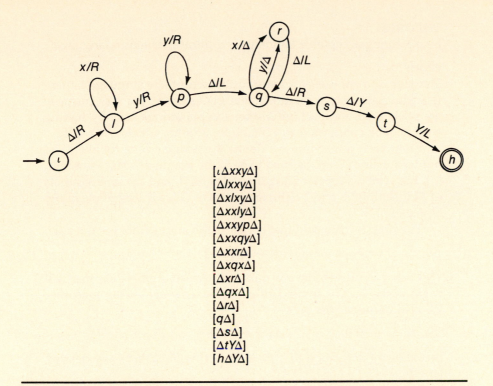

$[\iota\Delta xxy\Delta]$
$[\Delta lxxy\Delta]$
$[\Delta xlxy\Delta]$
$[\Delta xxly\Delta]$
$[\Delta xxyp\Delta]$
$[\Delta xxqy\Delta]$
$[\Delta xxr\Delta]$
$[\Delta xqx\Delta]$
$[\Delta xr\Delta]$
$[\Delta qx\Delta]$
$[\Delta r\Delta]$
$[q\Delta]$
$[\Delta s\Delta]$
$[\Delta tY\Delta]$
$[h\Delta Y\Delta]$

Figure 3.17   A skeletal transition diagram for a Turing machine and the sequence of configurations it produces as it processes the string *xxy*

that accepts strings by halting with its tape configured as $\underline{\Delta}Y\Delta\Delta\cdots$, then the process of accepting the string w could be summarized as a sequence of machine configurations beginning with $[\iota\triangle w\Delta]$ and terminating with $[h\triangle Y\Delta]$, where ι and h represent the machine's initial and halt states, respectively.

Figure 3.17 shows both a Turing machine that accepts the language $\{x^m y^n: m \in \mathbb{N}, n \in \mathbb{N}^+\}$ and the sequence of configurations produced as the machine processes the string *xxy*. This configuration sequence starts with a configuration containing the input string and ends with the configuration $[h\triangle Y\triangle]$. Thus, by reading backward, we obtain a sequence leading from the configuration $[h\triangle Y\triangle]$ to a configuration containing the input string. Such a sequence is quite similar to a derivation for the string. Indeed, if we constructed a grammar in which any derivation had to begin with the pattern $[h\triangle Y\triangle]$ and whose rewrite rules simulated the action of a machine transition in reverse, then we should be well on our way to constructing a grammar that would generate the strings that are accepted by the machine. This is the approach we follow to prove Theorem 3.3.

THEOREM 3.3
Every Turing-acceptable language is a phrase-structure language.

PROOF
Our task is to show that for any Turing-acceptable language L there
is a phrase-structure grammar that generates L. For this purpose
we select a Turing machine M that accepts strings only by halting
with its tape configured as $\triangle Y \triangle \triangle \cdots$ and for which $L(M) = L$.

From such a machine we define a grammar G as follows: The
nonterminals of G are defined to be S (the grammar's start symbol),
[,], the symbols representing the states of M, and the tape symbols
of M including $\triangle$ and Y. The terminals of G are the symbols in the
alphabet of M.

The only rewrite rule that contains the start symbol is the rule

$$S \rightarrow [h\triangle Y\triangle]$$

This rule guarantees that any derivation based on this grammar will
begin at the end of some configuration sequence of the machine.
We also introduce the rule

$$\triangle] \rightarrow \triangle\triangle]$$

that allows a derivation to expand the string $[h\triangle Y\triangle]$ to any desired
length.

Next, we introduce rewrite rules that simulate transitions in
reverse. For each transition of the form $\delta(p, x) = (q, y)$, we introduce the rewrite rule

$$qy \rightarrow px$$

(Thus, $[\triangle zqy\triangle]$ could be rewritten as $[\triangle zpx\triangle]$, which reflects the
fact that if the configuration of M were $[\triangle zpx\triangle]$, the application of
$\delta(p, x) = (q, y)$ would shift M to $[\triangle zqy\triangle]$.)

For each transition of the form $\delta(p, x) = (q, R)$, we introduce the
rule

$$xq \rightarrow px$$

(For example, $[\triangle xqyz\triangle]$ could be rewritten as $[\triangle pxyz\triangle]$.)

For each transition of the form $\delta(p, x) = (q, L)$ and each tape
symbol y of M, we introduce the rule

$$qyx \rightarrow ypx$$

(Thus, $[\triangle qyx\triangle\triangle]$ could be rewritten as $[\triangle ypx\triangle\triangle]$.)

We complete the list of rewrite rules in G by introducing three
rules that allow a derivation to remove the nonterminals [, ι, $\triangle$,

and] under certain circumstances. These rules are

$$[\iota\triangle \rightarrow \lambda$$
$$\triangle\triangle] \rightarrow \triangle]$$

and

$$\triangle] \rightarrow \lambda$$

(Consequently, if a derivation produced the initial configuration $[\iota\triangle xyx\triangle\triangle]$, it would be able to drop the nonterminals to produce the string xyx.)

Finally, we argue that $L(M) = L(G)$. If w were a string in $L(M)$, there would be a sequence of configurations of M starting with $[\iota\triangle w\triangle]$ and ending with $[h\triangle Y\triangle]$. Consequently, we could produce a derivation of the string w of the form

$$S \Rightarrow [h\triangle Y\triangle] \Rightarrow \cdots \Rightarrow [\iota\triangle w\triangle] \Rightarrow w\triangle] \Rightarrow w$$

We simply start by applying the rule $S \rightarrow [h\triangle Y\triangle]$, and then apply the rule $\triangle] \rightarrow \triangle\triangle]$ repeatedly until the string $[h\triangle Y\triangle\triangle\cdots\triangle]$ is as long as any configuration in the sequence that represents the computation of M. Next, we apply the rewrite rules corresponding to the transitions from the original configuration sequence in reverse order. This will produce the pattern $[\iota\triangle w\triangle\triangle\cdots\triangle]$, which we can reduce to w by applying the rules $\triangle\triangle] \rightarrow \triangle]$, $\triangle] \rightarrow \lambda$, and $[\iota\triangle \rightarrow \lambda$. As a result, w would be in $L(G)$. (As an example, Figure 3.18 displays the derivation corresponding to the sequence of configurations given in Figure 3.17.)

Conversely, if we were given a string in $L(G)$, its derivation would give rise to a sequence of configurations that in turn would show how the string could be accepted by M. Thus, any string in $L(G)$ is also in $L(M)$.

∎

The following theorem is all that we need now to justify our claim that the phrase-structure languages are exactly the Turing-acceptable languages.

THEOREM 3.4
Every phrase-structure language is a Turing-acceptable language.

PROOF
We begin by observing that, when applied to a nondeterministic multiple-tape Turing machine, the proof of Theorem 3.1 would pro-

$$
\begin{aligned}
S \Rightarrow{}& [h\Delta Y\Delta] \\
\Rightarrow{}& [h\Delta Y\Delta\Delta] \\
\Rightarrow{}& [h\Delta Y\Delta\Delta\Delta] \\
\Rightarrow{}& [\Delta t Y\Delta\Delta\Delta] \\
\Rightarrow{}& [\Delta s\Delta\Delta\Delta\Delta] \\
\Rightarrow{}& [q\Delta\Delta\Delta\Delta\Delta] \\
\Rightarrow{}& [\Delta r\Delta\Delta\Delta\Delta] \\
\Rightarrow{}& [\Delta qx\Delta\Delta\Delta] \\
\Rightarrow{}& [\Delta xr\Delta\Delta\Delta] \\
\Rightarrow{}& [\Delta xqx\Delta\Delta] \\
\Rightarrow{}& [\Delta xxr\Delta\Delta] \\
\Rightarrow{}& [\Delta xxqy\Delta] \\
\Rightarrow{}& [\Delta xxyp\Delta] \\
\Rightarrow{}& [\Delta xxly\Delta] \\
\Rightarrow{}& [\Delta xlxy\Delta] \\
\Rightarrow{}& [\Delta lxxy\Delta] \\
\Rightarrow{}& [\iota\Delta xxy\Delta] \\
\Rightarrow{}& xxy\Delta] \\
\Rightarrow{}& xxy
\end{aligned}
$$

Figure 3.18   The derivation of the string *xxy* corresponding to the configuration sequence in Figure 3.17

duce a nondeterministic one-tape machine that would accept the same language as the multiple-tape machine. (The transition to be simulated from a compound state of the form $(p, x_1, x_2, \cdots, x_k)$ may no longer be uniquely determined but all options are known prior to execution time and can therefore be built into the automaton by allowing nondeterminism.) Thus, for any nondeterministic multiple-tape Turing machine M there is a nondeterministic one-tape Turing machine M' such that $L(M) = L(M')$. This observation allows us to prove the current theorem by showing that for each grammar G there is a nondeterministic two-tape Turing machine N such that $L(G) = L(N)$. N could then be simulated by a nondeterministic one-tape Turing machine (by the above observation), which in turn could be simulated by a conventional Turing machine (by Theorem 3.2).

Next we observe that any rewrite rule in the grammar can be implemented by a Turing machine. That is, if a string of symbols v appears somewhere on the machine's tape and the grammar contains the rule $v \to w$, where w represents a (possibly empty) string of terminals and nonterminals, then by using right and left shifts together with write operations, the machine could replace the string v by the string w.

We now construct a nondeterministic two-tape machine that functions as follows: Use tape 1 to hold the input string being tested.

Write the grammar's start symbol on tape 2. Then repeatedly apply rewrite rules to the string on tape 2 in a nondeterministic fashion. (We say "nondeterministic fashion" because there could be more than one applicable rule at any one time.) If the contents of tape 2 becomes a string of only terminals, compare this string to the input string stored on tape 1. If the strings are identical, halt; otherwise, move one of the tape heads to the left until abnormal termination occurs.

In short, this process merely uses tape 2 to compute a derivation using rules from the grammar. If the input string is derivable from the grammar, it is possible that this string will be the one produced on tape 2. In this case the machine will accept the input by halting. If, however, the input is not derivable from the grammar, the string produced on tape 2 can never match the input, and it would be impossible for the machine to accept the string. Consequently, the language accepted by the machine is the language generated by the grammar.

■

In summary, the languages and machines we have studied form the hierarchy represented in Figure 3.19.

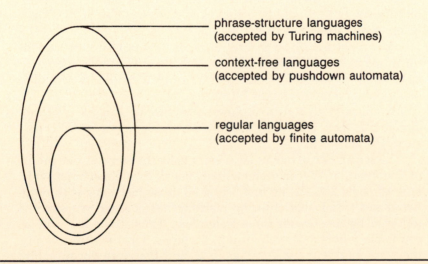

Figure 3.19 The language/machine hierarchy

The Scope of Phrase-Structure Languages

The equivalence between phrase-structure languages and Turing-acceptable languages means that Turing machines can be used to study the scope of phrase-structure languages. This is the spirit of the following theorem.

THEOREM 3.5

Associated with any alphabet Σ there is a language that is not a phrase-structure language.

PROOF

Let L be a phrase-structure language over the alphabet Σ. Then, by Theorem 3.4, there is a Turing machine M such that $L(M) = L$. We begin our proof by showing that there is such an M whose tape symbols are chosen from the set $\Sigma \cup \{\triangle\}$.

If M is a Turing machine such that $L(M) = L$ and the tape symbols of M include more than $\Sigma \cup \{\triangle\}$, we can construct another Turing machine M' with tape symbols from $\Sigma \cup \{\triangle\}$ such that $L(M') = L(M) = L$. Indeed, let x be any (nonblank) symbol in Σ. Then, arrange the nonblank tape symbols in M in a list and represent each entry of this list by a string of xs of length equal to the symbol's position in this list—the first entry is represented by x, the second by xx, etc. In this way, each nonblank tape symbol of M, and hence each symbol in M's alphabet as well, is represented by a unique string of xs. Thus, the tape contents of M can always be represented by short strings of xs separated by blanks. (A blank on the tape of M would be coded as two consecutive blanks, that is, an empty string of xs.)

Now construct M' so that it translates its input into this coded form, simulates the actions of M, and halts only if M is found to halt. Then M' will accept exactly the strings accepted by M while using only the tape symbols $\Sigma \cup \{\triangle\}$.

We conclude that given a phrase-structure language L over the alphabet Σ, there is a Turing machine M with tape symbols $\Sigma \cup \{\triangle\}$ such that $L(M) = L$.

The remainder of our proof is essentially the same as our proof of Theorem 1.1. We can systematically list all Turing machines with tape symbols $\Sigma \cup \{\triangle\}$ by first listing all those machines with only two states (recall that a Turing machine has at least two states), followed by those with three states, etc. Thus, there are only a countable number of such Turing machines. On the other hand, there are infinitely many strings in Σ^* and therefore uncountably many languages that can be formed from Σ. Consequently, there are more languages over Σ than there are Turing machines with tape symbols in $\Sigma \cup \{\triangle\}$. In turn, there must be languages over Σ that are not phrase-structure languages.

∎

It is here that our plot truly begins to thicken. Theorems 3.3, 3.4, and 3.5 tell us there are languages that do not have grammatical foundations, and moreover only those languages having grammatical foundations can be recognized by a Turing machine. If we accept Turing's thesis, that Turing machines capture the essence of any computation process, we must conclude that those languages without grammatical foundations cannot be recognized by any algorithmic process.

Not only does this conclusion imply that there are languages that we cannot hope to parse with a computer, but it also has ramifications relating to the search for natural language understanding systems—an extremely active area of current research. Indeed, it says that underlying the development of a natural language processing system is the requirement that the language being processed have a well-defined grammatical structure; if the natural language does not have a grammatical structure, we will not be able to process it algorithmically.

This requirement is also closely related to the general issue of natural intelligence versus artificial intelligence. If the human mind proceeds by executing algorithms, as many believe, then Turing's thesis dictates that there are languages that the human mind cannot parse. On the other hand, if natural intelligence is based on a level more powerful than algorithm execution, then Turing's thesis suggests that the dream of developing truly intelligent computing machines is destined to remain a dream forever.

We see, then, that the theory developed thus far has significant consequences. The only weak link is Turing's thesis—the *conjecture* that the concept of computing with a Turing machine is as powerful (although perhaps not as convenient) as any other computational model. As we mentioned earlier, this thesis is widely accepted among today's computer scientists. Much of this acceptance comes from the fact that Turing's thesis agrees with many other results and conjectures obtained by approaching the study of computation from other points of view. We consider some of these other approaches in the next chapter.

Exercises

1. Draw transition diagrams for all the Turing machines with tape symbols x and $\triangle$ that have only two states (an initial state and a halt state). What

does your ability to do this task have to do with the fact that the collection of all Turing machines whose set of tape symbols is $\{x, \triangle\}$ is countable?

2. Show that by adding a second stack to pushdown automata, we obtain a class of machines with the same language accepting powers as the class of Turing machines.

3. Using the construction process described in the proof of Theorem 3.3, develop a phrase-structure grammar that accepts the same language as accepted by the Turing machine whose transition diagram appears below. (The machine accepts strings by halting with its tape configured as $\triangle Y \triangle \triangle \cdots$.) Show a derivation for the string x using the grammar you obtain.

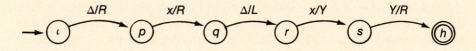

4. Show that the language $\{x^n y^{2n} z^{4n}: n \in \mathbb{N}\}$ is Turing-acceptable.

3.5 BEYOND PHRASE-STRUCTURE LANGUAGES

We have proved the existence of languages that are not phrase-structure languages (or equivalently not Turing-acceptable languages) but have not yet identified such a language explicitly. Filling this void is a major goal of this section; the introduction of universal Turing machines and the distinction between acceptable and decidable languages are important extensions of our discussion.

A Coding System for Turing Machines

To identify a language that is not Turing-acceptable (and thus not a phrase-structure language) we will need a coding system by which the Turing machines with alphabet Σ and tape symbols $\Sigma \cup \{\triangle\}$ can be represented as strings containing only 0s and 1s. Thus, we pause here to introduce such a system before proceeding with the major theme of this section.

Given a machine M to be represented, our coding system requires that we arrange M's states in a list whose first entry is the initial state and whose second entry is the halt state. Based on the order of this list, we can speak of the first state of M, the second state of M, and in general, the jth state of M. We agree to represent the jth state of M by a string of 0s of length j.

Thus, the initial state would be represented by 0, the halt state by 00, and the next state (if there is one) by 000.

Next, we represent the symbols L and R together with the symbols in Σ (the nonblank tape symbols of M) as strings of 0s. This we do by arranging the symbols in Σ in a list, and then representing L by 0, R by 00, the first symbol in the list by 000, the second symbol by 0000, and in general, the jth symbol by a string of 0s of length $j + 2$.

If we now agree to represent the blank symbol by the empty string, we obtain a system by which the symbols L and R, the states of M, and the tape symbols of M can be represented by strings of 0s. This in turn allows us to represent any transition of M as a string of 0s and 1s. After all, any transition (which must have the form $\delta(p, x) = (q, y)$) can be identified by a four-tuple (p, x, q, y) where p is the current state, x is the current symbol, q is the new state, and y is either a tape symbol (if the transition is a write operation), or either L or R (if the transition is a head move operation). Thus, the entire transition can be represented by four strings of 0s, which we separate by 1s. For example, the string 01000100100 would represent the transition $\delta(\iota, x) = (h, R)$, where x is the symbol represented by 000 and h is the machine's halt state. Since we represent a blank by the absence of 0s, the string 011001 represents the transition $\delta(\iota, \triangle) = (h, \triangle)$, where again h is the halt state of the machine.

Note that a list of all transitions available to some Turing machine with tape symbols $\Sigma \cup \{\triangle\}$ constitutes a complete description of that machine. Thus, we can represent any such machine as a list of transitions in coded form. We adopt the convention of attaching an extra 1 to the beginning of such a list as well as to the end, and we use a single 1 to separate the transitions in the list. Thus, the string 10110010001010001001001 (an introductory 1, followed by the transition code 011001000, a separating 1, the code 01000100100, and a final closing 1) represents the machine shown in Figure 3.20 with the two transitions $\delta(\iota, \triangle) = (h, x)$ and $\delta(\iota, x) = (h, R)$.

When representing a Turing machine in this manner, we agree to list the transitions in the following order: We first list all the transitions originating from state 0 (the initial state), then we list all the transitions originating from state 000, followed by those from state 0000, etc., until all states from which transitions can originate have been accounted for. Within the listing of transitions from a given state, we arrange the transitions according to the symbol required on the current tape cell, beginning with the transition requiring a blank as the current symbol, followed by the transition requiring the symbol whose code is 000, then the transition whose current symbol is 0000, etc. This uniformity makes it easier to test a string of 0s and 1s to see if it is a valid representation of some (deterministic and thus fully defined) Turing machine.

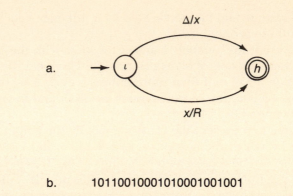

a.

b.   10110010001010001001001

Figure 3.20   a. A simple Turing machine
b. The same machine in coded form

A Non-Phrase-Structure Language

Using this coding convention, we find that every Turing machine with alphabet Σ and tape symbols $\Sigma \cup \{\triangle\}$ can be represented as a string of 0s and 1s, which in turn can be interpreted as a nonnegative integer written in binary. In fact, if we were to count in binary we would ultimately reach a pattern representing any given Turing machine with tape symbols $\Sigma \cup \{\triangle\}$. Of course, the binary representations of many nonnegative integers do not form valid machine representations. Let us agree to associate each of these integers with the simple machine shown in Figure 3.21. We then have a function from $\mathbb{N}$ *onto* the Turing machines with alphabet Σ and tape symbols $\Sigma \cup \{\triangle\}$. We use the notation M_i to represent the machine that this function associates with the integer i.

Based on this function we can now construct another function, this time from Σ^* onto the collection of Turing machines with alphabet Σ and tape symbols $\Sigma \cup \{\triangle\}$. This we do by merely associating any string w in Σ^* with the machine $M_{|w|}$, where $|w|$ represents the length of w. To simplify notation, we represent the machine associated with w under this function as M_w.

Note that the symbols in w are also in the alphabet of M_w. Thus, it makes sense to apply M_w to the input string w. We define the language L_0 to be the subset $\{w: M_w$ does not accept $w\}$ of Σ^*; a string w from Σ^* is in L_0 if and only if it is not accepted by its corresponding machine M_w.

Our task now is to show that L_0 is not Turing-acceptable. To this end we show that assuming the contrary leads to a contradiction. If L_0 were Turing-acceptable, it must be accepted by some Turing machine, and by an argument similar to that found in the proof of Theorem 3.5, we can assume that the alphabet of that machine is Σ and its set of tape symbols is $\Sigma \cup \{\triangle\}$. In

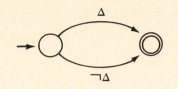

Figure 3.21   A simple Turing machine

turn, L_0 must be accepted by M_{w_0} for some string w_0 in Σ^*. (Every Turing machine with alphabet Σ and tape symbols $\Sigma \cup \{\triangle\}$ is M_w for some w in Σ^*.) Thus, $L_0 = L(M_{w_0})$.

We now ask whether or not the string w_0 is in $L(M_{w_0})$—either it is or it is not—but as we now see, both options lead to contradictions. Based on the definition of L_0 we know that $w_0 \in L(M_{w_0})$ implies $w_0 \notin L_0$, and that $w_0 \notin L(M_{w_0})$ implies $w_0 \in L_0$. But, since $L_0 = L(M_{w_0})$, both of these statements are contradictory. Faced with this paradox, we must conclude that our conjecture regarding the acceptability of L_0 is false. In other words, the language L_0 is not Turing-acceptable.

Universal Turing Machines

Our goal now is to show that the complement of L_0, the set $\{w: M_w$ accepts $w\}$, is Turing-acceptable. This will demonstrate that a Turing machine's ability to accept a language is not symmetric with the ability to reject that language's complement. That is, there are cases in which a Turing machine can be constructed that identifies the strings in a language, but no Turing machine can be constructed that identifies the strings not in the language.

Before we show that the complement of L_0 is Turing-acceptable, however, we need to introduce the concept of a **universal Turing machine.** This is nothing more than a "programmable" Turing machine that, depending on its program, is able to simulate any other Turing machine. As such, universal Turing machines are the abstract forerunners of today's programmable computers that fetch and execute the programs stored in their memories. Indeed, universal Turing machines are designed to execute programs that are stored on their tapes.

A program for a universal Turing machine is nothing more than the coded version of a Turing machine that performs the task desired of the universal machine. Suppose we wanted to program a universal Turing machine to perform a particular activity. We would first design a traditional Turing machine that performs that activity. Then, we would code this machine as a string of 0s and 1s, as we have already been doing. This code string would become the program for the universal machine.

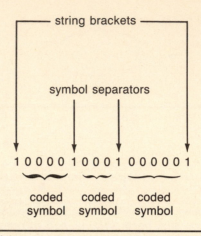

Figure 3.22   A string of three symbols in coded form

Next, we would code the data to be used as input for the particular computation desired. To do this recall that each nonblank tape symbol of the machine just coded was assigned a code word of three or more 0s. Consequently, any string of these symbols can be represented by the corresponding sequence of code words. In such a sequence, we separate adjacent code words by a single 1 and bracket the entire sequence with a 1 at each end (Figure 3.22). Note that the empty string would be represented by 11—an empty sequence of code words.

Having coded both the machine to be simulated and the string to be used as input, we place these codes on the input tape of the universal Turing machine as follows: The leftmost cell remains blank, next is the coded version of the machine to be simulated, followed by the coded input string. (The universal machine is able to detect the break between the coded machine and the data since the code string for the machine ends with a 1 and the code for the data begins with a 1. More precisely, each coded transition must begin with the code word for a state, which requires at least one 0. Thus, the end of the transition list can be detected by the presence of an illegal state code. See Figure 3.23.)

Once this information has been placed on the universal machine's tape, we position the machine's tape head over the leftmost cell of the tape and start the machine from its initial state. From this configuration, the universal Turing machine simply extracts and simulates the applicable transitions found on the early portion of its tape as it manipulates the string found on the latter part of its tape.

To be more precise, we might envision a universal Turing machine as a three-tape machine. The first tape is used to hold the input program and data as well as to hold any output, the second tape is used as a work tape

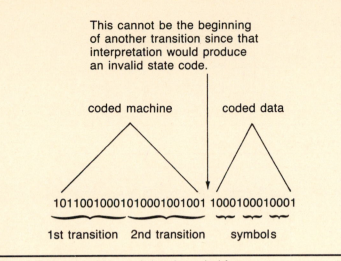

Figure 3.23 A Turing machine and data in coded form

on which the input data is manipulated, and the third tape is used to hold a representation of the current state of the machine being simulated.

Figure 3.24 describes such a machine as a composite of the building block machines presented earlier. Superscripts are used to indicate the target tape. (For example, R^1 moves the head on tape 1 to the right one cell, and R^2 moves the head on tape 2.) The major functions of the composite machine are as follows: First find the beginning of the coded input string, copy this string onto tape 2, and place the code for the initial state on tape 3. Then, proceed to search the list of coded transitions on tape 1 until an applicable transition is found. Once such a transition is found, simulate it on tape 2, and update the state code on tape 3 to reflect the new state. If the simulated state becomes the halt state, erase tape 1, copy the contents of tape 2 onto tape 1, position the head of tape 1 where the head of tape 2 was when the halt state was reached, and halt.

Although this presentation of a universal Turing machine has been in the context of a three-tape machine, we know that any three-tape Turing machine can be simulated by a one-tape Turing machine. We consider a universal Turing machine to be such a one-tape machine and denote it by T_u.

Acceptable Versus Decidable Languages

With the aid of a universal Turing machine, we can now construct a Turing machine that accepts the complement of the language L_0. We begin by

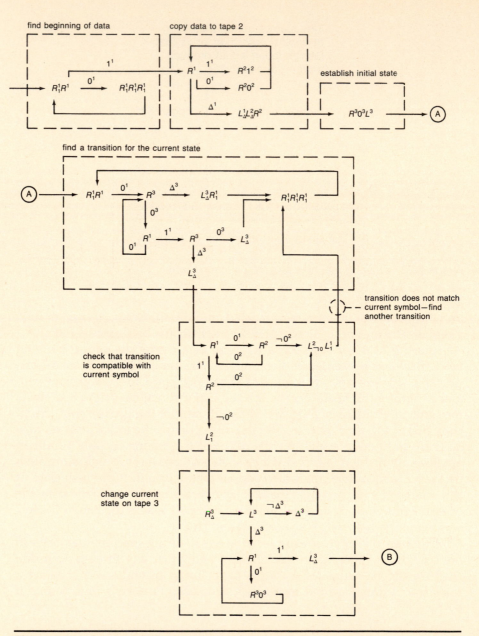

Figure 3.24 A universal Turing machine (continued on next page)

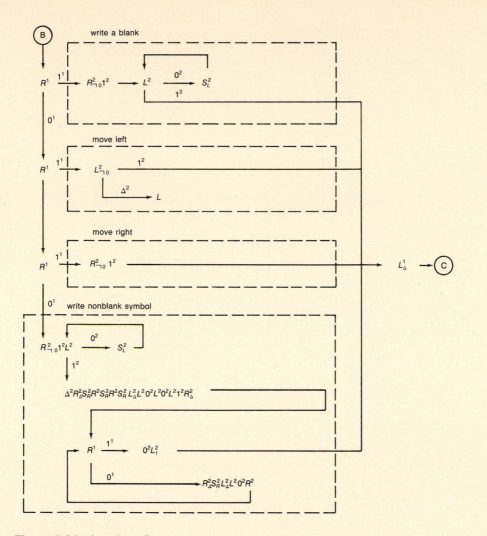

Figure 3.24 (continued)

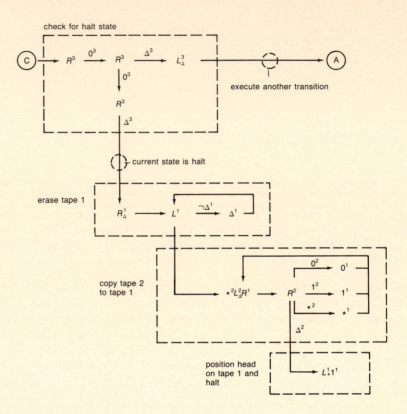

Figure 3.24   (continued)

constructing a Turing machine M_{pre} that processes an input string w from Σ^* as follows:

1. Generate a string of 0s and 1s representing the machine M_w. (This is a straightforward process since the desired representation for M_w is either the code for the default machine shown in Figure 3.21 or simply the binary representation for the length of w.)
2. Place the resulting string on the machine's tape followed by the coded version of w.

A machine that accepts the complement of L_0 can then be constructed by forming the composite machine $\rightarrow M_{pre} \rightarrow T_u$. Indeed, given input string w, this Turing machine would essentially apply M_w to w and halt if and only if M_w were found to accept w (see Figure 3.25). Thus, it accepts exactly the language $L_1 = \{w: M_w$ accepts $w\}$, which is the complement of L_0.

We have confirmed, then, that the complement of a Turing-acceptable language need not be Turing-acceptable: L_1 is Turing-acceptable but its com-

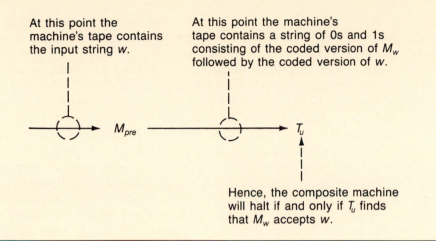

At this point the machine's tape contains the input string w.

At this point the machine's tape contains a string of 0s and 1s consisting of the coded version of M_w followed by the coded version of w.

M_{pre} T_u

Hence, the composite machine will halt if and only if T_u finds that M_w accepts w.

Figure 3.25   Applying the machine $\rightarrow M_{pre} \rightarrow T_u$ to the string w

plement L_0 is not. This lack of symmetry is not a mere curiosity but has significant repercussions. In our case it means that the ability to accept a language is not symmetric with the ability to reject its complement. There is a language L for which we can build a Turing machine that will respond with the message Y when given inputs from L, but no Turing machine can be constructed that can respond Y for all strings in L and respond N for all other strings. Languages for which this stronger condition holds are said to be **Turing-decidable** (or just **decidable**) in that a Turing machine can decide whether or not a string is in the language rather than merely accepting those strings in the language. (In less formal terms, we say that the Turing machine decides the language rather than merely accepting the language.) In summary, the language L_1 as defined above is acceptable but not decidable.

To obtain examples of decidable languages we need merely turn to the context-free languages, all of which are decidable. In support of this claim, let us sketch a general technique for constructing a Turing machine that will decide a given context-free language. We assume that L is a context-free language and that G is a context-free grammar, with start symbol S, that generates $L - \{\lambda\}$ and is in Chomsky normal form. Then, given a string w we can decide whether or not $w \in L$ by executing the following process.

If $w = \lambda$, answer yes or no depending on whether or not $\lambda \in L$. If $w \neq \lambda$, record the nonterminals of G as column headers of a table and fill in the table below these headers as follows: Under each nonterminal, record all the terminal strings of length one that can be derived from that nonterminal. This is merely the collection of terminals that appear as the right side of some rewrite rule whose left side is the nonterminal in question. (If the rules $N \rightarrow x$ and $N \rightarrow y$ are in G, then record the one-symbol strings x and y under the nonterminal N.) To construct the second row of the table, record under each nonterminal all the terminal strings of length two that can be derived from that nonterminal. (If $N \rightarrow PQ$ is a rule in G, record in column N the strings obtained by concatenating all the terminal strings of length one that can be derived from P with the one-symbol terminal strings that can be derived from Q. Note that these one-symbol strings are recorded in previous rows in the table.) In the third row of the table under each nonterminal, record all the terminal strings of length three that can be derived from that nonterminal. (If $N \rightarrow PQ$ is a rule in G, concatenate all the terminal strings of length one that can be derived from P with each terminal string of length two that can be derived from Q. Then, concatenate all terminal strings of length two that can be derived from P with those of length one that can be derived from Q. Again all the strings to be concatenated appear in table entries above the row being filled in.)

In general, in the nth row under each nonterminal N we record all the terminal strings of length n that can be derived from that nonterminal. These are found by finding each rule of the form $N \rightarrow PQ$ and then, for each i in $\{1, 2, \cdots, n - 1\}$, concatenating each terminal string of length i derivable from P with each terminal string of length $n - i$ derivable from Q (see Figure 3.26). We continue constructing this table until we have completed row number $|w|$. At this point we check to see if w has been recorded under the start symbol of G. If it has been, then $w \in L$; otherwise $w \notin L$. Hence, the decision process is finished.

To implement this procedure with a Turing machine, we could use a multiple-tape machine with one more tape than there are nonterminals in G. The first tape could be used to hold the input string as well as the final yes or no response. Each of the other tapes could be used to represent a column of the table. On each of these tapes entries from different rows could be separated by slashes. Thus, the process of deciding whether or not the string xyx is in the language generated by the grammar of Figure 3.26 would produce the tape contents shown in Figure 3.27, from which the machine could determine that xyx was not in the language.

Of course, there are also decidable languages that are not context-free. An example is the language $\{x^n y^n z^n : n \in \mathbb{N}\}$ that is not context-free but is decided by the Turing machine in Figure 3.28.

Finally, we should note that the terminology Turing-decidable and Turing-acceptable is not universal. We have already seen that a Turing-acceptable language is identical to a phrase-structure language. In other contexts, however, a Turing-acceptable language is often called a **recursively enumerable language.** This terminolgy is a consequence of the fact that the Turing-acceptable languages are exactly the languages whose strings can be enumerated—or in other words, listed—by a Turing machine. Furthermore, in those settings in which one speaks of recursively enumerable

$$S \rightarrow MN$$
$$M \rightarrow MP$$
$$N \rightarrow PN$$
$$M \rightarrow x$$
$$N \rightarrow y$$
$$P \rightarrow x$$
$$P \rightarrow y$$

	S	M	N	P
1		x	y	x y
2	xy	xx xy	xy yy	
3	xxy xyy	xxx xxy xyx xyy	xxy yxy xyy yyy	
4	xxxy xyxy xxyy xyyy	xxxx xxyx xyxx xyyx xxxy xxyy xyxy xyyy	xxxy xyxy xxyy xyyy yxxy yyxy yxyy yyyy	

Figure 3.26 A context-free grammar and the first four rows of the table constructed from it

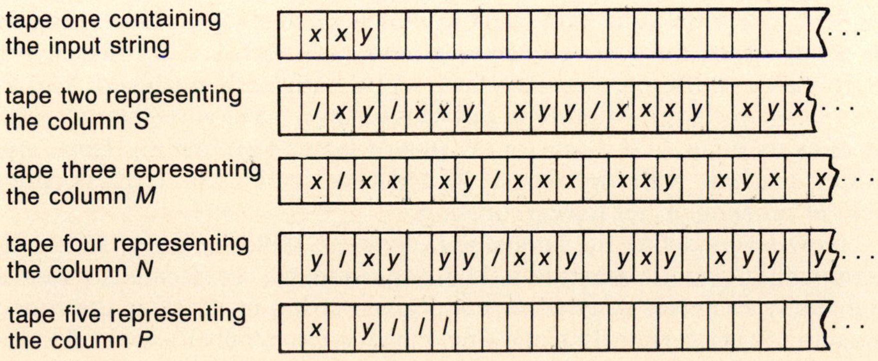

tape one containing the input string

tape two representing the column S

tape three representing the column M

tape four representing the column N

tape five representing the column P

Figure 3.27 A five-tape implementation of the table construction process of Figure 3.26

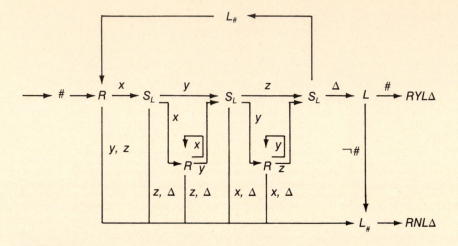

Figure 3.28   A Turing machine that decides the language $\{x^n y^n z^n: n \in \mathbb{N}\}$

languages, one normally refers the Turing-decidable languages as the **recursive languages.**

The Halting Problem

We close this section with an example of another language that is not Turing-decidable, not merely because we need another example, but because the following example, known as the halting problem, is a classic example in the theory of computation.

Recall that any Turing machine can be coded as a string of 0s and 1s. Let us denote this coded version of a Turing machine M by $\rho(M)$. If we now restrict our attention to machines with alphabet $\{0, 1\}$ and tape symbols $\{0, 1, \triangle\}$, then the code string $\rho(M)$ could be used as input to the machine M itself. We are not interested in whether or not such use of M bears any relationship to the purpose for which M was originally designed. We are merely interested in whether or not M ultimately halts when started with $\rho(M)$ as its input. If it does, we say that M is self-terminating. Thus, any Turing machine with alphabet $\{0, 1\}$ and tape symbols $\{0, 1, \triangle\}$ is either self-terminating or not self-terminating.

Now let us define the language L_h over $\{0, 1\}^*$ to be $\{\rho(M): M$ is self-terminating$\}$ and ask whether L_h is Turing-decidable. To decide L_h requires the ability to detect whether or not a given string in $\{0, 1\}^*$ is the coded version of a self-terminating machine, which is essentially the task of deciding whether a given machine halts when applied to a particular input; consequently, the problem of deciding L_h is known as the **halting problem.**

Unfortunately, the language L_h is not Turing-decidable. To convince ourselves of this, we assume to the contrary that there is a Turing machine M_h that decides L_h. Then, we modify M_h to obtain another machine M_h' that replies with the message 1 when M_h would have replied Y and with the message 0 when M_h would have replied N. Just as in the proof of Theorem 3.6, we can then argue that the tape symbols of M_h' need consist of only $\{0, 1, \triangle\}$. Thus, M_h' could be used to build the composite machine

$$\to M_h' \to R \xrightarrow{1} R \;\rceil$$

with tape symbols $\{0, 1, \triangle\}$, that halts if and only if M_h' reaches its halt state with output 0. Let us denote this composite machine by M_0.

From here our argument revolves around the question of whether M_0 is self-terminating or not self-terminating. Since it is a Turing machine with tape symbols $\{0, 1, \triangle\}$, it must be one or the other. Let us suppose that it is self-terminating. Then, when given input $\rho(M_0)$, M_h' would halt with output 1. This in turn means that M_0 would not halt if it were started with input $\rho(M_0)$. (Execution of M_0 would traverse the arc $R \xrightarrow{1} R$ and become trapped in the infinite process of repeatedly moving its tape head to the right. See Figure 3.29.) But this is the defining characteristic of a machine that is not self-terminating. Thus, our assumption that M_0 is self-terminating leads us to the contradiction that it is not self-terminating.

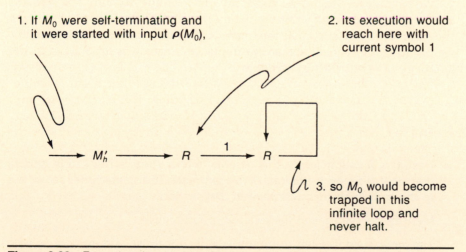

1. If M_0 were self-terminating and it were started with input $\rho(M_0)$,

2. Its execution would reach here with current symbol 1

3. so M_0 would become trapped in this infinite loop and never halt.

Figure 3.29 Executing the machine M_0 with input $\rho(M_0)$ under the assumption that M_0 is self-terminating

1. If M_0 were not self-terminating
   and it were started with input $\rho(M_0)$

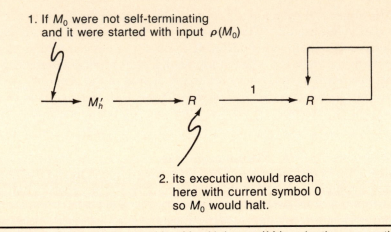

2. its execution would reach
   here with current symbol 0
   so M_0 would halt.

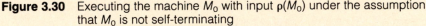

Figure 3.30   Executing the machine M_0 with input $\rho(M_0)$ under the assumption
that M_0 is not self-terminating

Since M_0 must be either self-terminating or not, we must at this point conclude that it is not self-terminating. But, if M_0 were not self-terminating, then when given input $\rho(M_0)$, M'_h would halt with output 0. This in turn would mean that M_0 would halt if it were started with input $\rho(M_0)$. (The execution of M_0 would not be able to traverse the arc $R \xrightarrow{1} R$. See Figure 3.30.) But this is the defining characteristic of a self-terminating machine. Thus, our assumption that M_0 is not self-terminating must also be false.

We have arrived at the inconsistency of a machine M_0 with tape symbols $\{0, 1, \triangle\}$ that is neither self-terminating nor not self-terminating, while at the same time any such machine must be one or the other. Consequently, we are forced to conclude that our initial assumption is false. That is, the language L_h is not Turing-decidable.

Exercises

1. Design a Turing machine that accepts exactly those strings of 0s and 1s that are valid representations of deterministic Turing machines according to the coding system described in this section.

2. Identify the paradox in the following statement:

   The cook in an isolated community cooks for those and only those who do not cook for themselves.

(Hint: Who cooks for the cook?) How does this question relate to this section?

3. Design a Turing machine that accepts the strings in the language $L = \{w^n : w = xy\}$ by halting with its tape configured as $\triangle Y \triangle \triangle \cdots$ and rejects strings not in L by halting with its tape configured as $\triangle N \triangle \triangle \cdots$.

   Explain why such a machine cannot be constructed in the case of all Turing-acceptable languages.

4. Present an argument that any language containing only a finite number of strings is Turing-decidable.

5. Extend the table in Figure 3.26 to resolve the question of whether the string $xyyyxy$ is generated by the grammar.

3.6 CLOSING COMMENTS

In this and the previous chapters we have introduced a hierarchy of languages together with the automata required to accept them. This hierarchy is a variation of the language hierarchy known as Chomsky's hierarchy (named for N. Chomsky, who pioneered the development of formal language theory in the 1950s). Figure 3.31 is a summary of the hierarchy we have presented. We have shown that each level in this hierarchy properly contains the next lower level. In fact, at each level we have given an explicit example of a language that resides at that level but not at the next lower level. An excellent review exercise at this time would be to collect these examples and add them to the diagram in Figure 3.31.

A major consequence of this chapter has been the introduction of Turing's thesis, which, translated into the context of Figure 3.31, says that those languages lying beyond the phrase-structure languages can never be parsed by a computational system. As pointed out at the end of Section 3.4, this thesis has far-reaching consequences. It is not surprising, then, that Turing's thesis has captured the attention of many researchers who have sought to support its claims as well as to challenge its validity.

In the next chapter, we investigate some of the results of these endeavors. For now we simply note that the wide range of terminology we have experienced (such as Turing-acceptable languages, phrase-structure languages, and recursively enumerable languages) is a result of the scope of Turing's thesis. The same apparent bound on the power of computational processes hypothesized by Turing has been witnessed and studied in a variety of disciplines, each one approaching the question of computability from a different perspective and with different terminology.

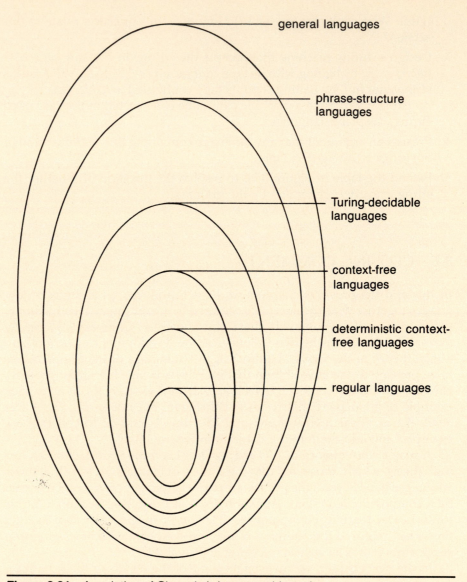

Figure 3.31   A variation of Chomsky's language hierarchy

Chapter Review Problems

1. Using the building blocks presented in Section 3.2, construct a composite Turing machine that converts its tape from the configuration $\triangle w\triangle\triangle\cdots$, where w is any string of xs and ys, into the configuration $\triangle w\triangle v\triangle\triangle\cdots$, where v is the string w written backward.

2. Using the building blocks presented in Section 3.2, construct a composite Turing machine that forms the concatenation of two strings v and w in $\{x, y\}^*$ by converting its tape from the configuration $\triangle v\triangle w\triangle\triangle\cdots$ into $\triangle vw\triangle\triangle\cdots$.

3. How might the result of executing $\rightarrow RL$ differ from that of $\rightarrow LR$?

4. Draw a transition diagram for the composite Turing machine $\rightarrow R_x\triangle L$.

5. Design a Turing machine M such that $L(M) = \{x^ny^{2n}z^n: n \in \mathbb{N}\}$.

6. Design a phrase-structure grammar G such that $L(G) = \{x^my^nx^my^n: m, n \in \mathbb{N}\}$.

7. Design a phrase-structure grammar G such that $L(G) = \{x^ny^{2n}z^n: n \in \mathbb{N}\} \cup \{x^ny^nz^n: n \in \mathbb{N}\}$.

8. Using the notation for representing the entire configuration of a Turing machine, as used in the proof of Theorem 3.3, trace the execution of the composite machine in Figure 3.3 when started with the tape configuration $\triangle\triangle yx\triangle\triangle\triangle\cdots$.

9. Using the notation for representing the entire configuration of a Turing machine, as used in the proof of Theorem 3.3, trace the execution of the machine whose transition diagram is shown below assuming the initial tape configuration $\triangle xyx\triangle\triangle\triangle\cdots$.

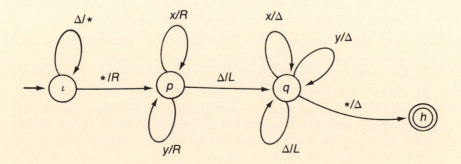

10. Is the language generated by the following grammar (with start symbol S) context-free? Describe the language.

$$S \rightarrow xN$$
$$N \rightarrow Sx$$
$$xNx \rightarrow y$$

11. Is the language generated by the following grammar (with start symbol S) context-free? Describe the language.

$$S \rightarrow SPQR$$
$$S \rightarrow \lambda$$
$$QP \rightarrow PQ$$
$$PQ \rightarrow QP$$
$$PR \rightarrow RP$$
$$RP \rightarrow PR$$
$$QR \rightarrow RQ$$
$$RQ \rightarrow QR$$
$$P \rightarrow x$$
$$Q \rightarrow y$$
$$R \rightarrow z$$

12. Design a Turing machine M such that $L(M) = \{x, y, z\}^* - \{x^n y^n z^n: n \in \mathbb{N}\}$.

13. Show that if the language L is Turing-acceptable, then there is a Turing machine that suffers an abnormal termination if and only if its input string is in L.

14. If the language L over Σ is Turing-acceptable, is there a Turing machine that halts for inputs in L and suffers an abnormal termination for inputs in $\Sigma^* - L$? Explain your answer.

15. a. Does the union of a finite number of phrase-structure languages form a phrase-structure language? Justify your answer.
    b. Does the union of a collection of phrase-structure languages always form a phrase-structure language? Justify your answer.

16. a. Does the intersection of a finite number of phrase-structure languages form a phrase-structure language? Justify your answer.
    b. Does the intersection of a collection of phrase-structure languages always form a phrase-structure language? Justify your answer.

17. We can express a grammar as one string of symbols in which rewrite rules are separated by slashes ($S \rightarrow xS/S \rightarrow \lambda$). Design a Turing machine that accepts only those strings that represent context-free grammars with terminals from the set $\{x, y\}$ and nonterminals from $\{S, M, N\}$.

18. Design a grammar G that is not context-free for which $L(G)$ is the context-free language $\{x^n y^n: n \in \mathbb{N}\}$.

19. Show that for each phrase-structure language L there are infinitely many grammars that generate L.

20. Design a Turing machine (perhaps a multiple-tape machine) that sorts a list of strings from $\{x, y, z\}^*$ into alphabetical order. Assume that the strings in the input list are separated by single blanks.

21. Show that the collection of non-phrase-structure languages has a greater cardinality than the collection of phrase-structure languages. (Hence, there are more languages that are not Turing-acceptable than there are languages that are Turing-acceptable.)

22. Show that for any alphabet Σ there is a language L over Σ such that neither L nor $\Sigma^* - L$ is Turing-acceptable.

23. Show that the collection of Turing-decidable languages over any alphabet is infinite but countable.

24. Show that if a Turing machine M accepts each string w in $L(M)$ after executing no more than $|w| + 1$ steps, then $L(M)$ must be regular.

25. Is a subset of a phrase-structure language always a phrase-structure language? Support your answer.

26. Show that the Kleene star of a Turing-acceptable language is also Turing-acceptable.

27. Show that the language $\{x^n: n$ is a prime positive integer$\}$ is Turing-acceptable. Is it decidable? Why or why not?

28. Show that the language $\{x^{n^2}: n \in \mathbb{N}\}$ is Turing-acceptable. Is it Turing-decidable? Why or why not?

29. Draw a transition diagram for a Turing machine that decides the language $\{x^m y^n: m, n \in \mathbb{N}$ and $m \geqslant n\}$.

30. Using the building blocks presented in Section 3.2, construct a Turing machine that accepts the language $\{x^m y^n x^m y^n: m, n \in \mathbb{N}\}$.

31. Apply the table construction algorithm described in Section 3.5 to decide whether or not the string $xxyyxxyyy$ is in the language generated by the following grammar, whose start symbol is S.

$$S \rightarrow SS$$
$$S \rightarrow MN$$
$$N \rightarrow SP$$
$$M \rightarrow x$$
$$N \rightarrow y$$
$$P \rightarrow y$$

What about the strings $xxxyyxyy$, $xyxyxyxy$, and $xyxxxyyy$?

32. Extend the table in Figure 3.26 to resolve the question of whether the string $xyyxyyy$ is generated by the grammar in that figure.

33. Suppose that $p(n)$ is a polynomial expression in n and M is a Turing machine that accepts each string w in $L(M)$ before executing more than $p(|w|)$ steps. Show that the language $L(M)$ is decidable.

34. Show that each Turing-acceptable language can be generated by a phrase-structure grammar in which no rewrite rule has a terminal appearing as a part of its left side.

35. Show that for any recursively enumerable language L, there is a Turing machine that when started with a blank tape will begin listing the strings in L on its tape in such a way that any string in L will ultimately appear on the tape.

36. Show that every infinite recursively enumerable language contains an infinite recursive language.

Programming Problems

1. Develop a Turing machine simulator. Design the simulator so that the description of the machine to be simulated is provided in a tabular form that can be replaced easily by the description of another machine.

2. Write a program to simulate the three-tape universal Turing machine described in this chapter.

3. Write a program for deciding whether or not strings are in the language $\{x^m y^n z^m : m, n \in \mathbb{N}\}$ by applying the table construction algorithm described in Section 3.5.

CHAPTER 4

Computability

Our study of automata as language accepters has led us to an apparent bound on the power of computational processes, a demarcation made explicit by Turing's thesis. A major supporting factor for this thesis is that the same apparent limit has surfaced in a variety of research areas. For example, we have seen that the power of Turing machines as language accepters corresponds to the generative power of grammars. In this chapter we investigate more instances in which the computational power of Turing machines corresponds to the capabilities of other computational systems.

We begin our investigation by reconsidering the question posed in the introductory chapter, regarding the expressive power of our favorite programming language. Recall that there must be functions that cannot be computed by any program written in that language. In turn, we posed the question regarding the extent to which this limitation was a result of the language's design or a reflection of the limitations of algorithmic processes in general. We wondered if the inability to compute a function by a program in the language means that the language is unable to express some algorithm or that there is simply no algorithm for computing the function.

To answer this question we will first identify a class of functions that apparently contains all the computable functions: all functions that can be computed by algorithmic means without regard for how the algorithm involved might be expressed or implemented. We will then show that all the functions in this class can be computed by Turing machines (thus supporting Turing's thesis), as well as by algorithms expressed in a very simple subset of most programming languages. From this we conclude that the limitations encountered with Turing machines and most programming languages reflect the limits of computational processes in general rather than the design of the machine or language being used.

4.1   FOUNDATIONS OF RECURSIVE FUNCTION THEORY

Until now our study of computational processes and their capabilities has been based on an operational approach rather than a functional one. We have concentrated on how a computation is performed, not on what a computation accomplishes. Now, however, our goal is to identify those functions that can be computed by at least one computational system, and thus we must separate our thoughts from any particular way in which a computation may be expressed or executed. That is, we wish to use the term *computable* to mean computable by some algorithm rather than computable by an algorithm that can be implemented in a particular system.

To obtain this generality, we adopt a functional approach to the study of computability in which we concentrate on the functions computed rather than the means of computing them. In particular, we will follow the approach taken by mathematicians in the study of recursive function theory. The basic theme is to start with a collection of functions, called the initial functions, that are so simple that their computability is beyond question, and then show that these functions can be combined to form more functions whose computability follows from that of the original functions. In this manner, we obtain a collection of functions that researchers believe to contain all functions that are computable in a general sense. Then, if a particular computational system, such as a programming language or a computational machine, encompasses all of these functions, we will conclude that the system is as powerful as possible. Otherwise, we will conclude that the particular system is unnecessarily restrictive.

Partial Functions

To reiterate, our goal for now is to identify those functions that are computable in a general sense (without regard to a particular computational system). This, of course, encompasses an extremely large class of functions dealing with a variety of domains and ranges. Hence, our first task is to establish a means of coping with this diversity. To this end we observe that any data can be coded as a string of 0s and 1s, and thus in the context of an appropriate coding system, any computable function can be considered as a function whose inputs and outputs are tuples of nonnegative integers. On the other hand, this does not mean that every computable function can be recognized as having the form

$$f:\mathbb{N}^m \to \mathbb{N}^n$$

where m and n are integers in $\mathbb{N}$. Indeed, the function div defined by

$$div(x, y) = \text{the integer part of } x/y,$$
$$\text{where } x, y \in \mathbb{N} \text{ and } y \neq 0$$

whose domain contains pairs of integers, should certainly fall within our collection of computable functions. But, div is not a function of the form

$$f:\mathbb{N}^2 \to \mathbb{N}$$

Indeed, it is not defined for pairs having 0 as their second component.

To account for functions whose domains do not include all of $\mathbb{N}^m$ for some m, let us introduce the concept of a **partial function.** A partial function on a set X is a function whose domain is a subset of X. Thus, we can speak of a partial function on X without implying that the function's domain is the entire set X. In particular, the function div defined above, although not a function on $\mathbb{N}^2$, is a partial function on $\mathbb{N}^2$.

Note that a reference to a partial function on X does not imply that the domain is necessarily a proper subset of X. To indicate that a partial function on X is, in fact, undefined for at least one element in X, we will refer to it as **strictly partial** or partial in the strict sense. In contrast, a partial function on X whose domain is the entire set X will be called a **total function** on X. Thus, both the functions div (as defined above) and $plus$ defined by

$$plus(x, y) = x + y$$

are partial functions on $\mathbb{N}^2$. More precisely, $plus$ is a total function on $\mathbb{N}^2$ while div is strictly partial on $\mathbb{N}^2$ (Figure 4.1).

We conclude that by applying appropriate coding systems, any computable function can be identified as a partial function of the form $f:\mathbb{N}^m \to \mathbb{N}^n$, for some m and n in $\mathbb{N}$. Hence, our search for all computable functions can be restricted to the partial functions from $\mathbb{N}^m$ into $\mathbb{N}^n$, where m and n are in $\mathbb{N}$.

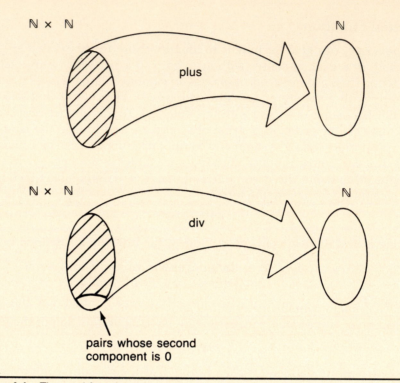

Figure 4.1   The total function *plus* and the strictly partial function *div*

Finally, since we will be referring to arbitrary *n*-tuples quite often, it is advantageous to adopt the simple notation $\bar{x}$ to represent a tuple of the form $(x_1, x_2, \cdots, x_n)$ in those cases where the details of the expanded form are not required.

Initial Functions

The foundation of the hierarchy of computable functions that we will be considering consists of the set of **initial functions.** One of these functions is the **zero function,** represented by ζ. It maps the zero-tuple (the empty tuple) to 0, written $\zeta(\ ) = 0$. Thus, ζ corresponds to the process of writing a 0 on a blank piece of paper or recording a 0 in an otherwise blank storage cell in a modern digital computer. Since either of these activities conforms to our intuitive concept of a computational process, we readily accept ζ as a function that should be classified as computable.

Another initial function, denoted by σ, maps one-tuples to one-tuples in such a way that $\sigma(x) = x + 1$, for each nonnegative integer x. In other words, σ produces the successor of its input value and is consequently called the **successor function.** Another way of thinking of σ is that it adds 1 to its input value. In this light, σ should also be classified as computable since we have long known a computational process for performing addition of integers.

To complete the class of initial functions we include the collection of functions known as **projections.** Each of these functions extracts as its output a particular component from its input tuple. We use the symbol π to represent a projection function along with a superscript to indicate the size of its input and a subscript to indicate which component is extracted. For example, the function π_2^3 maps $\mathbb{N}^3$ into $\mathbb{N}$ by associating each three-tuple with that tuple's second component. Thus, $\pi_2^3(7, 6, 4) = 6$, $\pi_1^2(5, 17) = 5$, $\pi_2^2(5, 17) = 17$, and $\pi_1^1(8) = 8$. (As a special case we agree that π_0^n maps n-tuples to zero-tuples so that $\pi_0^2(6, 5) = (\ )$.)

As with the other initial functions, it is easy to argue that the projections should fall within the class of computable functions. For instance, we could compute the function π_m^n by applying the procedure of scanning the input n-tuple until we reached the mth component and then extracting the integer found there.

The initial functions form the foundation of the hierarchy within recursive function theory. It is, admittedly, a very simple foundation containing functions that are unable to accomplish much on an individual basis. Thus, our next step is to investigate ways in which these functions can be used to construct more complex functions.

Primitive Recursive Functions

One way of constructing more complex functions from the initial functions is called **combination.** The combination of two functions $f:\mathbb{N}^k \to \mathbb{N}^m$ and $g:\mathbb{N}^k \to \mathbb{N}^n$ is the function $f \times g:\mathbb{N}^k \to \mathbb{N}^{m+n}$ defined by $f \times g(\bar{x}) = (f(\bar{x}), g(\bar{x}))$, where $\bar{x}$ is a k-tuple. That is, the function $f \times g$ takes inputs in the form of k-tuples and produces outputs in the form of $m + n$–tuples whose first m components consist of the output of f while the last n components constitute the output of g. Thus, $\pi_1^3 \times \pi_3^3(4, 6, 8) = (4, 8)$.

Assuming that we have ways of computing the functions f and g, we could compute $f \times g$ by first computing f and g separately and then combining their outputs to form the output of $f \times g$. We conclude, then, that the combination of computable functions should be considered computable.

Another method of forming more complex functions is **composition.** The composition of two functions $f:\mathbb{N}^k \to \mathbb{N}^m$ and $g:\mathbb{N}^m \to \mathbb{N}^n$ is the function $g \circ f:\mathbb{N}^k \to \mathbb{N}^n$ defined by $g \circ f(\bar{x}) = g(f(\bar{x}))$, where $\bar{x}$ is a k-tuple. Thus, to find the output of $g \circ f$, we first apply f to the input and then apply g to the output of f. For example, $\sigma \circ \zeta(\ ) = 1$ since $\zeta(\ ) = 0$ and $\sigma(0) = 1$.

As with combination, we argue that the composition of two computable functions should be classified as computable. After all, if we have ways of computing f and g, we could compute $g \circ f$ by first computing f and then using the output of that computation as input when computing g.

The last function construction technique to be considered at this time is called **primitive recursion.** Let us suppose we wanted to define a function $f:\mathbb{N}^2 \to \mathbb{N}$ such that $f(x, y)$ would be the number of nodes in a full, balanced tree in which every nonleaf node has exactly x children and every path from the root to a leaf contains y arcs. (Such a tree is said to have a depth of y.) Our first step might be to observe that each level of the tree contains exactly x^n nodes, where n is the level number (Figure 4.2). Thus, for a fixed value of x, to determine the number of nodes in a tree with depth $y + 1$, we need merely add $x^{y+1} = x^y x$ to the number of nodes in the tree of depth y. Combining this with the fact that a tree consisting of only a root node contains x^0 nodes allows us to define f recursively by the pair of formulas

$$f(x, 0) = x^0 \qquad\qquad (1)$$
$$f(x, y + 1) = f(x, y) + x^y x \qquad\qquad (2)$$

Based on this definition, we would compute $f(3, 2)$ as follows:

$$
\begin{aligned}
f(3, 2) &= f(3, 1) + 3^1 3 &\text{(by formula 2)} \\
&= f(3, 1) + 9 \\
&= f(3, 0) + 3^0 3 + 9 &\text{(by formula 2)} \\
&= f(3, 0) + 3 + 9 \\
&= f(3, 0) + 12 \\
&= 3^0 + 12 &\text{(by formula 1)} \\
&= 13
\end{aligned}
$$

In a more general context, what we have done is define f in terms of two other functions. One of these is $g:\mathbb{N} \to \mathbb{N}$ such that $g(x) = 1$ for each $x \in \mathbb{N}$; the other is $h:\mathbb{N}^3 \to \mathbb{N}$ such that $h(x, y, z) = z + x^y x$. Using these functions, f is defined recursively by the formulas

$$f(x, 0) = g(x)$$
$$f(x, y + 1) = h(x, y, f(x, y))$$

In this case we say that f is constructed from g and h using primitive recursion. In general, primitive recursion is a technique that allows us to construct a function f mapping $\mathbb{N}^{k+1}$ into $\mathbb{N}^m$ from two other functions g and h that map $\mathbb{N}^k$ into $\mathbb{N}^m$ and $\mathbb{N}^{k+m+1}$ into $\mathbb{N}^m$, respectively, as described by the equations

$$f(\overline{x}, 0) = g(\overline{x})$$
$$f(\overline{x}, y + 1) = h(\overline{x}, y, f(\overline{x}, y))$$

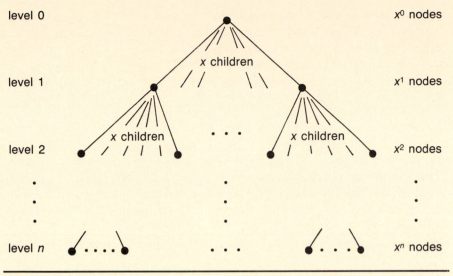

level 0 x^0 nodes

                    x children

level 1 x^1 nodes

      x children x children

level 2 x^2 nodes

level n x^n nodes

Figure 4.2   A level-by-level description of a balanced tree in which each nonleaf node has x children

where $\bar{x}$ represents an arbitrary k-tuple. That is, if the last component in the input tuple of f is 0, then the output of f is obtained by dropping this last component and applying g to the remaining k-tuple. If the last component in the input of f is not 0, then the output of f is determined by applying h to the $k + m + 1$–tuple that is formed by combining the first k entries of the original input, the predecessor of the original input's last component, and the result of applying f to the $k + 1$–tuple obtained by decrementing the last component of the original input by 1. Thus, the computation of $f(\bar{x}, 3)$ involves the computation of $f(\bar{x}, 2)$, which in turn requires the computation of $f(\bar{x}, 1)$, which requires the computation of $f(\bar{x}, 0)$, as represented in Figure 4.3.

Using primitive recursion along with other functions and operations already presented, we can define the function $plus{:}\mathbb{N}^2 \to \mathbb{N}$ (whose output is the sum of its input components) as follows:

$$plus(x, 0) = \pi_1^1(x)$$
$$plus(x, y + 1) = \sigma \circ \pi_3^3(x, y, plus(x, y))$$

Informally, this says that $x + 0$ is just x, whereas $x + (y + 1)$ is obtained (recursively) by finding the successor of $x + y$.

To complete our introduction of primitive recursion, we observe that a function constructed by primitive recursion from functions that are com-

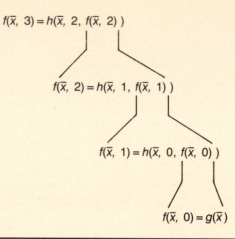

$$f(\overline{x}, 3) = h(\overline{x}, 2, f(\overline{x}, 2))$$

$$f(\overline{x}, 2) = h(\overline{x}, 1, f(\overline{x}, 1))$$

$$f(\overline{x}, 1) = h(\overline{x}, 0, f(\overline{x}, 0))$$

$$f(\overline{x}, 0) = g(\overline{x})$$

Figure 4.3   Computing $f(\overline{x}, 3)$, where $f(\overline{x}, y)$ is defined from g and h using primitive recursion

putable should itself be considered computable. In particular, if f is defined from computable functions g and h by primitive recursion, we could compute $f(\overline{x}, y)$ by first computing $f(\overline{x}, 0)$, then $f(\overline{x}, 1)$, then $f(\overline{x}, 2)$, etc., until we reached $f(\overline{x}, y)$.

We are now prepared to define the class of functions that resides above the initial functions in the hierarchy of recursive function theory. This is the class of **primitive recursive functions.** It consists of all those functions that can be constructed from the initial functions by applying a finite number of combinations, compositions, and primitive recursions. Clearly, this class is a proper extension of the initial functions since it contains the initial functions as well as the function *plus* which we constructed from σ and some projections. In fact, the class of primitive recursive functions is known to be extremely extensive. It includes most, if not all, of the total functions that are required in traditional computer applications. We support this claim in the next section by considering a variety of primitive recursive functions.

Finally, we should note that if $f: \mathbb{N}^m \to \mathbb{N}^n$ is a primitive recursive function, then f must be total. Indeed, the initial functions are total, and the construction techniques of combination, composition, and primitive recursion produce total functions when applied to total functions. Thus, the extensive nature of primitive recursive functions does not mean that this class completes our hierarchy of computable functions. For example, *div* is computable but not primitive recursive because it is not total. (In fact, we will find that there are computable total functions that are not primitive recursive.) Consequently, once we have expanded our repertoire of primitive recursive functions in the next section, we will continue our search for computable functions by looking beyond this class.

Exercises

1. What is the result of applying the function $(\pi_2^2 \times \pi_1^2) \circ (\pi_1^3 \times \pi_3^3)$ to the three-tuple $(5, 4, 7)$?

2. a. If $f:\mathbb{N} \to \mathbb{N}$ is defined by

$$f(0) = \zeta(\,)$$
$$f(y + 1) = (\sigma \circ \sigma) \circ f(y)$$

what is the value of $f(3)$?

   b. If $g:\mathbb{N} \times \mathbb{N} \times \mathbb{N} \to \mathbb{N}$ is defined by

$$g(x, y, 0) = \pi_1^2(x, y)$$
$$g(x, y, z + 1) = (\sigma \circ g)(x, y, z)$$

what is the value of $g(5, 7, 2)$?

3. Explain how the value of $plus(5, 2)$ could be computed based on the definition of $plus$ in this section.

4. Show that any permutation of an n-tuple is a primitive recursive function.

4.2 THE SCOPE OF PRIMITIVE RECURSIVE FUNCTIONS

The first goal of this section is to extend our repertoire of functions that we know to be primitive recursive. This will not only support the claim that the class of primitive recursive functions includes those total functions found in typical computer applications, but it will also provide specific examples that will be useful in the following sections. The second goal of this section is to clarify the distinction between the class of primitive recursive functions and the class of computable total functions.

Before we begin, we should establish some notational conveniences. Suppose we wanted to represent a function $h:\mathbb{N}^3 \to \mathbb{N}$ that returns the sum of the first and third components from its input. This function could be represented as $plus \circ (\pi_1^3 \times \pi_3^3)$. That is, to obtain $h(x, y, z)$ we extract the first and third components of the input using the projections π_1^3 and π_3^3, then combine the results into a pair $(\pi_1^3 \times \pi_3^3)$, and finally apply $plus$ to this pair. Thus, the notation $plus \circ (\pi_1^3 \times \pi_3^3)$ describes h quite adequately. On the other hand, such notation can become extremely cumbersome and hard to decipher, especially in comparison to the expression $h(x, y, z) = plus(x, z)$

or $h(x, y, z) = x + z$. We will often yield to these less formal forms for the sake of readability.

Examples of Primitive Recursive Functions

Let us now begin our investigation of primitive recursive functions by considering the collection of **constant functions,** each of which produces a fixed, predetermined output regardless of its input. The constant functions whose outputs are one-tuples are denoted by K_m^n, where n is a nonnegative integer that indicates the dimension of the function's domain and m is a nonnegative integer that indicates the function's output value. Thus, the function K_5^3 maps any three-tuple to the value 5 while K_3^5 maps any five-tuple to the value 3.

Constant functions of the form K_m^0 (that correspond to the process of writing the value m on a blank piece of paper) are easy to produce. We simply start with ζ and then, using composition, apply enough instances of σ to increment the output to the value m. For example, K_2^0 would be $\sigma \circ \sigma \circ \zeta$. We conclude that any constant function of the form K_m^0 is primitive recursive.

To show that functions of the form K_m^n with n greater than 0 are primitive recursive, we use induction on n. In general, if we know that K_m^i is primitive recursive for all i less than n, then K_m^n can be defined by

$$K_m^n(\overline{x}, 0) = K_m^{n-1}(\overline{x})$$
$$K_m^n(\overline{x}, y + 1) = \pi_{n+2}^{n+2}(\overline{x}, y, K_m^n(\overline{x}, y))$$

Constant functions whose outputs have more than one component are also primitive recursive since they are nothing more than combinations of functions of the form K_m^n. For example, the function that maps any triple to the pair (2, 5) is simply $K_2^3 \times K_5^3$.

(To avoid cumbersome notation, we can represent a constant function by the value of its output in those instances in which the dimension of its domain is either clear or not significant to the discussion. Thus, we will sometimes write 6 instead of K_6^2 or just (2, 5) instead of $K_2^3 \times K_5^3$.)

Using constant functions and the function *plus* from the previous section, we can show that multiplication is primitive recursive as follows:

$$mult(x, 0) = K_0^1(x)$$
$$mult(x, y + 1) = h(x, y, mult(x, y))$$

where $h(x, y, z) = plus(x, z)$, or in more readable form

$$mult(x, 0) = 0$$
$$mult(x, y + 1) = plus(x, mult(x, y))$$

Similarly, we can show that exponentiation is primitive recursive by defining $exp(x, y)$ as

$$exp(x, 0) = K_1^1(x)$$
$$exp(x, y + 1) = h(x, y, exp(x, y))$$

where $h(x, y, z) = mult(x, z)$. That is,

$$exp(x, 0) = 1$$
$$exp(x, y + 1) = mult(x, exp(x, y))$$

Next we consider the **predecessor function,** denoted by *pred*. This function maps one-tuples to one-tuples in such a way that 0 is mapped to 0, but values greater than 0 are mapped to their predecessor in the natural ordering of $\mathbb{N}$. (Thus, $pred(1) = 0$, $pred(2) = 1$, $pred(3) = 2$, etc.) To see that *pred* is primitive recursive, we note that it can be defined by

$$pred(0) = \zeta(\ )$$
$$pred(y + 1) = \pi_1^2(y, pred(y))$$

In a way, *pred* is the inverse of σ, and in fact, *pred* can be used to define subtraction in the same manner that we used σ to develop addition. In particular, we define the function *monus* (like minus, but different) by

$$monus(x, 0) = \pi_1^1(x)$$
$$monus(x, y + 1) = h(x, y, monus(x, y))$$

where $h(x, y, z) = pred(z)$. That is,

$$monus(x, 0) = x$$
$$monus(x, y + 1) = pred(monus(x, y))$$

Thus, $monus(x, y)$ is $x - y$ if $x \geq y$ and 0 otherwise. In recognition of the similar characteristics of the primitive recursive function *monus* and the concept of subtraction, you will often see $monus(x, y)$ written as $x \dotminus y$.

A popular computational task is to determine whether two values are equal. This process is modeled by the function $eq:\mathbb{N}^2 \to \mathbb{N}$, where

$$eq(x, y) = \begin{cases} 1 \text{ if } x = y \\ 0 \text{ if } x \neq y \end{cases}$$

The function *eq* is seen to be primitive recursive by recognizing that

$$eq(x, y) = 1 \dotminus ((y \dotminus x) + (x \dotminus y))$$

or, using a more formal notation, the function *eq* is

$$monus \circ (K_1^2 \times (plus \circ ((monus \circ (\pi_2^2 \times \pi_1^2)) \times monus \circ (\pi_1^2 \times \pi_2^2))))$$

For example,

$$eq(5, 3) = 1 \dotminus ((3 \dotminus 5) + (5 \dotminus 3))$$
$$= 1 \dotminus (0 + 2)$$
$$= 1 \dotminus 2$$
$$= 0$$

and

$$
\begin{aligned}
eq(5, 5) &= 1 \div (\,(5 \div 5) + (5 \div 5)\,) \\
&= 1 \div (0 \div 0) \\
&= 1 \div 0 \\
&= 1
\end{aligned}
$$

We can also "negate" any function $f\!:\!\mathbb{N}^n \to \mathbb{N}$ to produce another function $\neg f\!:\!\mathbb{N}^n \to \mathbb{N}$ that is 1 when f is 0 and 0 when f is not 0, by defining $\neg f$ to be $monus \circ (K_1^n \times f)$, i.e., $\neg f(x) = 1 \div f(x)$. For example,

$$
\neg eq(x, y) = \begin{cases} 1 \text{ if } x \neq y \\ 0 \text{ if } x = y \end{cases}
$$

is the primitive recursive function $monus \circ (K_1^2 \times eq)$.

Another collection of primitive recursive functions are those that can be defined by a table in which a finite number of possible inputs are listed explicitly along with their corresponding output values, and all other inputs are associated with a single common value. We will call such functions tabular functions. An example would be the function f defined by

$$
f(x) = \begin{cases} 3 \text{ when } x = 0 \\ 5 \text{ when } x = 4 \\ 2 \text{ otherwise} \end{cases}
$$

that can be summarized by the table in Figure 4.4. To convince ourselves that such functions are primitive recursive, we first recognize that the characteristic function κ_i of a single value i is primitive recursive. After all, the function

$$
\kappa_i(x) = \begin{cases} 1 \text{ if } x = i \\ 0 \text{ otherwise} \end{cases}
$$

can be expressed as $monus(I_i, I_{i-1})$, where

$$
I_i = eq \circ (\,(monus \circ (\pi_1^1 \times K_i^1)\,) \times K_0^1)
$$

i.e., $I_i(x) = eq(x \div i, 0)$. (See Figure 4.5.) Next we note that any tabular function is merely the finite sum of the product of constant, characteristic,

input	output
0	3
4	5
others	2

Figure 4.4   A tabular description of a function

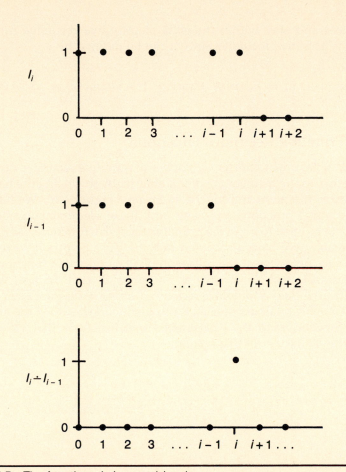

Figure 4.5 The functions l_i, l_{i-1}, and $l_i \dotdiv l_{i-1}$

and negated characteristic functions. For example, the function f defined by the table in Figure 4.4 is equivalent to

$$mult(3, \kappa_0) + mult(5, \kappa_4) + mult(2, mult(\neg\kappa_0, \neg\kappa_4))$$

As a final example, we show that the function $quo:\mathbb{N}^2 \to \mathbb{N}$ defined by

$$quo(x, y) = \begin{cases} \text{the integer part of } x \div y \text{ if } y \neq 0 \\ 0 \text{ if } y = 0 \end{cases}$$

is primitive recursive. (The notation quo is short for quotient.) For this purpose we first note that although primitive recursion is formally defined using the last component of the input tuple as the index, the use of projections and combinations allows us to apply primitive recursion based on other indices and stay within the class of primitive recursive functions. Thus, *quo* is primitive recursive since it can be defined by

$$quo(0, y) = 0$$
$$quo(x + 1, y) = quo(x, y) + eq(x + 1, mult(quo(x, y), y) + y)$$

Beyond Primitive Recursive Functions

Having taken the time to present a number of primitive recursive functions, we now return to the mainstream of this chapter by reviewing the hierarchy of computable functions introduced so far (see Figure 4.6). We have presented the initial functions and seen how these elementary computable functions can be used to build the primitive recursive functions, all of which are computable. We have also noted that the class of primitive recursive functions does not exhaust the collection of all computable functions since some computable functions, such as *div*, are not total. In fact, we have indicated that the class of primitive recursive functions does not even exhaust all the computable total functions. It is this distinction between the primitive recursive functions and the computable total functions that we wish to clarify in the remainder of this section.

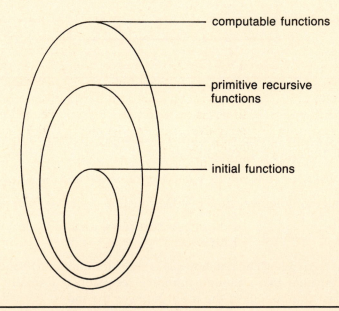

computable functions

primitive recursive functions

initial functions

Figure 4.6   The function hierarchy introduced so far

At one point in the development of recursive function theory there were those who conjectured that the class of primitive recursive functions might contain all computable total functions. However, such conjectures were squelched by the discovery of computable total functions that are not primitive recursive. One such example was presented by W. Ackermann in 1928. His example was the function $A:\mathbb{N}^2 \to \mathbb{N}$ (now known as Ackermann's function), defined by the equations

$$A(0, y) = y + 1$$
$$A(x + 1, 0) = A(x, 1)$$
$$A(x + 1, y + 1) = A(x, A(x + 1, y))$$

which he showed to be computable and total, yet not primitive recursive.

The proof of these claims is rather tedious and thus postponed to Appendix B. The fact is we do not need a specific example of a computable total function that is not primitive recursive for our classification study. All we really need is the knowledge that such a function exists, and in retrospect, the proof of this existence is straightforward as we now see.

THEOREM 4.1
There is a computable total function from $\mathbb{N}$ into $\mathbb{N}$ that is not primitive recursive.

PROOF
Each primitive recursive function from $\mathbb{N}$ into $\mathbb{N}$, being constructed from the initial functions by a finite number of combinations, compositions, and primitive recursions, can be defined by a finite string of symbols. Thus, we can assign an order to the primitive recursive functions by first arranging their definitions according to length (short strings first) and then arranging the strings of the same length by alphabetical order. In terms of this ordering, then, we can speak of the first primitive recursive function (denoted f_1), the second primitive recursive function (denoted f_2), and in general, the nth primitive recursive function (denoted f_n).

Let us now define the function $f:\mathbb{N} \to \mathbb{N}$ such that $f(n) = f_n(n) + 1$ for each $n \in \mathbb{N}$. Then, f is total and computable. (We could compute $f(n)$ by first finding the nth primitive recursive function f_n and then computing $f_n(n) + 1$.) However, f itself cannot be primitive recursive. (If it were, it would have to be f_m for some $m \in \mathbb{N}^+$. But then $f(m)$ would be equal to $f_m(m)$, which cannot be true since $f(m)$ is defined to be $f_m(m) + 1$.)

We conclude that f has the characteristics required by the theorem.

∎

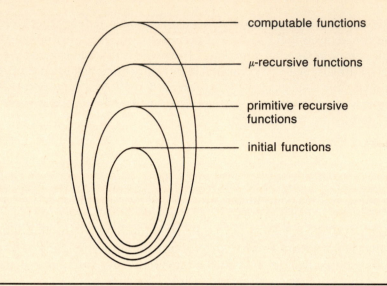

Figure 4.7   A refinement of Figure 4.6

The class of computable total functions is known as the class of **μ-recursive functions.** Thus, Theorem 4.1 says that Figure 4.6 can be refined as shown in Figure 4.7. In the following section we will explore that portion of Figure 4.7 which resides outside the μ-recursive functions.

Exercises

1. Show that the characteristic function of any finite subset of $\mathbb{N}$ is primitive recursive.
2. Show that the function $odd{:}\mathbb{N} \to \mathbb{N}$ defined by

$$odd(x) = \begin{cases} 1 \text{ if } x \text{ is odd} \\ 0 \text{ if } x \text{ is even} \end{cases}$$

   is primitive recursive.
3. Show that the function $dif{:}\mathbb{N}^2 \to \mathbb{N}$ defined by

$$dif(x, y) = \text{absolute value of } x - y$$

   is primitive recursive.
4. Show that the factorial function $f(x) = x!$ is primitive recursive.
5. Find $A(3, 1)$ where A is Ackermann's function.

4.3 PARTIAL RECURSIVE FUNCTIONS

Our study of computable functions has led us to the classes of initial functions, primitive recursive functions, and computable total functions, all of which are total. We now extend our study to include the computable partial functions.

Definition of Partial Recursive Functions

To extend our study of computable functions beyond the computable total functions we apply the construction technique known as **minimalization.** This technique allows us to construct a function $f{:}\mathbb{N}^n \to \mathbb{N}$ from another function $g{:}\mathbb{N}^{n+1} \to \mathbb{N}$ by declaring $f(\overline{x})$ to be the smallest y in $\mathbb{N}$ such that both $g(\overline{x}, y) = 0$ and $g(\overline{x}, z)$ is defined for all nonnegative integers z less than y. We represent such a construction by the notation $f(\overline{x}) = \mu y[g(\overline{x}, y) = 0]$, which is read, "$f(\overline{x})$ equals the smallest y for which $g(\overline{x}, y)$ is zero and $g(\overline{x}, z)$ is defined for all nonnegative integers z less than y."

As an example, suppose $g(x, y)$ is defined according to the table in Figure 4.8 and $f(x)$ is defined to be $\mu y[g(x, y) = 0]$. Then, $f(0) = 4$, $f(1) = 2$, and $f(2)$ is undefined. (Although 4 is the smallest value of y for which $g(x, y) = 0$, $g(x, z)$ is not defined for all values of z less than 4, and thus $f(2)$ is undefined.) As for the value of $f(3)$, the table does not provide enough information for us to determine whether it is defined.

We emphasize that, as in the preceding example, minimalization can produce functions that are undefined for some inputs. Another example is the function $f{:}\mathbb{N} \to \mathbb{N}$ defined by $f(x) = \mu y[plus(x, y) = 0]$. In this case f is 0 at 0, but f is undefined for all other inputs. (For $x > 0$, there is no y in $\mathbb{N}$ such that $x + y = 0$.) Still another example is the integer quotient function $div{:}\mathbb{N}^2 \to \mathbb{N}$ defined by

$$div(x, y) = \begin{cases} \text{integer portion of } x/y \text{ if } y \neq 0 \\ \text{undefined if } y = 0 \end{cases}$$

that can be constructed using minimalization as

$$div(x, y) = \mu t[(\,(x + 1) \div (mult(t, y) + y)\,) = 0]$$

On the other hand, minimalization sometimes produces total functions such as $f(x) = \mu y[monus(x, y) = 0]$, which is nothing more than the identity function: the smallest y such that $x - y = 0$ is x itself.

Let us now consider the computability of a function defined by minimalization. If the partial function g is computable, then $f(\overline{x}) = \mu y[g(\overline{x}, y) = 0]$ can be computed by computing the values $g(\overline{x}, 0)$, $g(\overline{x}, 1)$, $g(\overline{x}, 2)$, etc., until either the value 0 is obtained or a value z is reached for which $g(\overline{x}, z)$ is undefined. In the former case, the value of $f(\overline{x})$ is the value of y for which

$$g(0, 0) = 2 \qquad g(1, 0) = 3 \qquad g(2, 0) = 8 \qquad g(3, 0) = 2 \quad \dots$$
$$g(0, 1) = 3 \qquad g(1, 1) = 4 \qquad g(2, 1) = 3 \qquad g(3, 1) = 6 \quad \dots$$
$$g(0, 2) = 1 \qquad g(1, 2) = 0 \qquad g(2, 2) = \text{undefined} \quad g(3, 2) = 7 \quad \dots$$
$$g(0, 3) = 5 \qquad g(1, 3) = 2 \qquad g(2, 3) = 6 \qquad g(3, 3) = 2 \quad \dots$$
$$g(0, 4) = 0 \qquad g(1, 4) = 0 \qquad g(2, 4) = 0 \qquad g(3, 4) = 8 \quad \dots$$
$$g(0, 5) = 1 \qquad g(1, 5) = 0 \qquad g(2, 5) = 1 \qquad g(3, 5) = 4 \quad \dots$$

$$\vdots \qquad\qquad\qquad \vdots \qquad\qquad\qquad \vdots \qquad\qquad\qquad \vdots$$

Figure 4.8   The value of $g(x, y)$ for various xs and ys

$g(\overline{x}, y)$ was found to be 0; in the latter case, $f(\overline{x})$ is undefined. Thus, the process of minimalization applied to a computable partial function produces a computable partial function.

This observation allows us to extend our repertoire of computable functions beyond the bounds of primitive recursive functions to the class known as the **partial recursive functions.** More precisely, the class of partial recursive functions is the class of partial functions that can be constructed from the initial functions by applying a finite number of combinations, compositions, primitive recursions, and minimalizations. Thus, the function *div* defined previously is partial recursive but not primitive recursive.

Observe that the construction of a partial recursive function may require the application of combination, composition, or primitive recursion to strictly partial functions. In these cases, the definitions of these operations are extended in the obvious way. The combination of two partial functions f and g is defined at $\overline{x}$ if and only if both f and g are defined at $\overline{x}$, and the composition of f and g is defined at $\overline{x}$ if and only if g is defined at $\overline{x}$ and f is defined at $g(\overline{x})$. Likewise, f is defined from g and h by primitive recursion at $(\overline{x}, y)$ if and only if g is defined at $\overline{x}$ and h is defined at $(\overline{x}, z, f(\overline{x}, z))$ for all nonnegative integers z less than y.

Again we emphasize that the term partial does not imply that all the functions in the class of partial recursive functions are partial in the strict sense. Indeed, the class contains the μ-recursive functions, all of which are total (see Figure 4.9).

With the introduction of the partial recursive functions, we have reached the end of our hierarchy of computable functions. In the same spirit that Turing's thesis proposes that the class of Turing machines possesses the computational power of any computational system, the class of partial recursive functions is conjectured to contain all computable (partial) functions. This latter thesis is known as **Church's thesis,** although Church originally proposed it in a slightly different context. One case supporting Church's thesis is that no one has been able to prove it to be false: No one has found a partial function that is computable yet not partial recursive. However, a

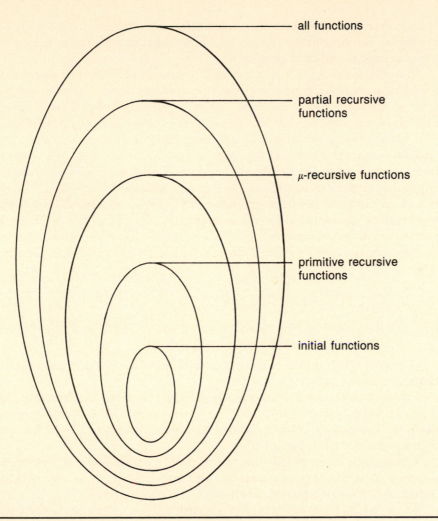

all functions

partial recursive
functions

μ-recursive functions

primitive recursive
functions

initial functions

Figure 4.9   The hierarchy of function classes in recursive function theory

more convincing argument is that Church's thesis and Turing's thesis are one and the same, a fact that we prove in the remainder of this section.

Turing-Computable Functions

Our first step in demonstrating the equivalence of Turing's thesis and Church's thesis is to show that Turing machines are powerful enough to compute any partial recursive function. This will imply that Church's thesis is no more general than Turing's. But, to establish this computational power of

Turing machines we must first reconsider the fundamentals of Turing machines, this time in the context of computing functions rather than solving language recognition problems.

Roughly speaking, a Turing machine computes a function by associating initial tape configurations with final tape configurations. To be more precise, let us agree that a tuple of strings, when represented on a Turing machine's tape, will appear as a list of strings separated by single blanks. The tuple $(xyx, yyxy)$ would be represented as $\triangle xyx \triangle yyxy \triangle \triangle \cdots$ and $(xyx, \lambda, yyxy)$ would appear as $\triangle xyx \triangle \triangle yyxy \triangle \triangle \cdots$. Using this convention, we can formally define the role of Turing machines as function computation devices as follows: A Turing machine $M = (S, \Sigma, \Gamma, \delta, \iota, h)$ is said to compute the partial function $f : \Sigma^{*^m} \to \Sigma_1^{*^n}$ (where Σ_1 is a set of nonblank symbols from Γ) if for each $(w_1, w_2, \cdots, w_m)$ in Σ^{*^m}, starting M with tape configuration $\underline{\triangle} w_1 \triangle w_2 \triangle \cdots \triangle w_m \triangle \triangle \cdots$ has one of the following consequences.

1. In those cases in which $f(w_1, w_2, \cdots, w_m)$ is defined, M halts with its tape containing $\triangle v_1 \triangle v_2 \triangle \cdots \triangle v_n \triangle \triangle \cdots$, where $(v_1, v_2, \cdots, v_n) = f(w_1, w_2, \cdots, w_m)$.
2. In those cases in which $f(w_1, w_2, \cdots, w_m)$ is not defined, M never halts (perhaps due to an abnormal termination).

A partial function that is computed by some Turing machine is said to be **Turing-computable.**

Figure 4.10 shows a Turing machine that computes the function that maps each triple of strings (w_1, w_2, w_3) to the pair (w_1, w_3). Another example is the machine $\to L$ that computes the partial function $f : \Sigma^* \to \Sigma^*$, which is undefined for all strings in Σ^*.

Clearly, not every partial function is Turing-computable. For example, suppose L_0 is the language over the alphabet $\Sigma = \{x, y\}$ as described in Section 3.5. Then the partial function $f : \Sigma^* \to \Sigma^*$ defined by

$$f(w) = \begin{cases} y \text{ if } w \in L_0 \\ \text{undefined otherwise} \end{cases}$$

is not Turing-computable. Indeed, the ability to compute this function would be equivalent to the ability to accept the language L_0, and we have seen that L_0 is not Turing-acceptable. In a similar manner, the function $f : \{0, 1\}^* \to \{0, 1\}^*$ defined by

$$f(w) = \begin{cases} 1 \text{ if } w = \rho(M) \text{ for a self-terminating machine } M \\ 0 \text{ otherwise} \end{cases}$$

is not Turing-computable since its computation would be equivalent to solving the halting problem.

Figure 4.10   A Turing machine that computes the function $f(w_1, w_2, w_3) = (w_1, w_3)$

Before proceeding, we should note that when computing a function by means of a Turing machine, we have not required that the Turing machine place its tape head over any particular tape cell before halting. We can, however, be more demanding in regard to a Turing machine's output configuration without restricting the class of functions that can be computed. In particular, if a partial function were computed by a Turing machine according to the previous definition, we could modify the machine so that it would return its tape head to the leftmost cell before halting. (This is essentially a matter of marking the leftmost cell, simulating the original machine, and returning the head to the marked cell if the simulation should reach the original machine's halt state.) Such an enhanced machine is often more convenient to work with than a less restricted one, and thus, we will resort to such machines when it is beneficial to do so.

Turing Computability of Partial Recursive Functions

Our goal now is to show that partial recursive functions are included in the class of partial functions that are Turing-computable.

Let us agree to represent nonnegative integers on a Turing machine's tape using binary notation. Thus, an n-tuple of nonnegative integers can be represented on a Turing machine's tape by listing its components separated by blanks. For instance, the pattern $\triangle 11 \triangle 10 \triangle 100 \triangle$ would represent the three-tuple (3, 2, 4), and $\triangle 10 \triangle 0 \triangle 11 \triangle 1 \triangle$ would represent the four-tuple (2, 0, 3, 1).

Based on this notation we can use Turing machines with alphabet {0, 1} to compute partial functions of the form $f: \mathbb{N}^m \to \mathbb{N}^n$, where m and n are nonnegative integers. In turn, Turing machines can be considered as possible instruments for computing the partial recursive functions. In fact, the following theorem shows that these machines can compute all the partial recursive functions.

THEOREM 4.2
Every partial recursive function is Turing-computable.

PROOF

We first show, in Figure 4.11, that the initial functions are Turing-computable. This figure describes explicit machines that compute the zero, successor, and projection functions.

Next, we show that the partial functions constructed from Turing-computable partial functions using combination, composition, primitive recursion, and minimalization are also Turing-computable. Let us begin with combination. If we have Turing machines M_1 and M_2 that compute the partial functions g_1 and g_2, respectively, we can construct a Turing machine M that computes $g_1 \times g_2$ as follows: Design M to be a three-tape machine that begins by duplicating its input on each of its other tapes. Then, M simulates M_1 using tape 2 and M_2 using tape 3. If each of these simulations reaches a valid termination, M erases its first tape, copies the contents of its other tapes onto tape 1 so that tape 1 contains the outputs of g_1 and g_2 separated by blanks, and halts.

To construct a Turing machine that computes the composition of two partial functions each of which is Turing-computable is extremely easy. If the machine M_1 computes g (by returning its tape head to the leftmost tape cell before halting) and M_2 computes f, then $\rightarrow M_1 M_2$ computes $f \circ g$.

We now consider primitive recursion. For this, suppose that f is defined by

$$f(\bar{x}, 0) = g(\bar{x})$$
$$f(\bar{x}, y + 1) = h(\bar{x}, y, f(\bar{x}, y))$$

where g is a partial function computed by the Turing machine M_1 and h is a partial function computed by M_2. (We can assume that M_1 and M_2 return their tape heads to the leftmost tape cell before halting.) Then, f can be computed by a Turing machine that proceeds as follows (see Figure 4.12):

1. If the last component of the input is 0, erase this component, return the tape head to the leftmost tape cell, and simulate machine M_1.
2. If the last component of the input is not 0, the tape must contain a sequence $\triangle, \bar{x}, \triangle, y + 1, \triangle, \triangle, \triangle, \cdots$ for some nonnegative integer y.
   a. Use the techniques of the copy and decrement machines of Section 3.2 to transform the tape contents into the sequence

$$\triangle, \bar{x}, \triangle, y, \triangle, \bar{x}, \triangle, y - 1, \triangle, \cdots, \triangle, \bar{x}, \triangle, 0, \triangle, \bar{x}, \triangle, \cdots$$

A machine to compute σ :

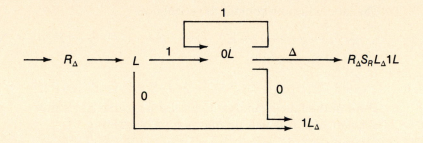

A machine to compute ζ:

$$\longrightarrow R0L$$

A machine to compute π_j^i :

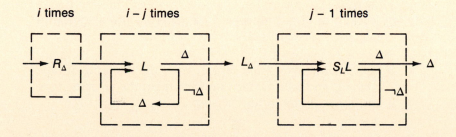

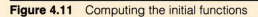

Figure 4.11   Computing the initial functions

Then, position the tape head over the cell that follows the 0, and simulate M_1.

b. The tape will now contain the sequence

$$\triangle, \overline{x}, \triangle, y, \triangle, \overline{x}, \triangle, y - 1, \triangle, \cdots, \triangle, \overline{x}, \triangle, 0, \triangle, g(\overline{x}), \triangle, \cdots$$

which is equivalent to

$$\triangle, \overline{x}, \triangle, y, \triangle, \overline{x}, \triangle, y - 1, \triangle, \cdots, \triangle, \overline{x}, \triangle, 0, \triangle, f(\overline{x}, 0), \triangle, \cdots$$

Position the tape head over the cell prior to the last $\overline{x}$ and simulate M_2. This will produce a tape containing

$$\triangle, \overline{x}, \triangle, y, \triangle, \overline{x}, \triangle, y - 1, \triangle, \cdots, \triangle, \overline{x}, \triangle, 1, \triangle, h(\overline{x}, 0, f(\overline{x}, 0)\,), \triangle, \cdots$$

that is equivalent to

$$\triangle, \overline{x}, \triangle, y, \triangle, \overline{x}, \triangle, y - 1, \triangle, \cdots, \triangle, \overline{x}, \triangle, 1, \triangle, f(\overline{x}, 1), \triangle, \cdots$$

c. Continue applying M_2 to the latter portion of the tape until M_2 is applied to

$$\triangle, \overline{x}, \triangle, y, \triangle, f(\overline{x}, y), \triangle, \triangle, \cdots$$

and the tape is reduced to the form $\triangle, h(\overline{x}, y, f(\overline{x}, y)\,)$, $\triangle, \triangle, \triangle, \cdots$. This is equivalent to $\triangle, f(\overline{x}, y + 1), \triangle, \triangle, \cdots$, the desired output.

Finally, we must argue that partial functions constructed from Turing-computable partial functions using minimalization are Turing-computable. This is quite straightforward. To compute $\mu y[g(\overline{x}, y) = 0]$, where g is computed by the Turing machine M, we could use a three-tape machine that proceeds as follows:

1. Write 0 on tape 2.
2. Copy $\overline{x}$ from tape 1 to tape 3 followed by the contents of tape 2.
3. Simulate M using tape 3.
4. If tape 3 contains 0, erase tape 1, copy the contents of tape 2 to tape 1, and halt. Otherwise, increment the value on tape 2, erase tape 3, and return to step 2.

■

We have shown, then, that the class of Turing machines possesses the power to compute all of the partial recursive functions.

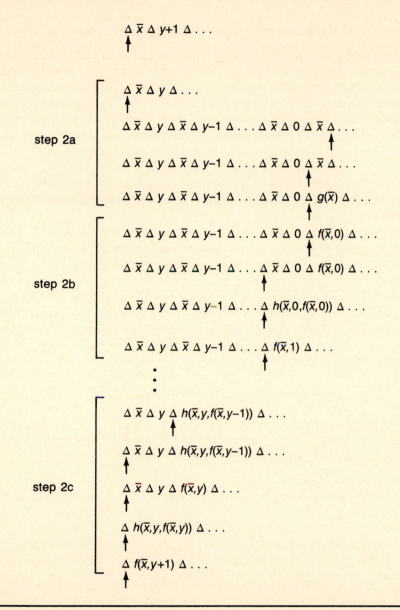

Figure 4.12 Snapshots of a Turing machine's tape during a primitive recursive computation

The Partial Recursive Nature of Turing Machines

To complete our proof that Turing's thesis is equivalent to Church's thesis, we must show that the computational power of Turing machines is restricted to the ability to compute partial recursive functions. To this end we consider a Turing machine $(S, \Sigma, \Gamma, \delta, \iota, h)$ and let $b = |\Gamma|$. The contents of such a machine's tape can be interpreted as a base b representation of a nonnegative integer, written in reverse order. We merely interpret $\triangle$ as the digit 0 and the nonblank tape symbols as nonzero digits. For example, if $\Gamma = \{x, y, \triangle\}$, then by interpreting x as 1 and y as 2, a tape containing $\triangle yx\triangle\triangle y\triangle\triangle\cdots$ would be equivalent to $021002000\cdots$, which when written in reverse order is $\cdots000200120$—the base three representation of 501. (See Figure 4.13.)

By interpreting machine tapes in this manner, we see that all a Turing machine really does is compute a partial function from $\mathbb{N}$ into $\mathbb{N}$. Given an input number represented by the initial tape configuration, the machine produces an output number represented by the final tape configuration. (For consistency we insist that the tape head start over the leftmost cell of the tape, but we make no restrictions on the final resting position of the tape head.) The fact that we have considered this process to be one of accepting a language or computing a function from tuples of symbols to tuples of symbols is merely a matter of interpretation of the tape rather than

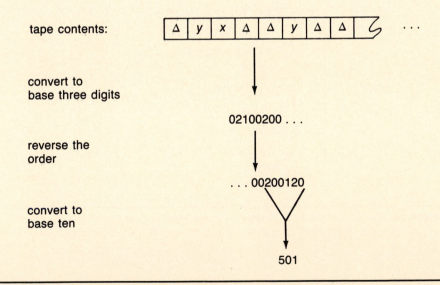

Figure 4.13   Interpreting the contents of a Turing machine's tape as a single numeric value

an action of the machine. Thus, we can show that Turing's thesis is no more general than Church's thesis by showing that the partial function from $\mathbb{N}$ into $\mathbb{N}$ computed by any Turing machine is partial recursive.

THEOREM 4.3
Any computational process performed by a Turing machine is actually the process of computing a partial recursive function.

PROOF

Let $M = (S, \Sigma, \Gamma, \delta, \iota, h)$ be a Turing machine and $f{:}\mathbb{N} \to \mathbb{N}$ be the partial function that is computed by M by interpreting the contents of the tape as base $b = |\Gamma|$ integer representations in reverse order. That is, for any $n \in \mathbb{N}$, $f(n)$ is defined only if M halts after being started with tape contents n, and in that case $f(n)$ is defined to be the number represented by the tape of the halted machine. We must show that f is partial recursive.

To this end, we associate the halt state of M with the integer 0, the initial state with 1, and the other states with the remaining nonnegative integers less than k, where k is the number of states in M. Thus, the states in M are represented by the integers $0, 1, \cdots, k - 1$.

At this point both the states in M and the symbols in M's alphabet are assigned numeric values.

Now define the following functions that summarize the information that would be contained in M's transition diagram.

$$mov(p, x) = \begin{cases} 2 \text{ if } M \text{ moves its tape head to the right} \\ \quad \text{ when in state } p \text{ with current symbol } x \\ 1 \text{ if } M \text{ moves its tape head to the left} \\ \quad \text{ when in state } p \text{ with current symbol } x \\ 0 \text{ otherwise} \end{cases}$$

$$sym(p, x) = \begin{cases} y \text{ if } M \text{ writes the symbol } y \\ \quad \text{ when in state } p \text{ with current symbol } x \\ x \text{ otherwise} \end{cases}$$

and

$$state(p, x) = \begin{cases} q \text{ if } M \text{ shifts to state } q \text{ when} \\ \quad \text{ in state } p \text{ with current symbol } x \\ k \text{ if either } p = 0 \text{ or } (p, x) \text{ is not a} \\ \quad \text{ valid state/symbol pair} \end{cases}$$

Each of these functions can be represented by a finite table as discussed in Section 4.2, and thus each is primitive recursive. In short, $mov(p, x)$ reports whether the action performed by M when faced with the state/symbol pair (p, x) is a move to the right, a move to the left, or a write operation; $sym(p, x)$ reports the symbol that M would leave in the current cell if (p, x) were the current state/symbol pair; and $state(p, x)$ reports the state to which M would shift if (p, x) were the current state/symbol pair. Note that $state(p, x)$ returns the nonvalid state number k (the states of M were numbered 0, 1, $\cdots$, $k - 1$) if the input state is the halt state or the input pair is not a valid state/symbol pair. This feature will guarantee that our final partial recursive function will be undefined for inputs that produce abnormal termination of M.

Next we observe that the configuration of M at any point in a computation can be represented by what we call a configuration triple, which is nothing more than a three-tuple (w, p, n) in which w represents the contents of the tape (as an integer written in base $b = |\Gamma|$), p is the integer representing M's current state, and n is a nonnegative integer that represents the position of the current cell, where the leftmost cell on the tape is cell 1, the first cell to the right is 2, the next cell 3, etc.

From the information in a configuration triple we can determine other aspects of the computation. For instance, from the triple (w, p, n) we can determine the current symbol to be $quo(w, b^{n-1}) \div mult(b, quo(w, b^n))$. (See Figure 4.14.) Moreover, this computation involves only functions that we have shown to be within the class of primitive recursive functions. Thus, the function $cursym: \mathbb{N}^3 \to \mathbb{N}$ defined by

$$cursym(w, p, n) = quo(w, b^{n-1}) \div mult(b, quo(w, b^n))$$

computes the current symbol from the information in a configuration triple and is also partial recursive.

Other computations based on information in a configuration triple are modeled by the functions $nexthead$, $nextstate$, and $nexttape$. In particular, $nexthead$ is defined by

$$nexthead(w, p, n) = n \div eq(mov(p, cursym(w, p, n)), 1) + eq(mov(p, cursym(w, p, n)), 2))$$

It produces the integer that represents the next tape head position. An abnormal termination caused by the tape head going off the end of the tape is indicated by a $nexthead$ output of 0. (Remember, the leftmost cell was numbered 1.)

The $nextstate$ function is defined by

$$nextstate(w, p, n) = state(p, cursym(w, p, n)) + mult(k, \neg nexthead(w, p, n))$$

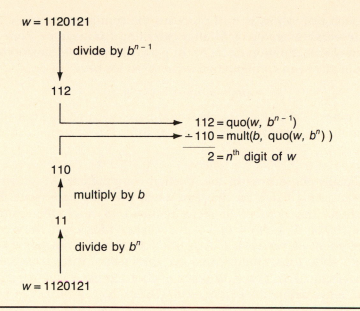

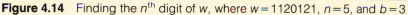

Figure 4.14 Finding the nth digit of w, where $w = 1120121$, $n = 5$, and $b = 3$

Normally, the second term in this sum is 0 so that *nextstate* returns a valid state number that represents the state to which M will shift if found in the configuration (w, p, n). However, if this shift is accompanied by an abnormal termination then the second term will produce the value k, so that *nextstate* will return a nonvalid state number.

The function *nexttape* is defined by

$$nexttape(w, p, n) = (w \div mult(b^n, cursym(w, p, n))) +$$
$$mult(b^n, sym(p, cursym(w, p, n)))$$

It produces the integer that represents the tape contents of M after executing a transition from the configuration (w, p, n).

The functions *nexthead*, *nextstate*, and *nexttape* are constructed from partial recursive functions using composition and combination and are therefore partial recursive. Moreover, by combining these functions, we obtain another partial recursive function $step: \mathbb{N}^3 \to \mathbb{N}^3$ that simulates a single step in a computation of M. It associates its input configuration triple with the output triple representing the next configuration of M. More precisely,

$$step = nexttape \times nextstate \times nexthead$$

Now, using primitive recursion we define a function $run: \mathbb{N}^4 \to$

$\mathbb{N}^3$ such that $run(w, p, n, t)$ produces the configuration triple that represents the status of M after executing t transitions from the starting configuration (w, p, n). In particular, after 0 transitions M would still be in configuration (w, p, n) so we have

$$run(w, p, n, 0) = (w, p, n)$$

and after $t + 1$ transitions, M would have executed one transition from the configuration $run(w, p, n, t)$ so

$$run(w, p, n, t + 1) = step(run(w, p, n, t))$$

Finally, the output of the function computed by M (given input w) is the value on the tape when the halt state (state 0) is reached. The number of steps required to reach this state is $\mu t[\pi_2^3(run(w, 1, 1, t)) = 0]$, i.e., the smallest t for which the second component of $run(w, 1, 1, t)$ is 0. (Note that the function run is total and thus there are no problems with computing $\mu t[\pi_2^3(run(w, 1, 1, t)) = 0]$ when such a t exists.) Following this lead, let us define the partial recursive function $stoptime:\mathbb{N} \to \mathbb{N}$ by

$$stoptime(w) = \mu t[\pi_2^3(run(w, 1, 1, t)) = 0]$$

Thus, if $f:\mathbb{N} \to \mathbb{N}$ is the partial function computed by M, then

$$f(w) = \pi_1^3(run(w, 1, 1, stoptime(w)))$$

Consequently, f is a partial recursive function.

∎

In summary, we have shown that the partial recursive functions are Turing-computable and that any Turing machine does nothing more than compute a partial recursive function. This means that Turing's thesis and Church's thesis, although stated in different contexts, are equivalent. The common idea in these theses is often called the Church–Turing thesis rather than just Turing's thesis or Church's thesis. More important than the blending of terminology, however, is the fact that the equivalence of these hypotheses means we have reached the same apparent bound on the power of computational processes from two distinct approaches—an operational approach and a functional approach—which reinforces our confidence in the conjectures.

Exercises

1. What is the value of $f(4)$ if f is defined by $f(x) = \mu y[monus(x, pred(y)) = 0]$? Is f total or strictly partial?

2. If $g(x, y)$ is primitive recursive and m is a positive integer, show that $f:\mathbb{N} \to \mathbb{N}$ defined by $f(x) = \mu y[g(x, y) = m]$ is partial recursive. (Thus, minimalization can be used to search for values other than 0 while remaining within the bounds of partial recursive functions.)

3. Design a Turing machine that computes the function $f:\Sigma^* \to \Sigma^*$ defined by $f(w) = w^R$, where $\Sigma = \{x, y\}$ and w^R is the string w written in reverse order.

4. For what strings is the partial function $f:\{x, y\}^* \to \{x, y\}^*$, as computed by the composite Turing machine $\to R \xrightarrow{x} yR_\triangle L_x LL$, defined? Describe the function.

4.4 THE POWER OF PROGRAMMING LANGUAGES

As an application of the theory presented in the previous sections, let us return to our question regarding the expressive power of programming languages. At issue is the question of what features must be included to guarantee that once a programming language is designed and implemented, we will not discover that there are problems whose solutions cannot be stated in the language, but could have been stated had we implemented an extended version of the language.

Our approach is to develop a simple bare-bones programming language in which a program for computing any partial recursive function can be expressed. This will insure (assuming the Church–Turing thesis) that as long as a programming language contains the features of our simple language, it will allow the expression of a solution to any algorithmically solvable problem.

A Bare-Bones Programming Language

Since our bare-bones language will be used to compute partial recursive functions, the only required data type is nonnegative integer. (As already noted, each item of data in a modern digital computer is represented as a nonnegative integer, even though the high-level language used may disguise this reality.) In turn, our simple language needs no type declaration statements. Rather, identifiers, consisting of letters and digits (beginning with a letter), are automatically declared to be of type nonnegative integer merely by their first occurrence in a program. (For convenience, we will sometimes use identifiers with subscripts with the understanding that this informality could be removed at the expense of clarity.)

Our language contains the following two assignment statements.

incr name;

and

decr name;

The first of these increments by 1 the value assigned to the identifier name, whereas the second decrements the value by 1 (unless the value to be decremented is already 0 in which case it remains 0).

The only other statement in our language is the control statement pair

while name ≠ 0 do;
.
.
.
end;

that indicates that the statements found between the while and end statements are to be repeated as long as the value assigned to the identifier name is not 0.

This, then, is our entire bare-bones language. It is extremely simple— so simple, in fact, that our first goal is to introduce some more powerful statements that can be simulated by sequences of bare-bones statements. We will then be able to use these additional statements to simplify bare-bones programs in the same manner in which macros are used to simplify assembly language programs. In particular, we will adopt the syntax

clear name;

as a shorthand for the sequence

while name ≠ 0 do;
    decr name;
end;

that has the effect of assigning the value 0 to the identifier name. Moreover, we will use

name1 ← name2;

to represent the program segment in Figure 4.15 that assigns the value of name2 to the identifier name1. (The value is first assigned to the auxiliary variable aux and then reassigned to both name1 and name2. This extra effort involving aux avoids the side effect of destroying the original assignment of name2.)

Partial Recursive Implies Bare-Bones Programmable

Our task now is to show that for any partial recursive function there is an algorithm for computing the function that can be expressed in our simple

```
clear aux;
clear name1;
while name2 ≠ 0 do;
     incr aux;
     decr name2;
end;
while aux ≠ 0 do;
     incr name1;
     incr name2;
     decr aux;
end;
```

Figure 4.15 The program segment represented by **name1 ← name2**

bare-bones language. For this purpose, we establish the convention that to compute a function from $\mathbb{N}^m$ into $\mathbb{N}^n$ we will write a program using identifiers $x_1, x_2, \cdots, x_m$ to hold the input values, and $z_1, z_2, \cdots, z_n$ to hold the output values.

Programs to compute the initial functions are easy to express in our language. The function ζ is handled by

$$\text{clear } z_1;$$

σ by

$$z_1 \leftarrow x_1;$$
$$\text{incr } z_1;$$

and π_j^m by

$$z_1 \leftarrow x_j;$$

We now turn our attention to the partial recursive functions in general. If F and G are programs that compute the partial functions $f:\mathbb{N}^k \to \mathbb{N}^m$ and $g:\mathbb{N}^k \to \mathbb{N}^n$, respectively, then the function $f \times g$ can be computed by concatenating the program G onto the end of the program F, modifying F and G so that they assign their outputs to the appropriate identifiers (F should assign its output to $z_1, \cdots, z_m$ while G assigns its output to $z_{m+1}, \cdots, z_{m+n}$), and adjusting F so that it does not destroy the input values before G gets its chance.

(Here, as in later cases, we assume that the programs involved do not have common auxiliary variable names that would result in undesirable side effects. If they did, we could change the names. All the auxiliary identifiers in program F could be prefixed by the letter F while those in G are prefixed by G.)

If F and G compute the partial functions $f:\mathbb{N}^k \to \mathbb{N}^l$ and $g:\mathbb{N}^l \to \mathbb{N}^m$, respectively, then $g \circ f$ can be computed by concatenating G onto the end of F and adjusting the output identifiers of F to agree with the input identifiers of G.

Now suppose that program G computes the partial function $g: \mathbb{N}^k \to \mathbb{N}^m$, H computes $h: \mathbb{N}^{k+m+1} \to \mathbb{N}^m$, and $f: \mathbb{N}^{k+1} \to \mathbb{N}^m$ is defined using primitive recursion by

$$f(\bar{x}, 0) = g(\bar{x})$$
$$f(\bar{x}, y + 1) = h(\bar{x}, y, f(\bar{x}, y))$$

Then, f can be computed by the program in Figure 4.16, where we assume (without loss of generality) that G and H do not have undesirable side effects.

We now show that if G is a program in our bare-bones language that computes the partial recursive function $g: \mathbb{N}^{n+1} \to \mathbb{N}$, then we can produce a program that computes $\mu y[g(\bar{x}, y) = 0]$. The program in Figure 4.17 does the job by computing $g(\bar{x}, 0)$, $g(\bar{x}, 1)$, $\cdots$ until an output of 0 is produced. (Note that G can be designed so that it does not alter the original assignments of its input variables.)

```
G
aux ← x_{k+1};
clear x_{k+1};
while aux ≠ 0 do;
        x_{k+2} ← z_1;
        x_{k+3} ← z_2;

              ⋮

        x_{k+m+1} ← z_m;
        H
        incr x_{k+1};
        decr aux;
end;
```

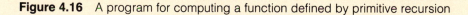

Figure 4.16   A program for computing a function defined by primitive recursion

```
clear x_{n+1};
G
while z_1 ≠ 0 do;
        incr x_{n+1};
        G
end;
z_1 ← x_{n+1}
```

Figure 4.17   A program for computing $\mu y[g(\bar{x}, y) = 0]$

At this point we have achieved our goal of showing that any partial recursive function can be computed by a program written in our simple bare-bones programming language. Thus, by the Church–Turing thesis, we are assured that any language providing the type nonnegative integer along with the ability to increment a value, decrement a value, and perform a while loop will have enough expressive power to express a solution to any problem having an algorithmic solution. Any additional features in a language provide convenience, not additional power.

Bare-Bones Programmable Implies Partial Recursive

Having discovered the surprising power of our simple language, one might conjecture that our language could provide a means of computing more than the partial recursive functions. Of course, if such a conjecture were true, it would contradict the Church–Turing thesis in that we would obtain a method of computing a class of functions larger than the partial recursive (Turing-computable) ones. Thus, we should not be surprised to learn that any computation expressed in our simple language can be modeled by a partial recursive function.

To prove the reality of this bound on our language's power, we first observe that any program in our simple language must involve at least one identifier since it must contain at least one of the three statement forms— incr, decr, and while—and each of these statements involves a variable. If a program contains k variables and we list these variables collectively as a k-tuple, then the computation expressed by the program actually computes a function from $\mathbb{N}^k$ to $\mathbb{N}^k$, where the input tuple is the k-tuple of values assigned to the variables when the program starts, and the output is the k-tuple of values assigned to these variables when the end of the program is reached. (If the program never terminates, then the function is not defined for that input tuple.) We proceed, now, to show that any such function must be partial recursive. Our approach is to induct on the number of statements in the program.

If there is only one statement in the program, there are three possibilities: it may be an incr, decr, or while statement. The former cases compute the primitive recursive functions σ and *pred*, respectively, whereas the latter case

$$\text{while } name \neq 0 \text{ do;}$$
$$\text{end;}$$

computes the function

$$f(name) = \begin{cases} 0 \text{ if } name = 0 \\ \text{undefined otherwise} \end{cases}$$

that is identical to the partial recursive function

$$f(name) = \mu y[plus(name, y) = 0]$$

Thus, all programs that contain only one statement from our simple language compute partial recursive functions.

Now we consider programs with n statements, where $n > 1$, while assuming that any program with fewer than n statements must compute a partial recursive function. If the program in question does not have the structure of one large while statement, then it is the concatenation of two shorter programs. By our induction hypothesis, each of these shorter programs computes a partial recursive function, but the overall program computes the composition of these functions. Thus, the complete program computes a partial recursive function.

To complete our argument we assume the program in question consists of one large while structure, which we represent as

$$\text{while } X \neq 0 \text{ do;}$$
$$B$$
$$\text{end;}$$

Since the body of this loop, B, contains fewer than n statements, our induction hypothesis implies that it computes a partial recursive function $h:\mathbb{N}^k \to \mathbb{N}^k$. Moreover, we may assume that the variable X identified in the while statement is one of the components, say the jth component, of the k-tuple manipulated by B. (If this variable were not manipulated by B the looping process, once started, would never terminate. Thus, the entire while structure would compute the partial recursive function that agrees with the identity function when X is 0, and is undefined for all other inputs.)

Using primitive recursion we now define the function $f:\mathbb{N}^{k+1} \to \mathbb{N}^k$ by

$$f(\overline{x}, 0) = ident(\overline{x})$$
$$f(\overline{x}, y + 1) = h(f(\overline{x}, y))$$

where *ident* is the identity function. (The identity function can be constructed as the combination of projections and is therefore primitive recursive.) Note that the value of $f(\overline{x}, y)$ is the k-tuple produced by initializing the variables in the loop body, B, to $\overline{x}$ and then performing the loop y times. The number of times the body of the while structure will actually be performed is $\mu y[\pi_j^k \circ f(\overline{x}, y) = 0]$. Thus, the function $g:\mathbb{N}^k \to \mathbb{N}^k$ computed by the entire while structure is defined by

$$g(\overline{x}) = f(\overline{x}, \mu y[\pi_j^k \circ f(\overline{x}, y) = 0])$$

Thus, the function computed by the while structure is partial recursive.

In closing, we should note that the study of computability by means of programming languages is yet another area of research whose results support the Church–Turing thesis. Indeed, no programming language has been designed with an expressive power greater than our simple language (although the more elaborate languages in use today are clearly superior in terms of readability).

Exercises

1. Show that the programming language consisting of statements of the form

    clear name;   incr name;   loop name times;

                                     .

                                     end;

   has the expressive power equal to the primitive recursive functions.

2. Write a program in the simple while language of this section that computes the function $f: \mathbb{N} \times \mathbb{N} \to \mathbb{N}$ defined by

$$f(x, y) = \begin{cases} 1 \text{ if } x > y \\ 0 \text{ otherwise} \end{cases}$$

3. Show how the programming structure

$$\text{if } x = 0 \text{ then } S_1 \text{ else } S_2$$

where S_1 and S_2 represent program segments, can be simulated in the simple while language of this section.

4. Show how the programming structure

$$\text{repeat } S \text{ until } x = 0$$

where S represents some program segment, can be simulated in the simple while language of this section.

4.5   CLOSING COMMENTS

In this chapter we have extended our study from that of language processing to include the computation of functions. Our major goal was to support Turing's thesis by showing that it agrees with conjectures developed in other research areas.

We first set out to identify the limitations of computational processes in general. To free our study from any particular computational system, we chose to consider a functional approach to computability rather than an operational one. That is, we concentrated on what computational processes accomplish rather than how they are performed. This led us to the class of partial recursive functions which, according to Church's thesis, is the class of all partial functions that can be computed by any computational system. We then showed that this apparent bound on the power of computational processes agrees with Turing's thesis.

Next, we considered the expressive power of traditional programming languages. At issue was our desire to determine whether a given language imposes unnecessary restrictions on the class of problems that can be solved by programs in that language. (Can every problem that can be solved algorithmically be solved by a program written in the language?) Our approach was to define a simple bare-bones programming language and show that any partial recursive function could be computed by a program written in that language. Thus, if we accept the Church–Turing thesis, we can conclude that any programming language containing the features of our bare-bones language will be general enough to allow any problem with an algorithmic solution to be solved by means of a program written in that language.

Finally, let us reconsider our entire study. We have approached the issue of computability from several directions—computational machines, generative grammars, recursive function theory, and programming languages. In each case we have discovered an apparent limit to the computational capabilities of that particular approach, and have shown that these limits agree with each other. The phrase-structure languages are the same as the Turing-acceptable languages, the Turing-computable functions are the same as the partial recursive functions, and the partial recursive functions are the same as the bare-bones computable functions. It therefore appears that we have identified the confines of computational processes in general, and of computers in particular. That is, we have found substantial support for the Church–Turing thesis: If a problem cannot be solved by a Turing machine, then it can never be solved by any computer because there is simply no algorithm for solving it. In other words, the limitations we have encountered are those of computational processes in general and not of technology.

Based on these observations, it is common to consider a problem to be a **solvable problem** (short for **Turing-solvable problem**) if and only if it can be solved by a Turing machine computation. Thus, the problem of accepting the language L_0, as defined in Section 3.5, and the halting problem are examples of unsolvable problems. Other unsolvable problems are discussed in Appendix C.

Chapter Review Problems

1. Find the value of
   a. $((\sigma \circ \zeta) \times \zeta)(\ )$
   b. $\pi_2^3 \times \pi_3^3 \times \pi_2^3(5, 6, 7)$
   c. $(\sigma \times \sigma) \circ \pi_2^2(4, 7)$
   d. $\zeta \circ \pi_0^3(4, 5, 6)$

2. Find the value of $f(5, 4)$ if the function f is defined by

   $$f(x, 0) = \sigma(x)$$
   $$f(x, y + 1) = (\pi_1^1 \circ f)(x, y)$$

3. Show that the function f defined by

   $$f(x, y, z) = \begin{cases} x \text{ if } z \text{ is even} \\ y \text{ if } z \text{ is odd} \end{cases}$$

   is primitive recursive.

4. Show that the function $tripleplus:\mathbb{N}^3 \to \mathbb{N}$ defined by $tripleplus(x, y, z) = x + y + z$ is primitive recursive.

5. Show that the function that assigns each triple of the form (x, y, z) to the ordered pair that results from interchanging x and y a total of z times is primitive recursive.

6. Find $f(0)$, $f(1)$, $f(2)$, and $f(3)$ if f is defined by $f(x) = \mu y[eq(x, y) = 0]$.
   Find $g(0)$, $g(1)$, $g(2)$, and $g(3)$ if g is defined by $g(x) = \mu y[\neg eq(x, y) = 0]$.

7. Compute $A(2, 2)$, where A is Ackermann's function.

8. Summarize the significance of Ackermann's function in the hierarchy of initial, primitive recursive, and partial recursive functions.

9. Give an example of a primitive recursive function that is not an initial function and an example of a partial recursive function that is not primitive recursive.

10. Show that the function $f:\mathbb{N} \to \mathbb{N}$ defined by

    $$f(x) = \begin{cases} x + 1 \text{ if } x \text{ is even} \\ x \text{ if } x \text{ is odd} \end{cases}$$

    is primitive recursive.

11. Show that if $f:\mathbb{N} \to \mathbb{N}$ is a one-to-one primitive recursive function, then the inverse function $g:\mathbb{N} \to \mathbb{N}$ defined by $g(f(x)) = x$ is partial recursive.

12. Digital computers are capable of testing for certain relationships between integers such as "equal to," "less than," "greater than," etc. Show, however, that there are relationships among integers that cannot be resolved by computers. (Hint: Use a cardinality argument.)

13. Show that the Pascal programming language provides a means of computing each partial recursive function. In what way is this power potentially restricted when the language is implemented on an actual machine?

14. Write a program in the bare-bones programming language of Section 4.4 that computes the function *plus* of Section 4.1.

15. Write a program in the bare-bones programming language of Section 4.4 that computes the factorial function.

16. Use a cardinality argument to show that there are functions from $\mathbb{N}$ into $\mathbb{N}$ that cannot be computed by an algorithm expressed in the bare-bones programming language of Section 4.4.

17. Write a program in the bare-bones programming language of Section 4.4 that computes the function $f:\mathbb{N} \rightarrow \mathbb{N}$ defined by $f(x) = \mu y[mult(x, y) > plus(x, y)]$. For what values is f not defined?

18. Show that the computational power of the bare-bones programming language of Section 4.4 is not reduced if the while structure is replaced with an if/then structure and the ability to express recursive procedures.

19. For what strings is the partial function $f:\{x, y\}^* \rightarrow \{x, y\}^*$, as computed by the composite Turing machine $\rightarrow R_x R_y L_\triangle$, defined? Describe the function.

20. Show that if we allow statements to be labeled and introduce a goto statement to the programming language in Exercise 1 of Section 4.4, we obtain a language with the same expressive power as our bare-bones language of Section 4.4.

21. Give an example of a function that is not partial recursive.

22. Suppose $g:\mathbb{N} \rightarrow \mathbb{N}$ and $h:\mathbb{N}^3 \rightarrow \mathbb{N}$ are primitive recursive. Show that the function $f:\mathbb{N} \rightarrow \mathbb{N}$ defined by

$$f(0, y) = g(y)$$
$$f(x + 1, y) = h(f(x, y), y, x)$$

is primitive recursive.

23. Show that if $f:\mathbb{N} \rightarrow \mathbb{N}$ is a function and M is a Turing machine that when given input n computes the value $f(n)$ in no more than 2^n steps, then f is primitive recursive.

24. Design a Turing machine that computes the function $f:\{x, y\}^* \times \{x, y\}^* \rightarrow \{x, y\}^* \times \{x, y\}^*$ such that $f(w_1, w_2) = (w_2, w_1)$.

25. Suppose $g:\mathbb{N}^2 \rightarrow \mathbb{N}$ is primitive recursive and $f:\mathbb{N}^2 \rightarrow \mathbb{N}$ is defined so that $f(x, y)$ is the smallest y less than z for which $g(x, y) = 0$ or 0 if no such y exists. Show that f is primitive recursive.

26. Show that the function $gcd:\mathbb{N}^2 \to \mathbb{N}$, where $gcd(x, y)$ is the greatest common divisor of x and y, is partial recursive.

27. Show that each partial recursive function can be constructed from the initial functions by applying a finite number of combinations, compositions, primitive recursions, and at most one minimalization.

28. Define $f:\mathbb{N} \to \mathbb{N}$ so that $f(0) = 0$, $f(1) = 1$, and $f(n + 2) = f(n) + f(n + 1)$. Show that f is primitive recursive.

29. Define $f:\mathbb{N} \to \mathbb{N}$ so that $f(x)$ is the sum of the divisors of x. For example, $f(5) = 1 + 5 = 6$ and $f(6) = 1 + 2 + 3 + 6 = 12$. Show that f is primitive recursive.

30. Give an argument to the effect that the programming languages Pascal, Modula-2, Ada, FORTRAN, and COBOL ultimately possess identical computational power. (Note, however, that this does not mean they are equivalent in their support for such popular design objectives as data abstraction, information hiding, modular design, and object implementation.)

31. Show that if the function $f:\mathbb{N}^2 \to \mathbb{N}$ is partial recursive, then the function $g:\mathbb{N} \to \mathbb{N}$, defined by $g(x) = f(x, 5)$, is partial recursive.

32. Suppose $f:\mathbb{N} \to \mathbb{N}$ and $g:\mathbb{N} \to \mathbb{N}$ are partial recursive functions. Show that there is a partial recursive function $h:\mathbb{N} \to \mathbb{N}$ such that $h(x)$ is defined at exactly those values of x for which either $f(x)$ or $g(x)$ is defined.

33. Suppose $f:\mathbb{N} \to \mathbb{N}$ and $g:\mathbb{N} \to \mathbb{N}$ are partial recursive functions. Is there a partial recursive function $h:\mathbb{N} \to \mathbb{N}$ such that

$$h(x) = \begin{cases} f(x) \text{ if } f(x) \text{ is defined} \\ g(x) \text{ if } g(x) \text{ is defined but } f(x) \text{ is not defined} \\ \text{undefined if neither } f(x) \text{ nor } g(x) \text{ is defined} \end{cases}$$

Programming Problems

1. Write a program to compute $g(x) = \mu y[\neg eq(f(x, y), 1) = 0]$ for various functions $f:\mathbb{N} \times \mathbb{N} \to \mathbb{N}$. What happens when executing your program if the function f is div (see Section 4.4) and you attempt to compute $g(2)$?

2. Write an interpreter for the bare-bones programming language in this chapter.

3. Write a program for computing Ackermann's function. What problems do you encounter when you try to execute your program?

CHAPTER 5

Complexity

Our study of computational processes has led us to classify problems into two broad categories—the solvable problems and the unsolvable problems. In this chapter we concentrate on the class of solvable problems. Our goal is to study the solutions of these problems from a practical, as opposed to a theoretical, perspective. In short, we will find that although solvable in theory, many of these problems require such a large amount of resources (such as time or storage space) that they remain unsolvable from any practical point of view.

239

5.1   THE COMPLEXITY OF COMPUTATIONS

A major objective in this chapter is to establish a scale on which we can classify problems according to their complexity. We will consider a problem to be complex if its solution requires the execution of a complex algorithm. In turn, an algorithm is considered complex if its application requires the execution of a complex computation. (We consider a computation to be the process performed when an algorithm is applied in a particular setting. For example, the traditional multiplication algorithm leads to different computations, with perhaps different complexities, when applied to different values.) To fulfill our goal of measuring the complexity of problems, we must therefore learn to measure the complexity of individual computations, from which we can determine the complexity of algorithms and finally determine the complexity of problems. We begin our study of complexity, then, by formalizing our intuitive concept of the complexity of a single computation.

Measuring Complexity

Let us first consider the concept of complexity itself. Although we may have an intuitive idea of what complexity is, we need a precise definition if we are to carry out a scientific investigation. Intuitively, a computation is complex if it is difficult to do. But how do we measure difficulty? A common approach, and the one we follow here, is to measure the difficulty of a computation indirectly by measuring the resources required to execute it—our motivation being that a difficult computation will require more resources than a less difficult one. We therefore define the complexity of a computation to be the amount of resources required to carry it out.

One resource often used in this context is time. We consider one computation to be more complex than another if the execution of the former takes more time than that of the latter. We call the amount of time required to perform a computation the computation's **time complexity.** It is the desire to minimize time complexity that leads one to use a binary search strategy rather than a sequential strategy when dealing with a long list. When searching a list of 1000 entries, a sequential search will interrogate an average of 500 entries per search, whereas a binary search requires at most ten. Thus, the expected time complexity of the binary search is less than that of the sequential approach.

Another resource often used to measure a computation's complexity is the amount of storage space required. This is based on the assumption that the more difficult a computation is, the more storage space will be required for its execution. We refer to the amount of storage space required by a computation as that computation's **space complexity.** Figure 5.1, in which

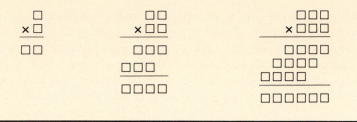

Figure 5.1   Space requirements of typical multiplication computations

squares represent storage spaces for individual digits, graphically compares the space complexity of the computations obtained by applying the traditional multiplication algorithm to one, two, and three digit integers.

It is easy to see that the time or space complexity of a particular computation can vary depending on the system on which the computation is performed. The time required to perform a computation on a modern computer is significantly less than that required to perform the same computation on the machines of the 1950s. Moreover, the amount of space required for data storage depends on the coding system being used. Any integer value greater than two requires more space when written in binary notation than it does when written in decimal.

To remove such variations from consideration, it is common to study complexity in the context of a fixed computational system. For our purposes, we will concentrate on the complexity of Turing machine computations. This choice not only provides a well-defined environment in which to work, but also leads to conclusions that are easily transported to other computational systems since Turing machines have many characteristics similar to those of modern digital computers.

Complexity of Turing Machine Computations

Let us refer to the execution of a single transition in a Turing machine as a step in the machine's computation and define the time complexity of a Turing machine computation to be the number of steps executed during the computation. For example, the time complexity of the computation performed by the Turing machine of Figure 5.2 when started with tape configuration $\triangle xxx\triangle\triangle\cdots$ would be 9. (It would require four steps to move the tape head to the first blank after the xs, one step to write an x at this location, and four more steps to return the head to its original position.) Or, if the tape were originally configured as $\triangle\triangle\triangle\cdots$, the computation performed would have time complexity 3.

Time complexity in the context of Turing machines will be a major example throughout this chapter, but we should recognize that other complexity measures are also important. For instance, the space complexity of Turing machine computations is also an important subject in ongoing research.

The space complexity of a Turing machine computation is defined to be the number of tape cells required by the computation. Thus, if the space complexity of a Turing machine computation were 9, the machine would use the first nine cells of the tape during the computation but would not require the rest of the tape to be present. The space complexity of the computation performed by the machine in Figure 5.2 when started with a tape configuration of $\triangle xxx\triangle\triangle\cdots$ is 5. (The tape head will move as far as the fifth cell on the tape before returning to the first cell and halting.) Likewise, when started with the tape configuration $\triangle\triangle\triangle\cdots$ the machine will execute a computation having space complexity 2 since only two tape cells will be used.

Observe that time and space complexity are distinct and therefore may not agree on the complexity of a given computation. A machine that never moves its tape head but writes a blank in its current cell 100 times before halting would perform a computation with time complexity of 100 but a space complexity of only 1. In fact, it is easy to see how this example could be extended to produce computations whose time and space complexities differ by any desired amount.

On the other hand, time and space complexity are not totally independent. In n steps the machine can access at most $n + 1$ tape cells. Consequently, *if the time complexity of a Turing machine computation is* n, *then the space complexity of that computation is no more than* n + 1.

We close by observing a rather peculiar consequence of our definitions. A Turing machine can accept a string by means of a computation whose space complexity is less than that required to hold the string itself. This is a result of the fact that a Turing machine does not have to read a string in order to accept it. For instance, the machine that merely writes a blank in its current cell while moving to its halt state will accept any string by a computation that accesses only a single tape cell and thus has a space complexity of only 1. However, if we require the machine to accept strings by halting with tape configuration $\triangle Y\triangle\triangle\cdots$, then the machine must erase the input string before halting. In these cases the accepting computation will have space complexity of at least the length of its input.

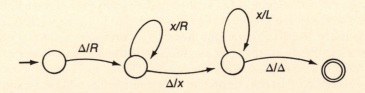

Figure 5.2   A simple Turing machine

Exercises

1. Show that a Turing machine that accepts strings by halting with its tape configured as $\triangle Y \triangle \triangle \cdots$ must perform a computation with time and space complexities of at least $3n$ and $n + 1$, respectively, when accepting a string of length n.

2. Design a Turing machine that accepts any string starting with the symbol x by means of a computation with time and space complexities of 2.

3. Determine the time and space complexities of the computation performed by the Turing machine

$$\rightarrow R \xrightarrow{\;x\;} R \;\begin{matrix} y \\ \end{matrix}$$

when processing the string xyx. What about the string $xyxx$?

4. Determine the time and space complexities of the computation performed by the Turing machine

$$\rightarrow R \rightarrow L_{\triangle}$$

when started with the initial tape configuration of $\triangle xxyyx \triangle \triangle \triangle \cdots$. What about the initial configuration $\triangle yyx \triangle xxy \triangle \triangle yyxx \triangle \triangle \triangle \cdots$?

5.2   THE COMPLEXITY OF ALGORITHMS

In general, different applications of the same algorithm will produce different computations. For instance, the computation actually performed by the binary search algorithm will depend on both the contents of the list being searched and the value sought, or as we have already observed, the traditional multiplication algorithm will lead to different computations when given different input values. Intuitively, whether or not we consider an algorithm to be complex should depend on whether or not these computations are complex. But what if some applications of an algorithm lead to simple computations while others lead to complex ones? Should we consider the algorithm to be simple or complex? This section addresses such questions in the context of time complexity.

Time Complexity of Turing Machines

We begin our study of algorithm complexity by considering algorithms in the context of Turing machines. Each Turing machine is nothing more than the implementation of a single algorithm, with the algorithm being represented in the form of the machine's transition diagram.

Let us consider a Turing machine for comparing two strings in $\{x, y, z\}^*$ of equal length. We assume that these strings are written on the machine's tape, one after the other, with an asterisk separating them. (To compare the strings $yxxz$ and $yxzx$, we would start the machine with the tape configuration $\triangle yxxz*yxzx\triangle\triangle\cdots$.) The task of the machine is to decide whether or not the string before the asterisk is identical to the string following the asterisk. It should halt with tape configuration $\triangle Y\triangle\triangle\cdots$ if the strings are equal and with configuration $\triangle N\triangle\triangle\cdots$ if they are not.

The technique used by our Turing machine is to compare corresponding entries in the strings repeatedly until each pair has been considered or a discrepancy has been discovered. This is done by reading the first symbol of the first string, and then moving the tape head to the first symbol of the second string to confirm that it is the same. If it is, the machine returns to the first string to observe the second symbol before moving back to the second string to check that its second entry is the same. Thus, the comparison process results in the tape head moving back and forth between the two strings as their entries are compared.

A composite diagram for the machine is shown in Figure 5.3. It is apparent that the time required by this machine to complete its task will depend on the input strings involved. In particular, it will take more time to recognize that two long strings are identical than to arrive at the same conclusion for shorter strings. This, in fact, is a common characteristic of algorithms: The time required to execute an algorithm tends to be a function of the length of the input. In our case the time required (measured in steps executed) to confirm that two strings of length n are identical is given by the formula

$$2n^2 + 10n + 9$$

This includes $2n^2 + 5n + 1$ steps to complete the comparison process itself, $5n + 4$ steps to move to the right end of the input and to erase the tape from right to left, three steps to write the symbol Y on the tape, and finally one last step to move to the halt state. (This last step is a consequence of the way we constructed composite machines in Chapter 3.) Thus, to confirm that two strings of length four are identical would have a time complexity of 81 (would require 81 steps), while the process of comparing two identical strings of length ten would have a time complexity of 309.

However, just because the strings being compared have length n does not mean that the computation performed by the machine will have time

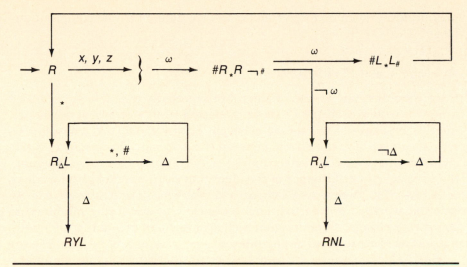

Figure 5.3 A Turing machine for comparing strings

complexity equal to $2n^2 + 10n + 9$. If the strings are not equal, the machine will stop comparing entries as soon as a discrepancy is reached. More precisely, if only the first r entries are identical, where $r < n$, the machine will perform a computation consisting of only $r(2n + 4) + 6n + 10$ steps. Thus, when comparing strings of length four in which the first two entries are equal but the third entries are different, the machine will execute only $2(8 + 4) + 24 + 10 = 58$ steps instead of 81. Moreover, if the strings differ in the first position, only 34 steps will be executed.

When evaluating the complexity of an algorithm, such variations in the algorithm's performance are normally handled by identifying worst-case and best-case situations. Then, any application of the algorithm is guaranteed to fall within this range. In our example, it is easy to see that when comparing strings of length n, the longest computation will occur when the strings are identical, whereas the shortest computation will occur when the strings differ in the first position. We conclude that the time complexity of any computation will be in the range of $6n + 10$ (best-case) to $2n^2 + 10n + 9$ (worst-case). (Actually, the machine will execute shorter computations in some cases of invalid inputs, such as a totally blank tape, but we are interested only in the performance of the machine for valid inputs.)

We see, then, that identifying the complexity of an algorithm is a rather nebulous undertaking. There are various possibilities to consider ranging from worst-case to best-case performances. For the sake of a formal definition, however, it is customary to take a pessimistic point of view and define the time complexity of an algorithm to be that of the algorithm's worst-case performance. Thus, although our string comparison algorithm may perform much better in some cases, we define its time complexity to be $2n^2 + 10n + 9$.

Average-Case Performance

If we were planning to use an algorithm repeatedly over a long period of time, we would probably be more interested in its average performance than its best-case or worst-case behavior. Furthermore, this average performance need not lie midway between the extremes. For instance, if the situations that produce an algorithm's best performance are extremely rare, then the actual performance of the algorithm over a period of time could tend toward the worst-case scenario and vice versa. Let us therefore evaluate the average (or expected) time complexity of our Turing machine for comparing strings, assuming that each arrangement of symbols of length n is just as likely to occur as any other.

Such expected values are computed by first multiplying the complexity of each possible computation by the probability of that computation occurring and then adding these products. If the application of an algorithm could result in m different computations with complexities $c_1, c_2, \cdots, c_m$ and probabilities of occurrence $p_1, p_2, \cdots, p_m$, then the expected complexity (the average complexity after repeated applications of the algorithm) would be

$$\sum_{i=1}^{m} p_i c_i$$

In our string comparison example, any application of the algorithm with strings of length n will result in one of the following $n + 1$ possibilities: finding no discrepancies between the strings, finding a discrepancy between the first entries, finding a discrepancy between the second entries, $\cdots$, or, finding a discrepancy between the last entries. We have already evaluated the complexity of each of these cases and found that when no discrepancy is present

$$2n^2 + 10n + 9$$

steps are required, whereas if the first discrepancy occurs in the $r + 1$ position, then

$$r(2n + 4) + 6n + 10$$

steps will be executed.

To find the probability of each of these cases occurring, we reason as follows. Since there are three symbols in the alphabet, the probability that the symbols in a given position in two strings will agree is only 1/3, while the probability that they will disagree is 2/3. Thus, when comparing two strings of length n, the probability that they will be identical is $(1/3)^n$, whereas

Position in which first discrepancy is found	Length of computation in that case	Probability of occurrence	Product of complexity and probability
1	34	$\frac{2}{3}$	$22 \frac{2}{3}$
2	46	$\frac{2}{9}$	$10 \frac{2}{9}$
3	58	$\frac{2}{27}$	$4 \frac{8}{27}$
4	70	$\frac{2}{81}$	$1 \frac{59}{81}$
no discrepancies	81	$\frac{1}{81}$	1

Expected complexity = $39 \frac{74}{81}$

Figure 5.4 Computing the average performance of the string comparison process

the probability that the first discrepancy will be found in the $r + 1$ position is $(1/3)^r(2/3)$ (the probability that the first r positions agree multiplied by the probability that the symbols in the $r + 1$ positions do not agree).

Using these conclusions, we can express the expected complexity of our string comparison algorithm as

$$\left(\frac{1}{3}\right)^n (2n^2 + 10n + 9) + \sum_{r=1}^{n-1} \left(\frac{1}{3}\right)^r \left(\frac{2}{3}\right)[r(2n + 4) + 6n + 10]$$

Thus, for strings of length four, we would expect the computations produced by the algorithm to contain an average of $39^{74}/_{81}$ steps (Figure 5.4) as compared to a best-case performance of 34 steps and a worst-case performance of 81 steps. In this case, then, the expected performance is close to the algorithm's best-case performance, a situation that should please a potential user of the algorithm.

Informal Algorithm Analysis

We turn now to the problems of evaluating the time complexity of algorithms in environments that are much less precise than that of Turing machines. In such environments, determining time complexity is not as straightforward as calculating the number of steps to be performed. Indeed, the ability to predict time complexity by this method relies on the assumption, known as the **uniform cost assumption,** that each step will require the same amount of time as each of the others. This is a reasonable assumption in the case of theoretical Turing machines, but when dealing with other systems, the uniform cost assumption may not be valid. For instance, in most modern machines the multiplication of two values often requires more time than the addition of the same values, and performing an I/O operation is much more time consuming than an operation performed within the central processing unit.

Fortunately, all that is usually needed in such settings is an estimation of an algorithm's time complexity that is accurate enough for the comparison of available options. For example, when choosing between two techniques for searching a list, one does not need precise knowledge of the time complexities involved, but instead needs only enough information to evaluate the relative merits of the techniques being proposed. In such cases one normally identifies the dominating steps in each technique, estimates the number of times these steps will be performed, and then bases the comparison on these estimates. This is what we did earlier when we compared the sequential technique for searching a list to the binary method. In particular, we estimated the number of list entries that would be interrogated by each approach and then based our comparison on these values.

Suppose, then, that we want to evaluate the time complexity of the insertion sort algorithm as expressed in the ALGOL/Pascal/Ada-like program segment shown in Figure 5.5. Recall that the insertion sort algorithm sorts a list by designating successive entries as the pivot entry (see the repeat loop of Figure 5.5) and as each pivot is designated, moving it into its proper place among its predecessors (see the while loop of Figure 5.5). The execution of the routine in Figure 5.5 would therefore be dominated by the process of comparing and moving list entries as directed by the while loop. In turn, we should expect the time required to execute the algorithm to be roughly proportional to the number of times the body of this loop is executed.

Let us determine how many times this loop body will be executed in a worst-case scenario. It is not hard to recognize that such a case will arise if the original list is in reverse order since in this case the while loop body will be executed for each predecessor of each pivot entry. Thus, when the pivot entry is the second entry, the loop body will be executed once; when the pivot is the third entry, it will be executed twice; and in general, when the pivot is the mth entry, the loop body will be executed $m - 1$ times. In short, if the list contained n entries, the while loop body would be executed a total of

$$1 + 2 + \cdots + n - 1 = \frac{n(n - 1)}{2} = \frac{1}{2}(n^2 - n)$$

times. We therefore estimate that the worst-case performance of the algorithm would have a time complexity proportional to $n^2 - n$, where n is the length of the input list.

Of course, since this is merely a rough approximation, we should use it only for developing a general understanding of the algorithm's efficiency rather than making precise claims about the algorithm's time requirements. For example, we cannot claim that the exact time required by the algorithm for sorting lists of length n will always be bounded by a particular constant

```
          program InsertSort (inout: List; in: ListLength)
     var
          PivotPosition, I: integer;
          Pivot: ListEntryType;
     begin
          if (ListLength ≥ 2) then
              begin
                PivotPosition : = 2;
                repeat
                  Pivot : = List[PivotPosition];
                  I : = PivotPosition;
                  while (I > 1 and List[I – 1] > Pivot) do
                    begin
                        List[I] : = List[I – 1];
                        I : = I – 1
                    end;
                  List[I] : = Pivot;
                  PivotPosition : = PivotPosition + 1
                until (PivotPosition > ListLength)
              end.
```

Figure 5.5 Insertion sort

multiple of $n^2 - n$, but we can claim that as the algorithm is applied to longer and longer lists, its worst-case performance will tend to increase in proportion to a quadratic expression in the length of the list. That is, if we double the length of the input list, we should expect the time requirements of the algorithm to increase by a factor of approximately four.

Such approximations are extremely useful when selecting among different approaches to a problem's solution in applied settings. If one solution is shown to have a time complexity proportional to n^2 while another has a complexity proportional to n^3, we would tend to pick the former solution, since for long inputs the latter solution has the potential of requiring much more time than the former.

You should be cautioned, however, against making such decisions too quickly. The particular application involved may be the best-case situation for the n^3 algorithm but close to the worst-case situation for the n^2 algorithm. Moreover, consider an algorithm that solves a particular problem in 2^n steps as compared to another algorithm that requires n^3 steps to solve the same problem. For large inputs the latter should prove to be much more efficient than the former, but for inputs in the range of two to ten the former solution will outperform the latter.

We conclude that the considerations required when making judgements about an algorithm's expected performance vary with the situation. In applied settings, best-case, worst-case, and even general average-case evaluations are often not sufficient. Rather, one must consider the actual environment in which the algorithm will be applied.

Finally, you should be aware that we have made statements concerning the time complexity of algorithms without having precise knowledge of the mechanism used for algorithm execution. Thus, the claims we are able to make are valid whether we use the slow machines of the 1950s, the fast machines of today, or the super machines of tomorrow. This fact will prove to be significant when we consider algorithms with time complexities so large that their execution is impractical, since this impracticality will prove to be a property of the algorithm and not of the technology. Merely executing the algorithm faster will have little effect on the algorithm's practicality.

Exercises

1. Modify the diagram in Figure 5.3 so that it answers N for all invalid inputs.
2. Evaluate the time complexity of the shift machines S_R and S_L as defined in Section 3.2.
3. What is the average-case time complexity of the Turing machine

$$\rightarrow R \xrightarrow{x} y$$

when given input strings from $\{x, y\}^*$?
4. Perform an average-case analysis of the time required by the insertion sort in Figure 5.5.

5.3 THE COMPLEXITY OF PROBLEMS

We turn now to the task of measuring the complexity of a problem. Intuitively, this measure should be associated with the complexity of the problem's solutions: A problem is difficult because it is difficult to solve. However, a problem should not be declared complex just because it has a difficult solution. There is a difficult way to solve just about every problem. A problem should be declared complex only when it does not have an easy solution. More precisely, we would like to say that the complexity of a problem is the complexity of that problem's simplest solution. Unfortunately, we will see that the abundance of solutions for a single problem makes identifying a simplest solution very difficult. In fact, it has been shown that many problems do not have a simplest solution.

The String Comparison Problem

A major obstacle when trying to establish the complexity of a problem by finding an optimal solution is that there seems to be a way of improving any solution we find. Consequently, the search for an optimal solution becomes an endless task of discovering better and better solutions. Let us investigate this phenomenon more closely by returning to the environment of Turing machines and the problem of comparing two strings in $\{x, y, z\}^*$ of the same length.

A solution to this problem was given in Figure 5.3. Its approach was to compare each symbol in the first string to the corresponding symbol in the second string until a discrepancy was found or until the ends of the strings were reached. You will recall that the time complexity of this algorithm (its worst-case performance) was $2n^2 + 10n + 9$, where n is the length of the input strings.

But this is not an optimal solution to the problem. We can produce a faster solution by designing a Turing machine that compares two symbols at a time. Such an approach is represented by the composite diagram of Figure 5.6. A machine based on this diagram would compare strings by interrogating two entries in the first string before moving its tape head to the other string to investigate its corresponding positions.

When compared to our original solution, this alternate approach reduces the number of times the tape head must move from one string to the other by a factor of approximately one-half, and we would expect a corresponding

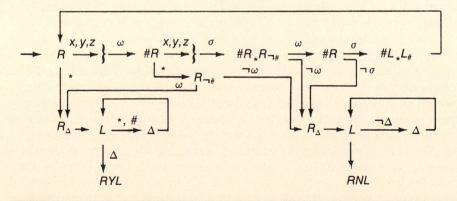

Figure 5.6 Another Turing machine for comparing strings of equal length

decrease in the time required by the computation. This suspicion is supported by the observation that the worst-case scenario of our alternate solution requires only

$$n^2 + 7n + 8$$

steps to confirm that two strings of length n are identical as compared to the

$$2n^2 + 10n + 9$$

steps required by our original solution. Figure 5.7 summarizes these expressions for various values of n.

Recognizing that we can improve our solution to the string comparison problem by comparing two symbols at a time opens the door to a multitude of improvements that could be made. If we compared k symbols at a time, where k is any integer bigger than 1, we would expect to obtain a new solution that improves our original solution by a factor of approximately $1/k$.

Moreover, this is just one technique from a host of methods for reducing time complexity. A more general technique is to expand the alphabet being used so that each pattern of k symbols in the original alphabet can be represented by a single symbol in the extended system. Then, we produce a new algorithm for solving the original problem that first recodes the input into this extended alphabet and then simulates the old algorithm in this recoded form. Note that a single operation in this recoded system can simulate numerous steps in the original algorithm. A single write operation could simulate all $2k - 1$ steps (k write steps and $k - 1$ move steps) required in the original algorithm to write symbols on k consecutive tape cells. Of course, the actual benefit of this technique varies with the situation, but as a general rule we can expect to reduce the time complexity by a factor of approximately $1/k$ in those cases in which the time required to recode the input is insignificant when compared to the remaining computation.

We conclude that an attempt to find a best solution (in terms of time complexity) for the string comparison problem leads to an endless chain of solutions, each more efficient than the preceding one. This is a common phenomenon. In fact, the theorem known as Blum's speedup theorem, which we will discuss in more detail later, states that some problems do not have a simplest solution. (Actually, Blum's speedup theorem states that there are problems for which any solution can be *significantly* improved.)

Thus, the classification of problems according to their complexity is a very difficult task—in fact, a task that we often do not complete. In some settings it suffices merely to establish an upper bound on the complexity of a problem, as we have done in the case of the string comparison problem. We have found a solution to the problem whose time complexity is $2n^2 +$

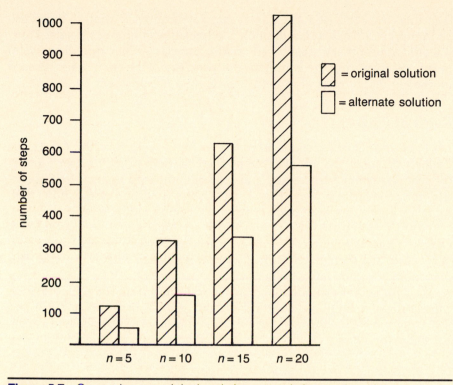

Figure 5.7 Comparing our original and alternate solutions to the string comparison problem

$10n + 9$. Thus, we know that the complexity of the problem is no greater than this. Moreover, if this solution is efficient enough for our needs, then we need not try to classify the problem more accurately.

In other cases, however, the known solutions to a problem may all be unbearably complex. In these cases our task is to find a significantly better solution or to show that no significantly better solution exists. We demonstrate this latter approach in Appendix D where we show that any solution to the string comparison problem using a (one-tape) Turing machine must have time complexity that is at least a quadratic expression in the length of the lists being compared. In other words, as the length of the strings being compared increases, the time required by any improved solution will grow in proportion to the solutions already obtained. This means that if these known solutions are too complex for an application, then any other solution to the problem will likely suffer the same fate.

What we have done, then, is classify the complexity of the string comparison problem (when solved by a one-tape Turing machine) as being in the class of quadratic functions. We have found a solution whose complexity is in this class, and we have shown that any improved solution must also be in that class. Such a classification is often sufficient for our needs. Thus, it would appear that a scale based on function classes may provide a useful means of measuring the complexity of problems. One such scale is based on the concept of rates of growth, which we now consider.

Rates of Growth

Let Ω be the set of functions from $\mathbb{N}$ into $\mathbb{N}$. Given a function f in Ω, we define $O(f)$ (read "big oh of f") to be the collection of all functions g in Ω for which there is a constant c and a positive integer n_0 such that $g(n) \leq cf(n)$ for all integers $n > n_0$. That is, $O(f)$ is the collection of functions that, for large inputs, are bounded above by a constant multiple of f.

Next, if f and g are functions in Ω, we say that f and g are equivalent if $O(f) = O(g)$. We denote the set of functions that are equivalent to f by $\Theta(f)$, read "big theta of f." Each class $\Theta(f)$ is called a **rate of growth.** This terminology is motivated by the fact that for any $g \in \Theta(f)$, the graphs of $g(n)$ and $f(n)$, when extended far enough, must lie within the same corridor. More precisely, there are constants c_1 and c_2 such that $g(n) \leq c_1 f(n)$ and $f(n) \leq c_2 g(n)$ for all integers n that are larger than some fixed positive integer n_0. Thus, for $n \geq n_0$,

$$\frac{1}{c_2} f(n) \leq g(n) \leq c_1 f(n)$$

That is, the graph of $g(n)$ must ultimately lie in the corridor between $\frac{1}{c_2}f(n)$ and $c_1 f(n)$ as shown in Figure 5.8. Hence, although the graph of $g(n)$ may oscillate within this corridor, from a global perspective the two functions f and g must grow at the same rate for large values of n. (Note that c_1 and c_2 can be chosen so that $f(n)$ also lies within the corridor.)

We now show that the absolute value of any polynomial of degree d is in $\Theta(n^d)$. Given the polynomial $\sum_{i=0}^{d} a_i n^i$, with $a_d \neq 0$, then for each n in $\mathbb{N}^+$,

$$\frac{n^d}{|\sum_{i=0}^{d} a_i n^i|}$$

can be rewritten as

$$\frac{1}{|a_d + a_{d-1}\frac{1}{n} + \cdots + a_0 \frac{1}{n^d}|}$$

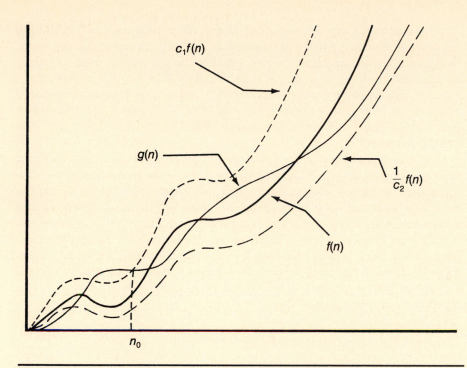

Figure 5.8   Two functions f and g with the same rate of growth

which becomes arbitrarily close to $\dfrac{1}{|a_d|}$ for large values of n. Thus, there is a positive integer n_0 such that

$$\frac{1}{2|a_d|} \leq \frac{n^d}{|\sum_{i=0}^{d} a_i n^i|} \leq \frac{3}{2|a_d|}$$

for all $n \geq n_0$. The left of these inequalities implies that

$$\left| \sum_{i=0}^{d} a_i n^i \right| \leq 2n^d |a_d|$$

while the right inequality implies

$$n^d \leq \frac{3}{2|a_d|} \left| \sum_{i=0}^{d} a_i n^i \right|$$

Consequently, $O(\sum_{i=0}^{d} a_i n^i) = O(n^d)$ as required.

The reason for considering rates of growth is now at hand. Although we cannot identify a particular function as being the time complexity of our string comparison problem, we can say that the problem can be solved by an algorithm whose complexity is in the class $\Theta(n^2)$ and that any better solution must also have complexity in $\Theta(n^2)$. Indeed, we have demonstrated a solution whose time complexity is a quadratic function and have shown (see Appendix D) that any solution must have a time complexity that is at least a quadratic.

Thus, it appears that rates of growth may provide a classification scheme coarse enough to overlook the imprecisions that arise when trying to determine the complexity of a problem. Following this lead, let us define the time complexity of a problem to be the class $\Theta(f)$ if the problem can be solved by an algorithm with time complexity f, and any better solution also has time complexity in $\Theta(f)$. Then, we establish an order among the rates by defining $\Theta(f) \leq \Theta(g)$ to mean $O(f) \subseteq O(g)$. Similarly, we write $\Theta(f) < \Theta(g)$ to mean $\Theta(f) \leq \Theta(g)$ and $\Theta(f) \neq \Theta(g)$. For example, $\Theta(n^2) < \Theta(n^3)$; a problem with complexity $\Theta(n^3)$ would be considered more complex than a problem with complexity $\Theta(n^2)$.

Limitations of the Rates-of-Growth Scale

The rates-of-growth scale has been used successfully for classifying the complexity of numerous problems in a variety of settings. However, it is still not coarse enough to provide a system in which problems in general can be classified. One reason is that there are problems for which any solution can be improved indefinitely in such a way that each new solution falls within a different rate of growth. This result is known as Blum's speedup theorem, which was discovered by M. Blum in 1967. Roughly speaking, this theorem states that, in the context of Turing machines (and thus in a variety of other computational systems as well), for any μ-recursive function $g:\mathbb{N} \rightarrow \mathbb{N}$ there is a problem for which any solution, with some time complexity $t(n)$, can be improved to obtain a new solution with time complexity $g(t(n))$ for all but a finite number of values in $\mathbb{N}$. (In turn, this new solution can be improved to obtain a time complexity of $g(g(t(n)))$, and so forth.)

To make this more meaningful, let us pick $\lfloor log_2 \rfloor$ as the function g. (The notation $\lfloor log_2 x \rfloor$ denotes the largest integer in $\mathbb{N}$ that is less than or equal to $log_2 x$ if such an integer exists; otherwise, $\lfloor log_2 x \rfloor$ is 0.) Blum's speedup theorem says that there is a problem for which any solution with time complexity $t(n)$ can be improved to obtain another solution with time complexity $\lfloor log_2(t(n)) \rfloor$. To be more precise, any solution with time complexity 2^n could be improved to form another solution with time complexity $\lfloor log_2(2^n) \rfloor = n$, which is a significant improvement. This new solution could also be improved to obtain still another solution with complexity

$\lfloor log_2\, n \rfloor$—an improvement of the same relative magnitude as before.

Currently, problems having speedup characteristics as described in Blum's speedup theorem have not surfaced outside the realm of theoretical computer science, and hence such problems are of little concern in applied settings. The major drawback to classifying problems by rates-of-growth is that such classifications are sensitive to changes in the underlying computational system—if we change from one computational system to another, the time complexity of a problem will likely fall within a different rate-of-growth. Thus, the complexity of a problem when measured as a rate-of-growth is not a property of the problem alone, but is a property of the underlying computational system as well.

This phenomenon is apparent in the case of our string comparison problem, which we have shown to have time complexity $\Theta(n^2)$ in the context of one-tape Turing machines. However, we can find a better solution if we change to a two-tape machine, such as the two-tape Turing machine represented in Figure 5.9. This machine scans its input tape from left to right

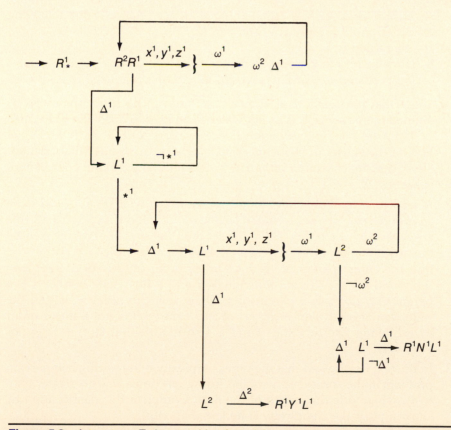

Figure 5.9 A two-tape Turing machine for solving the string comparison problem

until it finds the asterisk separating the two input strings. Then, it copies the second string onto its second tape while erasing it from its first tape. Next, the machine scans the strings on its two tapes from right to left, comparing entries in corresponding positions and erasing the entries on tape 1 as it compares them. If unequal entries are found, the machine erases the rest of tape 1 and responds with the answer N before halting. Otherwise, the machine responds with Y and halts.

In the worst-case scenario in which the two input strings, with length n, are identical, the number of steps executed by this machine would be

$$9n + 11$$

We conclude that the time complexity of the string comparison problem is no greater than $\Theta(n)$ in the environment of two-tape Turing machines—a significant improvement over the one-tape environment.

Exercises

1. A relation on a set X is called an equivalence relation if the following conditions hold for any x, y, and z in X:
    a. x is related to x.
    b. If x is related to y, then y is related to x.
    c. If x is related to y and y is related to z, then x is related to z.

    Show that the relation of equivalence among the functions in Ω, as defined in this section, is an equivalence relation in this technical sense.

    Let X be a set with an equivalence relation, and for each $x \in X$, let $E(x)$ be the subset of elements that are related to x under that relation. Show that the collection $\{E(x): x \in X\}$ is a mutually disjoint collection of subsets of X.

2. A set whose members have an order associated with them is said to be an ordered set. The set is said to be linearly ordered if any two elements are related by the order. Thus, the set of integers is linearly ordered by the order $\leq$ since given any two integers x and y, either $x \leq y$ or $y \leq x$. But, the order "parent of" is not a linear order on the set of people in the world since there are individuals x and y for which neither x is a parent of y nor y is a parent of x. Show that the order $\leq$ within the collection of equivalence classes of the form $\Theta(f)$ is not a linear order by exhibiting two functions f and g such that neither $\Theta(f) \leq \Theta(g)$ nor $\Theta(g) \leq \Theta(f)$.

3. In the text we showed that the time complexity of our string comparison problem in the context of two-tape Turing machines was no greater than $\Theta(n)$, where n is the length of the lists. Complete the classification by showing that the complexity is no less than $\Theta(n)$.

4. Show that $\Theta(log_2\ n) < \Theta(n)$.

5.4 TIME COMPLEXITY OF LANGUAGE RECOGNITION PROBLEMS

In this section we return to the study of language recognition problems, with our emphasis now on complexity rather than merely on computability. We are interested in whether or not the processing of a language is a practical undertaking rather than merely possible in theory. A significant consequence of this study is the introduction of a classification scheme for measuring problem complexity that is much coarser than rates-of-growth and is a major topic of current research. We begin with some general observations regarding polynomial-time computations.

Polynomial-Time Computations

Suppose a (single- or multiple-tape) Turing machine M computes the partial function $f:\Sigma_1^* \to \Sigma_2^*$. We say that M computes the function in polynomial-time if there is a polynomial $p(x)$ such that for each $w \in \Sigma_1^*$ for which $f(w)$ is defined, M computes $f(w)$ in no more than $p(|w|)$ steps.

An important property of functions that can be computed by Turing machines in polynomial-time is that the composition of two such functions is also computable in polynomial-time. To justify this claim, suppose that f_1 and f_2 are partial functions computed by Turing machines M_1 and M_2, respectively. Furthermore, suppose $p_1(x)$ and $p_2(x)$ are polynomial expressions such that for any inputs v and w, M_1 computes $f_1(v)$ in no more than $p_1(|v|)$ steps and M_2 computes $f_2(w)$ in no more than $p_2(|w|)$ steps. Now consider the time required for the composite machine $\to M_1M_2$ to compute the function $f_2 \circ f_1$. Given input v, M_1 will pass control to M_2 after executing no more than $p_1(|v|)$ steps. Thus, the string produced by M_1 and given to M_2 as input can have length no greater than $p_1(|v|) + 1$. (We can assume that $|v| < p_1(|v|)$ for all inputs v of f_1.) In turn, M_2 will halt after executing no more than $p_2(p_1(|v|) + 1)$ steps. Thus, the entire computation performed by $\to M_1M_2$ will require no more than $p_1(|v|) + p_2(p_1(|v|) + 1)$ steps, which is a polynomial expression in $|v|$.

It is also true that the class of functions that can be computed in polynomial-time using multiple-tape Turing machines is the same as that for traditional (single-tape) machines. This follows by reconsidering the proof of Theorem 3.1, in which we showed how a single-tape Turing machine could simulate any computation of a multiple-tape machine. We need merely make two additional observations. First, the simulation process described in the proof of Theorem 3.1 can be extended so that the single-tape machine translates its tape back into single-tape format in such a way that its tape is configured as tape 1 on the multiple-tape machine before halting. This means that the single-tape machine produces the same output as the multiple-tape version. Second, if the multiple-tape machine performs its task in polynomial-time, the single-tape simulation will also be performed in polynomial-time.

With these observations behind us, we turn to the topic of this section: the complexity of language recognition problems.

The Class P

If M is a Turing machine, we say that M accepts the language L in polynomial-time if $L = L(M)$ and there is a polynomial $p(n)$ such that the number of steps required to accept any $w \in L(M)$ is no greater than $p(|w|)$. We define P to be the class of languages that can be accepted by Turing machines in polynomial-time.

Our interest in the class P stems from an intuitive notion that it contains those languages that can be accepted in a reasonable amount of time. Consider, for example, a Turing machine M that accepts any string $w \in L(M)$ in an amount of time proportional to the polynomial $|w|^2$, as compared to another machine M' that accepts each string $w \in L(M')$ in time proportional to the exponential $2^{|w|}$. If we doubled the length of the input of M, say from ten to 20, the time required by the corresponding computation would increase by no more than a factor of four, whereas a similar change in the input of M' would result in an increase by a factor of $2^{10} = 1024$. Thus, as the length of the strings being tested becomes larger, we would expect M to be much less time consuming than M'. Indeed, if the execution of each step required one microsecond, then M could process a string of length 50 in less than a second, whereas M' would require more than 35 years to process the same string (see Figure 5.10).

Another important characteristic of P is that it remains stable over a wide range of computational systems. If we change the computational sys-

Time complexity

n = length of input	n^2	2^n
10	.0001 second	.0001 second
20	.0004 second	1.05 second
30	.0009 second	17.92 minutes
40	.0016 second	12.74 days
50	.0025 second	35.75 years
60	.0036 second	36.6 centuries
70	.0049 second	374.8 million years

Figure 5.10   The polynomial time complexity n^2 compared to the exponential time complexity 2^n

tem being used, the class of languages that can be accepted in polynomial-time tends to remain the same. This should not be too surprising. After all, the class P consists of all languages that can be accepted in time $O(n^d)$ for some $d \in \mathbb{N}^+$, and hence a classification based on polynomial versus non-polynomial time complexity is much coarser than one that distinguishes between different rates-of-growth.

The following theorem provides additional testimony to the robustness of P. It shows that the class of languages that can be accepted in polynomial-time does not change if we shift from machines that indicate acceptance by merely halting to those that indicate acceptance by halting with tape configuration $\triangle Y \triangle \triangle \cdots$.

THEOREM 5.1
If a Turing machine accepts the language L in polynomial-time, then there is another Turing machine that also accepts L in polynomial-time but indicates acceptance by halting with tape configuration $\triangle Y \triangle \triangle \cdots$.

PROOF
In Section 3.3 we argued that, given a Turing machine M that accepts the language L, we could construct another machine of the form

$$\rightarrow R_\triangle S_R R*L_\triangle L\#R \rightarrow M_0 \rightarrow R_* \rightarrow \triangle L \xrightarrow{\urcorner \#}$$
$$\downarrow \#$$
$$\triangle RYL$$

that also accepts L but does so by halting with its tape configured as $\triangle Y \triangle \triangle \cdots$. (Recall that M_0 is essentially a copy of M except for a few extra steps in those cases where the current symbol is either $\#$ or $*$.) Our task now is to show that if M accepts L in polynomial-time, then this new machine must also accept L in polynomial-time.

Suppose, then, that p is a polynomial and that for each $w \in L$, M accepts w in time $p(|w|)$. It is straightforward to show that the component of our composite machine preceding M_0 will complete its task in no more than $q(|w|)$ steps, where q is a polynomial. Moreover, the output of this stage will be the tape configuration $\#\triangle w*\triangle\triangle\triangle \cdots$ so that M_0 will simulate the actions of M as though M were given the input w. In most cases M_0 will perform one step for every step of M being simulated. The exceptions are in those cases in which M_0 finds the symbol $\#$ or $*$, but in these cases M_0 executes no more than four extra steps. Thus, if M would have completed its task in time $p(|w|)$, then M_0 will complete its task in time $4p(|w|)$.

We conclude that once M_0 passes control to the remaining component of our composite machine, the soiled portion of the tape will be no longer than $k = |w| + 3 + 4p(|w|)$; that is, the length of the soiled portion when M_0 began plus the maximum number of cells that M_0 may have soiled itself. But, this means that the last stage of our composite machine will require no more than $3k + 4$ steps to erase the tape, write a Y, and return to the leftmost cell. In turn, the entire composite machine will accept the language L in polynomial-time.

∎

Note that Theorem 5.1 can easily be extended to multiple-tape machines. If a language L can be accepted by a multiple-tape Turing machine in polynomial-time, there is a multiple-tape Turing machine that computes the partial function defined by

$$f(w) = \begin{cases} Y \text{ if } w \in L \\ \text{undefined if } w \notin L \end{cases}$$

in polynomial-time. But, we have already shown that there must then be a single-tape Turing machine that computes this same function in polynomial-time. Consequently, *shifting from traditional (single-tape) Turing machines to multiple-tape machines does not increase the class of languages that can be accepted in polynomial-time*. This is yet another result supporting the robustness of the class P.

Polynomial-Time Decidable Languages

We say that a language L over an alphabet Σ can be decided in polynomial-time if there is a Turing machine M that decides the language L and a polynomial $p(x)$ such that for each $w \in \Sigma^*$, starting M with input w results in a computation of no more than $p(|w|)$ steps. Since the process of deciding a language over some alphabet Σ is merely that of computing a particular function from Σ^* into $\{Y, N\}$, our knowledge of polynomial-time computations allows us to conclude that the class of languages that can be decided in polynomial-time by multiple-tape Turing machines is identical to the class that can be decided in polynomial-time by single-tape machines.

Our goal now is to show that this class of languages is the same as P. That is, if we restrict consideration to polynomial-time computations, the ability to accept a language by a Turing machine is equivalent to the ability to decide the language by a Turing machine. We begin our proof of this with the following lemma, which essentially says that a polynomial function can be computed in polynomial-time.

LEMMA

For any polynomial $p(x)$ with coefficients in $\mathbb{N}$, there is a polynomial $q(x)$ and a Turing machine that when started with an input string of length n, will halt after no more than $q(n)$ steps with its tape configured as $\triangle w \triangle \triangle \cdots$, where w is a string of 1s of length $p(n)$.

PROOF

We induct on the degree of $p(x)$. If this degree is zero, $p(x) = a_0$ for some constant a_0. In this case the desired Turing machine needs merely to mark its leftmost cell with a special marker (one step), erase the input string while scanning from left to right ($2n + 1$ steps), move its tape head back to the special marker ($n + 1$ steps), write a string of a_0 1s to the right of the special marker ($2a_0$ steps), return its head to the special marker (a_0 steps), and replace the special marker with a blank (one step). This requires a total of $3n + (3a_0 + 4)$ steps, which is a polynomial in n as required.

Now we assume that the lemma holds for polynomials of degree less than r and that $p(x) = \sum_{i=0}^{r} a_i x^i$. By rearranging the expression for $p(x)$, we obtain

$$p(x) = \left(\sum_{i=1}^{r} a_i x^{i-1} \right) x + a_0$$

But, $\sum_{i=1}^{r} a_i x^{i-1}$ (which we denote by $p_1(x)$) is a polynomial with coefficients in $\mathbb{N}$ of degree less than r. Thus, there must be a Turing machine M that, given an input of length n, will produce an output of $p_1(n)$ 1s in no more than $q(n)$ steps, where $q(x)$ is a polynomial expression. We construct the Turing machine to compute $p(n)$ by making the following modifications to M.

First, add a second and third tape to M. Then, alter M so that it copies its input onto this second tape before computing $p_1(n)$. (This copying process will require $2n + 2$ steps to scan the input on the first tape until a blank is reached and then return the head to the leftmost cell, in addition to $2n$ steps to move the head on the second tape to the right while writing the input string, and another n steps to return this head back to the leftmost cell. Thus, this modification adds $5n + 2$ steps to the overall computation performed by M.)

Second, further modify M so that after computing $p_1(n)$, the machine continues by copying the string of $p_1(n)$ 1s from its first tape onto the third tape, returning its tape head on the first tape to the leftmost cell while erasing that tape, then producing a string of $np_1(n)$ 1s on the first tape by concatenating copies of the third tape as the symbols on the second tape are scanned, and finally adding a_0 more 1s to the string on the first tape before returning the tape head on tape 1 to the leftmost cell. See Figure 5.11. Executing this process will require

$$4np_1(n) + 6p_1(n) + 2n + 3a_0 + 3$$

steps.

In summary, the modified version of M, when given an input of length n, will produce an output string of 1s on its first tape of length

$$\left(\sum_{i=1}^{r} a_i n^{i-1} \right) n + a_0$$

while requiring no more than

$$[5n + 2] + q(n) + [4np_1(n) + 6p_1(n) + 2n + 3a_0 + 3]$$

steps. But, since $q(n)$ and $p_1(n)$ are polynomials in n, this polynomial expression is also a polynomial in n. Hence, the modified machine satisfies the conditions of the theorem. ∎

We now use this lemma to show that the ability to accept a language in polynomial-time with a Turing machine is equivalent to the ability to decide the language in polynomial-time.

THEOREM 5.2

If a language L can be accepted by a Turing machine in polynomial-time, then there is a Turing machine that decides L in polynomial-time.

PROOF

We can assume that the machine that accepts L in polynomial-time never suffers an abnormal termination because otherwise we could modify it so that it begins any computation by shifting its input to the right (using S_R from Section 3.2), writing a special marker on the leftmost cell of the tape, and then moving its tape head to the

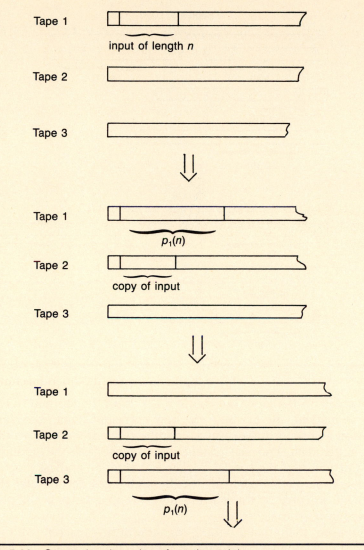

Figure 5.11   Computing the value of a polynomial
(continued on next page)

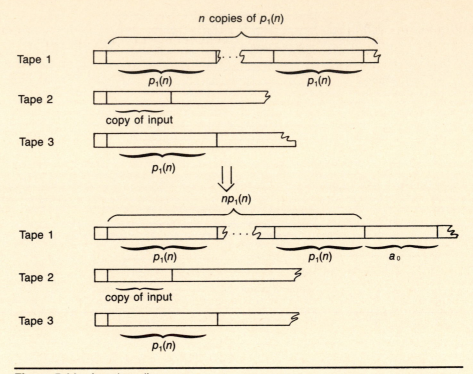

Figure 5.11 (continued)

second cell on the tape (see Figure 5.12). With the left end of the tape so marked, the machine can now carry out its normal computation except in those cases where the original machine would have suffered an abnormal termination. In those cases the modified machine will read the special marker and enter an endless loop. It is straightforward to confirm that these changes do not alter the language accepted by the machine and this acceptance is still performed in polynomial-time.

Suppose, then, that $L = L(M)$ for some Turing machine M, that there is a polynomial $p(x)$ such that for each $w \in L$, M accepts w in no more than $p(|w|)$ steps, and that M never suffers an abnormal termination. With this machine as a base, our approach is to construct a two-tape Turing machine M' that decides L in polynomial-time. It will then follow that there is a one-tape Turing machine that decides L in polynomial-time. (If a function from Σ^* into $\{Y, N\}$ can be computed by a multiple-tape machine in polynomial-time, then it can be computed by a single-tape machine in polynomial-time.)

We construct our two-tape machine M' as a composite of two smaller machines, M_1 and M_2, that perform the following operations.

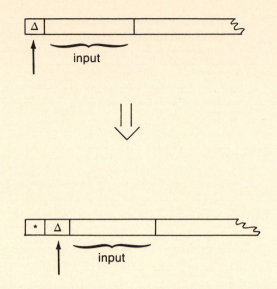

Figure 5.12 Shifting a machine's input to avoid abnormal termination

M_1 copies the input string w onto its second tape and then replaces that string on tape 2 with a string of 1s of length $p(|w|)$. (See Figure 5.13.) Note that this can be done in polynomial-time according to the preceding lemma.

M_2 simulates the actions of M with the following modification: After executing each step of M, M_2 advances its tape head on tape 2 one cell to the right. If this simulation should reach the halt state of M, then M_2 halts with its first tape configured as $\triangle Y \triangle \triangle \cdots$. If, however, it reaches a blank on its second tape, it halts with its first tape configured as $\triangle N \triangle \triangle \cdots$. Note that M_2 can perform this process in polynomial-time since, when given input w, it simulates no more than $p(|w|)$ steps of M, must erase no more than $p(|w|)$ cells on its first tape, and then must write only Y or N before halting.

In summary, M' simulates at most $p(|w|)$ steps of M when given input w. If $w \in L$ then M would have accepted w by this time, and thus M' will halt with an affirmative response. Otherwise, M' will halt with a negative response.

■

An immediate consequence of Theorem 5.2 is that the language L_1 from Section 3.5 is not in P. Recall that this language was shown to be Turing-

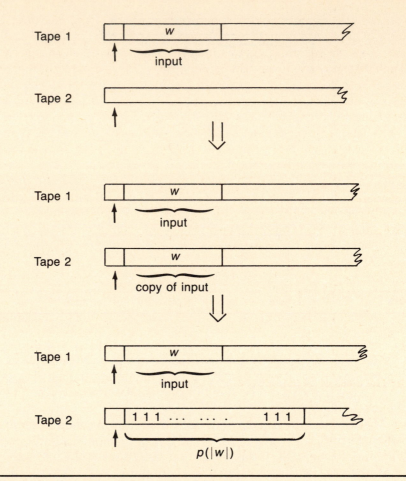

Figure 5.13   The computation performed by M_1

acceptable but not Turing-decidable. Thus, Theorem 5.2 says that L_1 cannot be accepted by any Turing machine in polynomial-time.

Decision Problems

Another consequence of Theorem 5.2 is that it allows us to expand our notion of the class P. As defined, P is a collection of languages, but as a result of Theorem 5.2, it is often considered to be a class of decision problems. Let us explain.

A decision problem is a problem that can be stated in the form of a question whose answer is either yes or no. An example is the string comparison problem of Section 5.2, in which the question is whether or not two strings are identical. When coded as input to a Turing machine, each instance of such a problem is represented by a collection of strings of symbols. In turn, by accepting a convention by which individual strings can be concatenated into one long string (perhaps by using separating markers), we are able to consider all decision problems to have single string inputs over some alphabet. In this context, the collection of strings for which the answer to a decision problem is yes constitutes a language. Moreover, the task of deciding this language is the same as that of solving the decision problem. (Deciding the language $\{w*w: w \in \{x, y, z\}^*\}$ is the same as solving the string comparison problem.)

Thus, solving decision problems and deciding languages are one and the same; in this light Theorem 5.2 says that the class P corresponds to the class of decision problems that can be solved by Turing machines in polynomial-time. In fact, this correspondence is so strong that we often shift between considering P as a class of languages and a class of decision problems without hesitation.

In summary we have established the following equivalent characterizations of the class P:

1. The class of languages that can be accepted by Turing machines in polynomial-time.
2. The class of languages that can be decided by Turing machines in polynomial-time.
3. The class of decision problems that can be solved by Turing machines in polynomial-time.

Furthermore, each of these characterizations can also be stated in terms of multiple-tape Turing machines.

Exercises

1. Suppose problem A can be solved by an algorithm with time complexity n^2, while problem B requires an algorithm with time complexity 2^n. Moreover, suppose current technology allows instances of problem A with input lengths of 100 to be solved in one hour. What size instances of problem A could be solved in one hour if technology produces a machine that runs 100 times faster than current machines? Answer the same question for problem B. What do your answers have to say about the practicality of solving problems with polynomial-time solutions as opposed to those with only exponential time solutions?

2. Show that the time complexity of accepting any regular language by a Turing machine is $\Theta(n)$, where n is the length of the input string, and thus every regular language is in P.

3. Show that a Turing-acceptable language that cannot be accepted by a Turing machine in fewer than 2^n steps, where n is the length of the input string, is not in P.

4. State each of the following decision problems as language recognition problems.
   a. Given two inputs m, $n \in \mathbb{N}$, decide whether there is a prime number between m and n.
   b. Given two input strings of symbols, decide whether they are permutations of each other.
   c. Given a positive integer and a finite list of positive integers, decide whether there is a subset of the list whose sum is the first integer.

5.5   TIME COMPLEXITY OF NONDETERMINISTIC MACHINES

In Chapter 3 we saw that the traditional (one-tape) Turing machines, the multiple-tape Turing machines, and the nondeterministic Turing machines possess the same language recognition power in the sense that any language accepted by a machine from one class can be accepted by a machine from any other class. Moreover, we have now seen that this equivalence in power still holds between one-tape and multiple-tape Turing machines when restricted to polynomial-time computations. It is natural, then, to ask what effect polynomial-time restrictions have on nondeterministic Turing machines. It is this question that concerns us now.

The Class NP

We say that a nondeterministic Turing machine M accepts the language L in polynomial-time provided $L = L(M)$ and there is a polynomial $p(x)$ such that for any $w \in L$, M can accept w by a computation involving no more than $p(|w|)$ steps. Furthermore, we define NP to be the class of languages that can be accepted by nondeterministic Turing machines in polynomial-time.

Since every deterministic Turing machine is contained in the class of nondeterministic Turing machines, we can immediately claim that $P \subseteq NP$. But, the question of whether $P = NP$ is not yet resolved. In fact, this is perhaps the most important research problem in computer science today. There are numerous decision problems throughout computer science (some of which are listed in Appendix E) that can be restated in terms of recognizing languages that are known to be in NP but whose membership, or lack of membership, in P is not yet determined. Thus, if $P = NP$, these problems would appear to have practical algorithmic solutions, but if $P \neq NP$, the chances of finding efficient algorithmic solutions to these problems would be significantly reduced.

We must admit, however, that the association between solving decision problems and accepting the languages in NP is not as well established as in the case of P. Recall that the close association between solving decision problems and accepting languages in P was a consequence of the fact that the ability to accept a language in polynomial-time is equivalent to the ability to decide the language in polynomial-time. Researchers have not yet resolved the relationship between accepting and deciding languages in polynomial-time in the context of nondeterministic Turing machines (Figure 5.14). Thus, the fact that a language in NP is associated with a particular decision problem may not imply that the problem can be completely solved in polynomial-time by a nondeterministic machine.

Let us summarize with an example. Consider the following problem known as the traveling salesman decision problem, which occurs repeatedly under various disguises in numerous settings.

> Given a set of cities, the distance separating each pair of cities, and a total allowable travel distance d, is there a way to travel among the cities such that each city is visited, the path ends at the starting city, and the total distance traveled does not exceed d?

Associated with this decision problem is the problem of deciding the language L_S, which consists of those strings representing instances of the traveling salesman problem with affirmative answers. This language is accepted by the nondeterministic Turing machine that, when given an instance

Polynomial-time deterministic computations

$$
\begin{array}{ccc}
\text{solvable} & & \\
\text{decision} & = & \text{decidable} & = & \text{acceptable} \\
\text{problems} & & \text{languages} & & \text{languages}
\end{array}
$$

Polynomial-time nondeterministic computations

$$
\begin{array}{ccc}
\text{solvable} & & \\
\text{decision} & = & \text{decidable} & \overset{?}{=} & \text{acceptable} \\
\text{problems} & & \text{languages} & & \text{languages}
\end{array}
$$

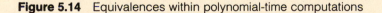

Figure 5.14 Equivalences within polynomial-time computations

of the traveling salesman problem, generates a path through the cities in a nondeterministic manner in which each path is a potential output, and then tests the path generated. If the path is found to be short enough, the machine halts; otherwise, it enters an endless loop.

Moreover, this machine would accept L_S in polynomial-time since any path can be generated and tested in time bounded by some polynomial expression of the number of cities. (If there are n cities, then generating a path consists of piecing together n inter-city routes, while testing the path consists of adding the corresponding n inter-city distances.) We conclude that L_S is in NP.

However, the fact that L_S is in NP merely means that L_S can be *accepted* by a nondeterministic Turing machine in polynomial-time. This may not imply that it can be *decided* in polynomial-time. It is this latter, more stringent requirement that is needed to solve the traveling salesman decision problem. Thus, knowing that L_S is in NP sheds some light on the complexity of the corresponding problem but may not tell the whole story. It may be that the traveling salesman problem cannot be completely solved in polynomial-time by any variation of a Turing machine.

On the other hand, if we could prove that $P = NP$, then L_S would belong to P; in turn, we could decide it in polynomial-time by a deterministic Turing machine and thus solve the traveling salesman decision problem in the same amount of time.

Polynomial Reductions

Appendix E contains only a few of the many problems that have been determined to lie in the class NP but whose membership in P has not yet been resolved. Thus, to show that only one such problem actually belongs to P would be a very small step toward resolving the relationship between the classes P and NP. There is, however, a way of attacking the classification of many problems at the same time. This approach is based on the concept of NP-completeness, which in turn is founded on the idea of polynomial reductions, which we now define.

A **polynomial reduction** (also known as a polynomial transformation) from some language L_1 over alphabet Σ_1, to another language L_2 over alphabet Σ_2, is a function $f:\Sigma_1^* \rightarrow \Sigma_2^*$ that can be computed by a Turing machine in polynomial-time, and for which $w \in L_1$ if and only if $f(w) \in L_2$ for each $w \in \Sigma_1^*$. If there is a polynomial reduction from language L_1 to language L_2, we say that L_1 reduces to L_2 and write $L_1 \propto L_2$.

Such reductions allow questions regarding string membership in one language to be converted into questions about string membership in another language. In particular, if $f:\Sigma_1^* \rightarrow \Sigma_2^*$ is a polynomial reduction from L_1 to L_2 computed by the Turing machine M_f, and if M_2 is a Turing machine with

$L(M_2) = L_2$, then the language accepted by the composite machine $\rightarrow M_f M_2$ is L_1. Furthermore, the fact that M_f computes f in polynomial-time means that the time complexity of the composite machine $\rightarrow M_f M_2$ is comparable to that of M_2—a claim that is justified by the following theorem.

THEOREM 5.3

If $L_1 \propto L_2$ and L_2 is in P, then L_1 is in P.

PROOF

Since $L_1 \propto L_2$, there is a polynomial reduction f from L_1 to L_2 that can be computed by some Turing machine M_f in polynomial-time. In particular, there is a polynomial $p(x)$ such that M_f computes $f(w)$ in time $p(|w|)$ for each $w \in L_1$. In turn, the length of $f(|w|)$ cannot be more than $p(|w|) + |w|$. (M_f can write no more than $p(|w|)$ symbols in $p(|w|)$ steps. Thus, the output of M_f, when given input w, can be no longer than $p(|w|)$ plus the length of the original input, $|w|$.)

Now let M_2 be a Turing machine that accepts L_2 in polynomial-time. Then, there is a polynomial $q(x)$ such that M_2 accepts each v in L_2 in no more than $q(|v|)$ steps. But, then the composite machine $\rightarrow M_f M_2$ accepts each $w \in L_1$ in no more than $p(|w|) + q(p(|w|) + |w|)$ steps, which is a polynomial in $|w|$ as required. That is, $\rightarrow M_f M_2$ accepts L_1 in polynomial-time, so L_1 is in P.

∎

As an example, the function $f : \{x, y\}^* \rightarrow \{x, y, z\}^*$ defined by $f(v) = vzv$ is a polynomial reduction from the language

$$L_1 = \{w : w \text{ is a palindrome in } \{x, y\}^*\}$$

to the language

$$L_2 = \{wzw^R : w \in \{x, y\}^* \text{ and } w^R \text{ is the string } w \text{ written backward}\}$$

It is easy to confirm that $v \in L_1$ if and only if $f(v) \in L_2$. Moreover, f can be computed in polynomial-time by applying the copy routine of Figure 3.8 followed by the writing of a z in the blank between the two pieces. Consequently, if we had a Turing machine that accepted L_2 in polynomial-time, we could use it along with this polynomial reduction to construct a machine that accepts L_1 in polynomial-time.

A major application of Theorem 5.3 is as a tool for showing that certain languages are in P. If we can show the existence of a polynomial reduction from some language L_1 to another language L_2, then we can prove that both languages are in P by merely showing that L_2 is in P.

In addition, if we restate Theorem 5.3 as "If $L_1 \propto L_2$ and L_1 is not in P, then L_2 is not in P," we obtain a tool for showing that languages are not in P. That is, if we demonstrate the existence of a polynomial reduction from L_1 to L_2, then both languages can be shown to lie outside of P by showing that L_1 lies outside of P.

We conclude that polynomial reductions provide a means of attacking the classification of more than one problem at the same time.

Cook's Theorem

The theorem we are about to prove, known as Cook's theorem in honor of its discoverer S. A. Cook, allows us to reap the utmost leverage from Theorem 5.3. It identifies a language (a decision problem) in the class NP to which any other language in NP can be reduced by some polynomial reduction. Thus, if this language should ever be shown to lie in P, all languages in NP must belong to P. But, before turning our attention to the statement and proof of Cook's theorem, we must introduce some additional terminology.

Let $V = \{v_1, v_2, \cdots, v_n\}$ be a finite set of Boolean variables (called propositions by logicians), and define a **truth assignment** for V to be a function from V into the set {true, false}. Moreover, let us represent the negation of a variable v_i by $\bar{v}_i$. Thus, if a truth assignment assigns v_i the value true, then $\bar{v}_i$ will be false, and vice versa. Variables and negations of variables are called **literals.**

We define a **clause** over V to be a nonempty set of literals associated with V. If a clause contains two or more literals, we envision them connected by the word "or" such as "v_1 or $\bar{v}_3$ or v_4." A clause is said to be **satisfied** by a truth assignment if at least one of its literals is true under that truth assignment. (The truth assignment that assigns v_1 to true and v_2 to false satisfies the clauses "v_1 or v_2" and "$\bar{v}_1$ or v_2 or $\bar{v}_2$" but not the clause "$\bar{v}_1$ or v_2.")

We can now state the decision problem associated with Cook's theorem as follows:

Given a finite set V of variables and a collection of clauses over V, is there a truth assignment that satisfies the clauses?

This problem is known as the problem of **satisfiability** or just **SAT** for short.

We can code any instance of SAT as a single string in the following manner. If $\{v_1, v_2, \cdots, v_m\}$ is the set of variables, denote each literal by a string of length m according to the following scheme: each literal v_i is represented by a string of all 0s except for a p (short for positive) in the ith position; each literal $\bar{v}_i$ is represented by a string of all 0s except for an n (short for negative) in the ith position. Then, each clause is represented by a list of its literals, separated by slashes. Finally, the entire instance of SAT is represented by a list of these clauses in which each clause is bracketed by parentheses. The instance of SAT containing variables v_1, v_2, and v_3 and clauses "v_1 or $\bar{v}_2$," "v_2 or v_3," and "$\bar{v}_1$ or $\bar{v}_3$ or v_2" would be represented by the string

$$(p00/0n0)(0p0/00p)(n00/00n/0p0)$$

We denote the language that consists of those strings representing instances of SAT that have satisfying truth assignments by L_{SAT}. Thus, $(p00/0n0)(0p0/00p)(n00/00n/0p0)$ is in L_{SAT} because the corresponding instance of SAT can be satisfied by the truth assignment that assigns v_1 to false, v_2 to false, and v_3 to true. The string $(0p0/00p)(00n/0p0/n00)(p00/0n0)$ is also in L_{SAT} since it represents the same instance of SAT as the previous string. But, the string $(p00/0p0)(n00/0p0)(p00/0n0)(n00/0n0)$ is not in L_{SAT} since there is no truth assignment that satisfies "v_1 or v_2," "$\bar{v}_1$ or v_2," "v_1 or $\bar{v}_2$," and "$\bar{v}_1$ or $\bar{v}_2$" simultaneously.

Let us now represent truth assignments by strings of ps and ns in which a p in the ith position indicates that variable v_i is true and an n in the ith position indicates that v_i is false. Then it is straightforward to test whether or not a particular truth assignment satisfies a coded instance of SAT. We need merely scan the string representing the problem instance from left to right while checking each clause to see that it contains a literal in which the p or n matches the corresponding position in the truth assignment (see Figure 5.15).

Based on this technique we can construct a nondeterministic Turing machine that accepts L_{SAT} in polynomial-time. Note that a variation of Theorem 3.1 tells us that a multiple-tape machine is good enough. In particular, we could construct a two-tape nondeterministic Turing machine that would 1) start each computation by checking that its input is a string representing a collection of clauses, 2) write, in a nondeterministic manner, a string of ps and ns of length equal to the number of variables in the clauses on its second tape, and 3) move the tape head on the first tape across the input string while testing to see that the truth assignment on its second tape satisfies the clauses being scanned (Figure 5.16).

This process can easily be implemented in a manner in which the time complexity of accepting computations is bounded by a polynomial of the length of the input string. We conclude that L_{SAT} is in NP.

We are now prepared to state and prove Cook's theorem.

THEOREM 5.4
If L is any language in NP, then $L \propto L_{SAT}$.

PROOF
Since L is in NP, there is a nondeterministic Turing machine M and a polynomial $p(x)$ such that for each $w \in L$, M accepts w in no more

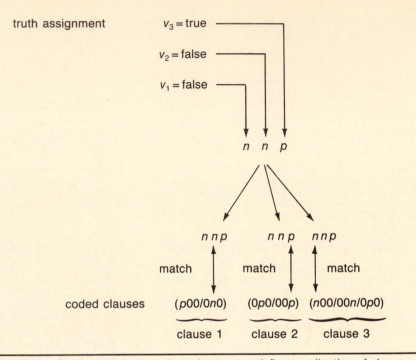

truth assignment

$v_3 = \text{true}$

$v_2 = \text{false}$

$v_1 = \text{false}$

n n p

n n p   n n p   n n p

match   match   match

coded clauses   (p00/0n0)   (0p0/00p) (n00/00n/0p0)

clause 1   clause 2   clause 3

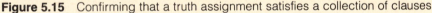

Figure 5.15   Confirming that a truth assignment satisfies a collection of clauses

than $p(|w|)$ steps. In addition, we can assume that $|w| < p(|w|)$ for all $w \in L$, and, as in Theorem 5.2, we can assume that M never suffers an abnormal termination.

We construct a polynomial reduction f from L to L_{SAT} based on the structure of M. More precisely, for each $w \in L$, $f(w)$ will be a collection of clauses that can be simultaneously satisfied if and only if there is a computation by which M accepts w. The clauses in $f(w)$ will be designed to represent the following four statements:

1. At any time during the computation the machine M is in one and only one state, the tape head is over one and only one tape cell, and each tape cell contains one and only one symbol.
2. The machine starts its computation from its initial state, with its tape head over the leftmost tape cell and with its tape containing a blank, followed by the input string w, followed by blanks.
3. At each step in the computation, the tape head position, current state, and tape contents change according to the machine's program.
4. The computation reaches the machine's halt state.

Starting
configuration

Tape 1: $\Delta(p00/0n0)(0p0/00p)(n00/00n/0p0)\Delta\Delta \ldots$
↑
Tape 2: $\Delta\Delta\Delta \ldots$
↑

Truth assignment
has been written
on tape 2

Tape 1: $\Delta(p00/0n0)(0p0/00p)(n00/00n/0p0)\Delta\Delta \ldots$
↑
Tape 2: $\Delta nnp\Delta\Delta \ldots$
↑

First clause is
found to be
satisfied

Tape 1: $\Delta(p00/0n0)(0p0/00p)(n00/00n/0p0)\Delta\Delta \ldots$
↑
Tape 2: $\Delta nnp\Delta\Delta \ldots$
↑

Second clause is
found to be
satisfied

Tape 1: $\Delta(p00/0n0)(0p0/00p)(n00/00n/0p0)\Delta\Delta \ldots$
↑
Tape 2: $\Delta nnp\Delta\Delta \ldots$
↑

Third clause is
found to be
satisfied

Tape 1: $\Delta(p00/0n0)(0p0/00p)(n00/00n/0p0)\Delta\Delta$
↑
Tape 2: $\Delta nnp\Delta\Delta \ldots$
↑

Machine halts
having found all
clauses to be
satisfied

Tape 1: $\Delta(p00/0n0)(0p0/00p)(n00/00n/0p0)\Delta\Delta \ldots$
↑
Tape 2: $\Delta nnp\Delta\Delta \ldots$
↑

Figure 5.16 Testing satisfiability using a two-tape nondeterministic Turing
machine

Clearly, a set of clauses that represent these statements can be satisfied simultaneously if and only if w is a string in $L(M)$. Thus, to
define $f(w)$, we need merely translate these statements into clauses.

We begin this translation process by representing the states of
M as $q_1, q_2, \cdots, q_r$, where q_1 and q_2 are the initial and the halt states,
respectively. We also agree to represent the blank symbol by x_1 and
the nonblank tape symbols of M by $x_2, x_3, \cdots, x_m$.

The variables involved in $f(w)$ are identified in Figure 5.17. As
indicated there, each variable stands for a statement about the computation performed by M when given input w. These statements
are posed in the context of an imaginary clock that starts counting
at 0 and ticks off time units at the same rate that M performs steps
in its computation. After M performs its first step the clock will
read 1, after the second step the clock will read 2, and so forth.

Variable	Range of subscripts	Corresponding statement	Number of variables of this type
$Hd_{i,\,j}$	$0 \le i \le p(n)$ $1 \le j \le p(n)+1$	M's tape head is over cell j at time i.	$[p(n)+1]^2$
$St_{i,\,j}$	$0 \le i \le p(n)$ $1 \le j \le r$	M is in state q_j at time i.	$r\,[p(n)+1]$
$Cont_{i,\,j,\,k}$	$0 \le i \le p(n)$ $1 \le j \le p(n)+1$ $1 \le k \le m$	Cell j contains symbol x_k at time i.	$m[p(n)+1]^2$

Figure 5.17   The variables used in the instance of SAT represented by $f(w)$

Thus, the clock essentially counts the steps executed by M. We say "essentially" because the clock will continue ticking after M halts, in which case the clock reading would no longer correspond to the number of steps executed. In fact, this is why we introduce the clock: If a computation halts after ten steps it would not make sense to refer to its configuration after executing 12 steps, but we could speak of its configuration after 12 clock ticks. (Once M halts, it remains in its halt configuration for all future ticks of the clock.)

Since M can accept any $w \in L(M)$ in no more than $p(|w|)$ steps, the meaningful part of M's computation will be completed in no more than $p(|w|)$ steps. Thus, the statements represented by the variables in $f(w)$ refer to clock readings in the range from 0 to $p(|w|)$. Likewise, in $p(|w|)$ steps the machine will not be able to move its tape head beyond cell number $p(|w|) + 1$, where we consider the cells to be numbered from left to right starting with 1. Consequently, the variables in $f(w)$ refer only to tape cells 1 through $p(|w|) + 1$.

We are now prepared to translate statements 1 through 4 into clauses. Statement 4 is the simplest since it can be represented by the one variable clause

$$St_{p(n),\,2}$$

Statements 1 and 2 are a bit more involved but still straightforward. They are translated in figures 5.18 and 5.19, respectively. The clauses representing statement 1 are based on the observation that if x, y, and z are variables, then the clause

$$x \text{ or } y \text{ or } z$$

Constraint	Clauses	Number of such clauses
M's tape head must be over at least one cell at any time.	$Hd_{i,\,1}$ or $Hd_{i,\,2}$ or . . . or $Hd_{i,\,p(n)+1}$ for each i in $\{0, 1, \ldots, p(n)\}$	$p(n) + 1$
M's tape head can be over only one cell at any time.	$\overline{Hd_{i,\,j}}$ or $\overline{Hd_{i,\,k}}$ for each i in $\{0, 1, \ldots, p(n)\}$ and each j and k in $\{1, 2, \ldots, p(n)+1\}$ with $j < k$	$\dfrac{(p(n)+1)^2\,p(n)}{2}$
M must be in at least one state at any time.	$St_{i,\,1}$ or $St_{i,\,2}$ or . . . or $St_{i,\,r}$ for each i in $\{0, 1, \ldots, p(n)\}$	$p(n) + 1$
M can be in only one state at any time.	$\overline{St_{i,\,j}}$ or $\overline{St_{i,\,k}}$ for each i in $\{0, 1, \ldots, p(n)\}$ and each j and k in $\{1, 2, \ldots, r\}$ with $j < k$	$(p(n)+1)\,\dfrac{r(r-1)}{2}$
Each tape cell must contain at least one symbol at any time.	$Cont_{i,\,j,\,1}$ or $Cont_{i,\,j,\,2}$ or . . . or $Cont_{i,\,j,\,m}$ for each i in $\{0, 1, \ldots, p(n)\}$ and each j in $\{1, 2, \ldots, p(n)+1\}$	$(p(n)+1)^2$
Each tape cell can contain at most one symbol at any time.	$\overline{Cont_{i,\,j,\,k}}$ or $\overline{Cont_{i,\,j,\,l}}$ for each i in $\{0, 1, \ldots, p(n)\}$, each j in $\{1, 2, \ldots, p(n)+1\}$, and each k and l in $\{1, 2, \ldots, m\}$ with $k < l$	$(p(n)+1)^2\dfrac{m(m-1)}{2}$

Figure 5.18   Clauses representing statement 1

reflects the requirement that at least one of the variables must be true, and the clauses

$$\overline{x} \text{ or } \overline{y}$$
$$\overline{x} \text{ or } \overline{z}$$
$$\overline{y} \text{ or } \overline{z}$$

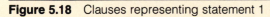

capture the requirement that only one of the variables can be true.

Let us now consider statement 3. We translate it according to the transitions that can be performed by M. Recall that these tran-

$St_{0, 1}$

$Hd_{0, 1}$

$Cont_{0, 1, 1}$

$Cont_{0, 2, k_1}$

$Cont_{0, 3, k_2}$

$\vdots$

$Cont_{0, n+1, k_n}$

$Cont_{0, n+2, 1}$

$\vdots$

$Cont_{0, p(n)+1, 1}$

Figure 5.19   Clauses representing statement 2

sitions can be classified into three categories: those that move the tape head to the right, those that move the tape head to the left, and those that change the contents of the current cell.

Each transition in the first category requires that the machine be in a particular state q_s with a particular symbol x_k in its current cell, and results in a shift to a new state q_t while the tape head is moved to the right. Thus, for each of these transitions, each i in $\{0, 1, \cdots, p(n) - 1\}$, and each j in $\{1, 2, \cdots, p(n)\}$, we introduce the three clauses

$$\overline{St}_{i, s} \text{ or } \overline{Hd}_{i, j} \text{ or } \overline{Cont}_{i, j, k} \text{ or } Hd_{i+1, j+1}$$
$$\overline{St}_{i, s} \text{ or } \overline{Hd}_{i, j} \text{ or } \overline{Cont}_{i, j, k} \text{ or } St_{i+1, t}$$
$$\overline{St}_{i, s} \text{ or } \overline{Hd}_{i, j} \text{ or } \overline{Cont}_{i, j, k} \text{ or } Cont_{i+1, j, k}$$

Collectively, these clauses correspond to the statement: "If at time i, M is in state q_s with its tape head over cell j that contains symbol x_k, then at time $i + 1$ the tape head will be over cell $j + 1$, the machine will be in state q_t, and the contents of cell j will still be x_k."

Likewise, each transition in the second category requires that M be in some state q_s with its current cell containing x_k, and results in a shift to state q_t while its tape head moves to the left. Hence, for each of these transitions, each i in $\{0, 1, \cdots, p(n) - 1\}$, and each j in $\{2, 3, \cdots, p(n) + 1\}$, we introduce the three clauses

$$\overline{St}_{i, s} \text{ or } \overline{Hd}_{i, j} \text{ or } \overline{Cont}_{i, j, k} \text{ or } Hd_{i+1, j-1}$$
$$\overline{St}_{i, s} \text{ or } \overline{Hd}_{i, j} \text{ or } \overline{Cont}_{i, j, k} \text{ or } St_{i+1, t}$$
$$\overline{St}_{i, s} \text{ or } \overline{Hd}_{i, j} \text{ or } \overline{Cont}_{i, j, k} \text{ or } Cont_{i+1, j, k}$$

These clauses collectively correspond to the statement: "If at time i, M is in state q_s with its tape head over cell j that contains symbol x_k, then at time $i + 1$ the tape head will be over cell $j - 1$, the machine will be in state q_t and the contents of cell j will still be x_k."

Each transition in the third category requires that the machine be in some particular state q_s with a particular symbol x_k in the current cell, and results in a shift to state q_t while some symbol x_l is written in the current cell. Thus, for each such transition, each i in $\{0, 1, \cdots, p(n) - 1\}$, and each j in $\{1, 2, \cdots, p(n)\}$, we introduce the three clauses

$$\overline{St}_{i, s} \text{ or } \overline{Hd}_{i, j} \text{ or } \overline{Cont}_{i, j, k} \text{ or } Hd_{i+1, j}$$
$$\overline{St}_{i, s} \text{ or } \overline{Hd}_{i, j} \text{ or } \overline{Cont}_{i, j, k} \text{ or } St_{i+1, t}$$
$$\overline{St}_{i, s} \text{ or } \overline{Hd}_{i, j} \text{ or } \overline{Cont}_{i, j, k} \text{ or } Cont_{i+1, j, l}$$

These clauses correspond to the statement: "If at time i, M is in state q_s with its tape head over cell j that contains symbol x_k, then at time $i + 1$ the tape head will be over cell j, which will contain symbol x_l, and M will be in state q_t."

We see, then, that each transition in M contributes no more than $3(p(n) + 1)^2$ to the total number of clauses.

To assure that cell contents change only in accordance with these rules we add the collection of clauses of the form

$$Hd_{i, j} \text{ or } \overline{Cont}_{i, j, k} \text{ or } Cont_{i+1, j, k}$$

for each i in $\{0, 1, \cdots, p(n) - 1\}$, each j in $\{1, 2, \cdots, p(n) + 1\}$, and each k in $\{1, 2, \cdots, m\}$. These clauses represent the statement: "If the tape head is not over cell j at time i, then cell j will remain unchanged at time $i + 1$." Note that there are only $mp(n)(p(n) + 1)$ clauses in this collection.

Finally, we add the clauses of the form

$$\overline{St}_{i, 2} \text{ or } St_{i+1, 2}$$

for i in $\{0, 1, \cdots, p(n) - 1\}$. These clauses say that once in its halt state, the machine will remain in its halt state.

Collecting all the clauses described together, we obtain a set of clauses that is satisfied by those and only those truth assignments that correspond to computations by M that accept the string w in time $p(|w|)$. Thus, we have obtained an instance of SAT that is satisfiable if and only if $w \in L$. In turn, the coded version of this instance is the string $f(w)$ we desire, since according to this definition we have $w \in L$ if and only if $f(w) \in L_{SAT}$.

It remains to show that $f(w)$ can be computed in polynomial-time. To this end we note that the computation of $f(w)$ is essentially the process of listing the clauses represented by $f(w)$. But, the number of clauses to be listed, the number of literals in each clause, and the lengths of the strings representing each literal are each bounded by a polynomial in $|w|$. Thus, the string $f(w)$ can be computed in polynomial-time.

∎

Since the discovery of Cook's theorem, many other languages in NP have been found to possess the same pivotal properties as L_{SAT}. That is, there are now a large number of languages in NP (including those identified in Appendix E) that are known to be polynomial reductions of any other language in NP. These languages are said to be **NP-complete.**

The classification of the NP-complete languages is an important topic of research today. If any one of these languages can be accepted by a deterministic Turing machine in polynomial-time, then NP must be equal to P, and many problems that appear to be so time consuming as to be intractable will have been shown to be tractable after all. Conversely, if any language in NP can be shown to lie outside of P, then all the NP-complete languages must also lie outside of P, and we will know that continuing to search for efficient solutions to these problems is useless. Unfortunately, researchers have as yet been unable to determine which of these options is true.

Exercises

1. Show that the following decision problem is in NP.

    Given a test integer and a finite set of integers from $\mathbb{N}$, is there a subset whose sum is equal to the test value?

2. Find a polynomial reduction from the language over $\{x, y\}$ that consists of the strings containing at least two xs, into the language over $\{y, z\}$ that consists of the strings containing at least three zs.

3. Based on the definitions in this section, identify the following strings that are in L_{SAT}.
    a. $(p00/0n0/00p)(0p0/00n)(n00/0p0/00n)$
    b. $(0n00/00n0)(n000/00n0)(n000/000n)(0n00/000n)$
    c. $(p00)(0p0)(00p)(n00/0n0)(0n0/00n)(n00/00n)$
    d. $(p0/0p)(n0/0p)(p0/0n)(n0/0n)$

4. It is customary to denote the class of languages whose complements are in NP by co-NP. Show that if co-$NP \neq NP$ then $P \neq NP$.

5.6   CLOSING COMMENTS

It is fitting to close this final chapter with a review of the entire text. We began by introducing finite automata and regular languages in the context of lexical analysis. From there, the goal of developing more powerful language recognition techniques led us to the study of pushdown automata and context-free languages. Seeking still more powerful techniques, we then turned to Turing machines and general phrase-structure languages. There, we appeared to bump up against the limits of algorithmic processes—we had reached the boundary identified by the Church–Turing thesis.

With this thesis before us, we turned our attention to the power of computational processes in an effort to learn more about the limitations we had encountered. Here, we expanded our use of automata (Turing machines in particular) from that of mere language accepting devices to that of more general purpose machines that compute functions. We identified the class of functions that could be computed by Turing machines as the Turing-computable functions, and found that this class was identical to the class of partial recursive functions as well as to the functions computable by our simple bare-bones programming language. This identification of classes gave significant credence to the Church–Turing thesis, since it showed that the apparent limitations discovered in other disciplines are equivalent.

Having investigated the boundary between computability and noncomputability, we restricted our attention to problems that are theoretically solvable by algorithms, our goal being to classify the practicality of the computations involved. Here we encountered significant difficulties, because the vast number of possible solutions to a problem can make the task of identifying the most efficient solution extremely difficult. In fact, there are problems whose various solutions form an infinite chain of significantly more efficient algorithms. Consequently, any general scheme for classifying problems according to the complexity of their "best" solutions must be implemented on a very coarse scale.

This realization led us to consider the class P, which consists of those languages that can be accepted (those decision problems that can be solved) in polynomial-time by a Turing machine. Intuitively, we consider this to be the class of problems that have practical computational solutions. (For large inputs, the solution of problems outside this class becomes much more time consuming than those within P.) Unfortunately, the classification of problems, even on this broad scale, continues to thwart the efforts of researchers in the field. A major obstacle is the class NP, which consists of those languages that can be accepted in polynomial-time by nondeterministic Turing machines. Whether or not the classes P and NP are identical is one of the most prominent questions in computer science today, since its solution appears to play an important role in determining the applications in which computers can ultimately be used.

Chapter Review Problems

1. Determine the time and space complexities of the computation performed by the Turing machine

$$\rightarrow R_\triangle \rightarrow L \xrightarrow{x} y \underset{y}{}$$

   when processing the strings *xyxxy*, *xxx*, and *yyy*.

2. Design a Turing machine that accepts only strings containing one or more *x*s followed by one or more *y*s. What is the time complexity of your solution? How accurately can the time complexity of this language recognition problem be determined?

3. Find the time complexity (worst-case) of the Turing machine below assuming inputs are chosen from $\{x, y\}^*$.

$$\rightarrow R \xrightarrow{x} R \xrightarrow{x} y$$

4. Find the average-case time complexity of the Turing machine in the previous problem assuming inputs are chosen from $\{x, y\}^*$.

5. Show that the language over alphabet Σ that consists of strings of the form ww^R, where $w \in \Sigma^*$ and w^R is the string w written backward, can be accepted by a nondeterministic multiple-tape Turing machine with time complexity $\Theta(n)$.

6. Show that $\Theta(n^d) < \Theta(n!)$ for any $d \in \mathbb{N}$.

7. Show that $\Theta(log_a n) = \Theta(log_b n)$.

8. Show that $\underset{d \in \mathbb{N}^+}{\cup} O(n^d) \neq \underset{d \in \mathbb{N}^+}{\cup} \Theta(n^d)$.

9. Is the language L_{SAT}, as defined in Section 5.5, context-free? Support your answer.

10. Find a polynomial reduction from the language over $\{z, y\}$ that consists

of those strings containing at least three zs, into the language over $\{x, y\}$ that consists of those strings containing at least two xs.

11. Show that if L_1 and L_2 are languages in P (other than $\varnothing$ and Σ^*), then $L_1 \propto L_2$ and $L_2 \propto L_1$.

12. Show that the language $\varnothing$ is in P, and for any alphabet Σ, the language Σ^* is in P.

13. Suppose that x is a symbol in the alphabet Σ. Show that $\varnothing \propto \Sigma^* - \{x\}$ but there is no polynomial reduction from $\Sigma^* - \{x\}$ to $\varnothing$.

14. Show that the time complexity of accepting the language that consists of strings of the form ww^R, where $w \in \{x, y\}^*$ and w^R is w in reverse order, is $\Theta(n^2)$, when using a one-tape Turing machine.

15. Suppose $T:\mathbb{N} \rightarrow \mathbb{N}$ is a total computable function. Show that there is a Turing-acceptable language that cannot be accepted by any Turing machine with a time complexity in $O(T)$.

16. Suppose $T:\mathbb{N} \rightarrow \mathbb{N}$ is a total computable function. Show that there is a Turing-acceptable language that cannot be accepted by any Turing machine with a space complexity in $O(T)$.

17. Which of the following functions are in $O(n^3)$? Which are in $\Theta(n^3)$?
    a. $3n^2 + 2n + 1$ b. $n!$
    c. $\lfloor \log_2 n \rfloor$ d. $5n^3 + 2n^2$

18. Find integers c_0 and n_0 such that $4n^2 + 3n < c_0(2n^2 + n)$ for all integers n greater than n_0.

19. Show that $\Theta(2^n) < \Theta(2^{2^n})$.

20. Show that if the languages L_1 and L_2 are in P, then $L_1 \cup L_2$, $L_1 \circ L_2$, and L_1^* are also in P.

21. Show that the intersection of any two languages in NP is always a language in NP.

22. Find a polynomial reduction $f:\{x, y, z\}^* \rightarrow \{x, y\}^*$ from the language $\{wzw^R: w \in \{x, y\}^*$ and w^R is the string w in reverse order$\}$ to the language $\{w: w$ is a palindrome in $\{x, y\}^*\}$.

23. Find a polynomial reduction from the language $\{x, y\}^*$ to the language that consists of strings containing an even number of xs.

24. Find a polynomial reduction $f:\{x, y\}^* \rightarrow \{x, y\}^*$ from the language of strings containing an even number of ys to the language of strings containing an odd number of xs.

25. Show that the language consisting of all palindromes in $\{x, y\}^*$ is in P.

26. Restate the following decision problems as language recognition problems.
    a. Decide whether the name Carol is in a given list.
    b. Decide whether a collection of integers whose sum is 100 can be chosen from a given list of integers.
    c. Decide whether a complete computer system can be constructed from the items in a list of computer components.

27. Is there a language recognition problem whose solution requires exponential time when using a one-tape Turing machine, but which can be solved in polynomial-time on a multiple-tape Turing machine? Explain your answer.

28. Give an example of a language that
    a. is in P
    b. is not in P
    c. is in NP and may not be in P

29. Design a (one-tape) nondeterministic Turing machine that accepts L_{SAT} in polynomial-time.

30. Show that if there is an NP-complete language that is in co-NP, then $NP = $ co-NP.

31. Show that if L is in NP, then L is Turing-decidable.

32. Is every context-free language in P? Justify your answer.

Programming Problems

1. Write a program for accepting the language L_{SAT}. Why should you expect your program to be time consuming for large inputs?

2. Write a program for solving the traveling salesman decision problem.

APPENDIX A

More About Constructing *LR*(1) Parse Tables

In Chapter 2 we saw how an *LR*(1) parse table is based on a finite automaton that is constructed from the pertinent context-free grammar, but we did not discuss the details of this construction. Our goal now is to give an explanation of this process. Our approach is to show how the transition diagram in Figure 2.37 was constructed from the grammar

$$S \rightarrow zMNz$$
$$M \rightarrow aMa$$
$$M \rightarrow z$$
$$N \rightarrow bNb$$
$$N \rightarrow z$$

with start symbol *S*. By applying the same steps, suitable automata can be constructed from other (nonambiguous) context-free grammars in which no rules have right-hand sides consisting of the empty string.

The first step is to introduce a new start symbol that we denote by *S'* and the new rewrite rule

$$S' \rightarrow S$$

Note that these changes do not change the language generated by the grammar. They do, however, ensure that the start symbol appears in only one, very simple rewrite rule.

Next, we introduce the marker ∧ for indicating the status of the parsing process. For example, using this marker we could write

$$S \rightarrow z{\scriptstyle\wedge}MNz$$

to indicate the status of having found the leading *z* in the pattern *S* and thus being prepared to look for the remaining pattern *MNz*. The use of this marker allows us to summarize the stages of recognizing the pattern *S* as follows:

$$S \rightarrow \text{.}zMNz$$
$$S \rightarrow z\text{.}MNz$$
$$S \rightarrow zM\text{.}Nz$$
$$S \rightarrow zMN\text{.}z$$
$$S \rightarrow zMNz\text{.}$$

Let us agree that a marked rewrite rule is in initial form if its marker is at the far left of the rule's right-hand side. Likewise, a marked rule is in terminal form if its marker is at the far right end of the right-hand side. Thus, the first rule in the preceding list is in initial form, whereas the last one is in terminal form.

Next, we need to define what we mean by the closure of a set of marked rewrite rules. We form such a closure by first finding all the nonterminals that appear immediately to the right of a marker in some rule in the set. Then, we add to the set the initial forms of all rewrite rules in the grammar whose left-hand sides consist of those nonterminals. If some of these added rules have nonterminals appearing immediately to the right of a marker, we add the initial forms of all rewrite rules for those nonterminals as well. We continue this process until no new nonterminals appear immediately to the right of a marker. (Note that this process must stop because there are only finitely many nonterminals in the grammar.) The result is said to be the closure of the original set. For example, the closure of the set containing the two rules

$$S \rightarrow zM\text{.}Nz$$

and

$$M \rightarrow a\text{.}Ma$$

based on our example grammar is the collection

$$S \rightarrow zM\text{.}Nz$$
$$N \rightarrow \text{.}bNb$$
$$N \rightarrow \text{.}z$$
$$M \rightarrow a\text{.}Ma$$
$$M \rightarrow \text{.}aMa$$
$$M \rightarrow \text{.}z$$

The second and third rules were added because *N* appeared immediately to the right of a marker, and the last two were added because *M* appeared immediately to the right of a marker.

With these definitions behind us, we are prepared to describe the process by which the transition diagram in Figure 2.37 was constructed. It is as follows:

1. Form the closure of the set containing the single marked rule $S' \rightarrow$ $_\wedge S$. Establish this set as the initial state in the transition diagram.

2. While possible without redundancy do the following:

   a. Select a symbol s (terminal or nonterminal) appearing immediately to the right of the marker in a rule in some established state A.
   b. Let X denote the collection of all marked rules in A that have s immediately to the right of their markers.
   c. Let Y be the set of marked rules obtained by moving the marker in each rule in X to the right of the symbol s.
   d. If the closure of Y has not yet been established as a state, do so now.
   e. Draw an arc labeled s from state A to the closure of Y.

3. Let each state represented by marked rules in terminal form be accept states in the automaton.

Let us clarify this process by following it through the early part of the construction of Figure 2.37. We begin by establishing the set containing the two marked rules

$$S' \rightarrow {}_\wedge S \qquad \text{and} \qquad S \rightarrow {}_\wedge zMNz$$

as the transition diagram's initial state. (This is the closure of the set that consists of the marked rule $S' \rightarrow {}_\wedge S$ as requested in the first step in our construction process.)

According to step 2, there will be two arcs leaving this state: one labeled S and the other labeled z because these symbols appear immediately to the right of some marker in this state. The arc labeled z will lead to the state established by forming the closure of the set that consists of

$$S \rightarrow z_\wedge MNz$$

This is the set consisting of

$$S \rightarrow z_\wedge MNz$$
$$M \rightarrow {}_\wedge aMa$$
$$M \rightarrow {}_\wedge z$$

The arc labeled S will lead to the state established by forming the closure of the set that consists of

$$S' \rightarrow S_\wedge$$

(Note that this state will be an accept state in the completed transition diagram.)

Our construction to this point is summarized in Figure A.1. If we were to continue the construction, the state represented by

$$S \rightarrow z_{\wedge}MNz$$
$$M \rightarrow {}_{\wedge}aMa$$
$$M \rightarrow {}_{\wedge}z$$

would have three arcs leaving it: one labeled *M* leading to the closure of the set consisting of $S \rightarrow zM_{\wedge}Nz$; another labeled *a* leading to the closure of the set consisting of $M \rightarrow a_{\wedge}Ma$; and the third labeled *z* leading to the closure of the set consisting of $M \rightarrow z_{\wedge}$.

The completed diagram would appear as in Figure A.2. You should compare this to the diagram in Figure 2.37. They are the same except that Figure 2.37 has its states labeled by numbers rather than sets of marked rewrite rules.

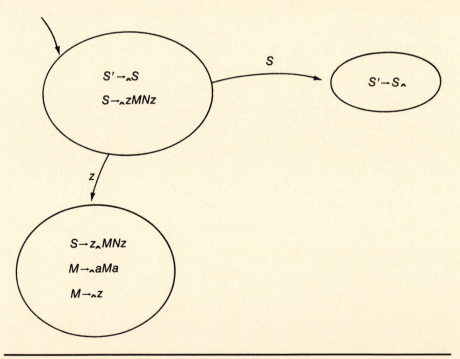

Figure A.1   The first stages of constructing Figure 2.34

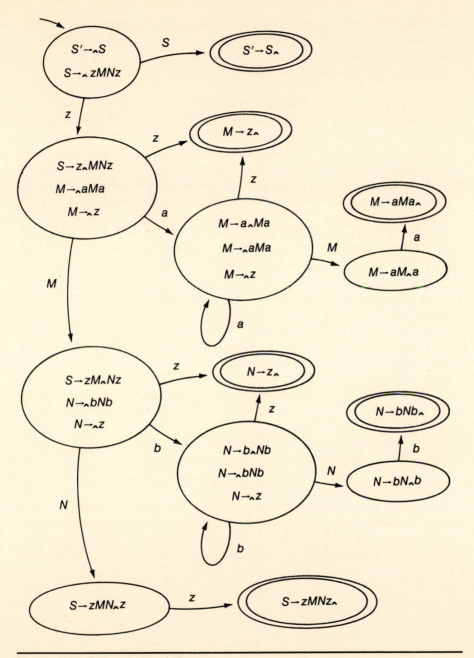

Figure A.2   The completed diagram

We should close by giving some intuition behind this construction process. The status of starting the process of parsing a string based on our altered grammar is represented by

$$S' \to {}_{\wedge}S$$

which represents the initial stage of recognizing the pattern S'. The position of our marker indicates that this will involve finding a string that matches the pattern S—the symbol to the right of our marker. In turn, the details of this process are more fully described by considering the initial forms of all those rules that describe possible structures for S, which in our case is the single marked rule $S \to {}_{\wedge}zMNz$. Indeed, the initial state in the parsing process is totally described by the two marked rewrite rules

$$S' \to {}_{\wedge}S$$

and

$$S \to {}_{\wedge}zMNz$$

That is, to find a pattern conforming to the structure S', we must look for a pattern of the form S (first marked rule), which means we must find a pattern that begins with z (second marked rule).

You should note that obtaining the above description of the initial state of the parsing process is nothing more than the process of computing the closure of the set that contains the single marked rule $S' \to {}_{\wedge}S$. In fact, forming the closure of a set of marked rules is exactly the process of more fully describing the options available to a parser when in the state represented by the original set.

If we now found a z in the input string, our status in recognizing the pattern S would become

$$S \to z_{\wedge}MNz$$

which means our immediate problem would become that of finding a match for the pattern M. According to the grammar, this can be done in one of two different ways: using the rule $M \to aMa$ or the rule $M \to z$. Thus, the beginning of our search for a pattern matching the structure M is captured by the marked rules

$$M \to {}_{\wedge}aMa$$

and

$$M \to {}_{\wedge}z$$

Again, the complete state description is obtained by forming the closure of its preliminary description.

We see, then, that the process of parsing a string based on our altered grammar begins in the state described by

$$S' \rightarrow \char"02 S$$
$$S \rightarrow \char"02 zMNz$$

and when a z is found, moves to the state described by

$$S \rightarrow z\char"02 MNz$$
$$M \rightarrow \char"02 aMa$$
$$M \rightarrow \char"02 z$$

You should observe that this is the arc drawn by our formal construction process.

Note that since the accept states in the completed transition diagram are derived from marked rules in terminal form, the strings accepted by the automaton will be exactly those strings that should lead to a reduction in the corresponding *LR*(1) parser. Thus, each time the automaton accepts a string, the parser knows to perform a reduce operation. Moreover, the reduction to be performed is based on the rewrite rule whose terminal form produced the accept state.

APPENDIX B

More About Ackermann's Function

The goal of this appendix is to prove that Ackermann's function, defined by the equations

$$A(0, y) = y + 1 \tag{A1}$$
$$A(x + 1, 0) = A(x, 1) \tag{A2}$$
$$A(x + 1, y + 1) = A(x, A(x + 1, y)) \tag{A3}$$

is total and computable, yet not primitive recursive. The fact that it is total follows by induction on the input pairs in lexicographic order, as we now see.

For all pairs of the form $(0, y)$, $A(0, y)$ is defined by Equation A1. Suppose now that $A(x, y)$ is defined for all (x, y) less than $(m + 1, 0)$ in lexicographic order. Then, $A(m + 1, 0) = A(m, 1)$ by Equation A2, so $A(m + 1, 0)$ is defined. Finally, suppose that $A(x, y)$ is defined for all (x, y) less than $(m + 1, n + 1)$ in lexicographic order. Then, $A(m + 1, n + 1) = A(m, A(m + 1, n))$ by Equation A3, and by induction, A is defined for both $(m + 1, n)$ and $(m, A(m + 1, n))$. Consequently, $A(m + 1, n + 1)$ is also defined.

The computability of A follows from our proof that A is total. Indeed, the definition of $A(x, y)$ is a description of a process for computing the corresponding output value.

The following proof—that Ackermann's function is not primitive recursive—although long, is really quite simple. We show that for any primitive recursive function f mapping n-tuples to one-tuples there is a positive integer N such that, for each $\bar{x}$ in $\mathbb{N}^n$,

$$f(\bar{x}) < A(N, \Sigma(\bar{x}))$$

where $\Sigma(\bar{x})$ represents the sum of the components of $\bar{x}$. (The sum of the components of a zero-tuple is 0.) From this, the fact that Ackermann's function is not primitive recursive follows almost immediately. If A were primitive recursive, then the function $f = A \circ (\pi_1^1 \times \pi_1^1)$ would also be primitive recursive. Thus, there would be a positive integer N such that $f(x) < A(N, x)$ for all x in $\mathbb{N}$. In particular, by picking $x = N$, we would have $f(N) < A(N, N)$. But, $f(N) = A \circ (\pi_1^1 \times \pi_1^1)(N) = A(N, N)$ so we would arrive at the contradictory statement $A(N, N) < A(N, N)$. We must conclude, then, that Ackermann's function is not primitive recursive.

We see, then, that our goal will be obtained by proving the existence of a positive integer N, having the properties described above, for each primitive recursive function. For this purpose, we now establish some properties of Ackermann's function as stated in the following lemmas.

LEMMA 1
For all z in $\mathbb{N}$,

    a. $A(1, z) = z + 2$
    b. $A(2, z) = 2z + 3$

PROOF

a. We induct on z. When $z = 0$, we have

$$
\begin{aligned}
A(1, 0) &= A(0, 1) && \text{(by Equation A2)} \\
&= 1 + 1 && \text{(by Equation A1)} \\
&= 0 + 2 &&
\end{aligned}
$$

If the equation holds for $z \leq n$, then

$$
\begin{aligned}
A(1, n + 1) &= A(0, A(1, n)) && \text{(by Equation A3)} \\
&= A(0, n + 2) && \text{(by induction hypothesis)} \\
&= (n + 2) + 1 && \text{(by Equation A1)} \\
&= (n + 1) + 2 &&
\end{aligned}
$$

b. Again, we induct on z. When $z = 0$, we have

$$
\begin{aligned}
A(2, 0) &= A(1, 1) && \text{(by Equation A2)} \\
&= A(0, A(1, 0)) && \text{(by Equation A3)} \\
&= A(0, A(0, 1)) && \text{(by Equation A2)} \\
&= A(0, 2) && \text{(by Equation A1)} \\
&= 3 && \text{(by Equation A1)}
\end{aligned}
$$

Suppose now that the equality holds for $z \leq n$. Then,

$$
\begin{aligned}
A(2, n + 1) &= A(1, A(2, n)) && \text{(by Equation A3)} \\
&= A(1, 2n + 3) && \text{(by induction hypothesis)} \\
&= (2n + 3) + 2 && \text{(by Lemma 1a)} \\
&= 2(n + 1) + 3 &&
\end{aligned}
$$

■

LEMMA 2
For all x and y in $\mathbb{N}$, $y + 1 \leqslant A(x, y)$.

PROOF
We proceed by induction. If $x = 0$, the inequality holds for all y by Equation A1.

Now suppose the inequality holds for $x = n$. To prove the inequality for $x = n + 1$, we induct on y, beginning at $y = 0$.

$$0 + 1 \leqslant 1 + 1$$
$$\leqslant A(n, 1) \qquad \text{(by induction hypothesis)}$$
$$= A(n + 1, 0) \qquad \text{(by Equation A2)}$$

so the inequality holds for $x = n + 1$ and $y = 0$. Moreover, if the inequality holds for $x = n + 1$ and $y = m$, then

$$(m + 1) + 1 \leqslant A(n + 1, m) + 1 \qquad \text{(by induction hypothesis)}$$
$$\leqslant A(n, A(n + 1, m)) \qquad \text{(by induction hypothesis)}$$
$$= A(n + 1, m + 1) \qquad \text{(by Equation A3)}$$

so the inequality holds for $x = n + 1$ and $y = m + 1$.

∎

LEMMA 3
Ackermann's function satisfies the following inequalities for all x and y in $\mathbb{N}$.

   a. $A(x, y) < A(x, y + 1)$
   b. $A(x, y + 1) \leqslant A(x + 1, y)$
   c. $A(x, y) < A(x + 1, y)$

PROOF
a. We induct on x. For $x = 0$, the inequality follows from Equation A1. If $0 < x$, then

$$A(x, y) < A(x, y) + 1$$
$$\leqslant A(x - 1, A(x, y)) \qquad \text{(by Lemma 2)}$$
$$= A(x, y + 1) \qquad \text{(by Equation A3)}$$

b. We induct on y. For $y = 0$ the inequality follows from Equation A2. If $0 < y$ and the inequality holds for values less than y, then

$$A(x, y + 1) \leqslant A(x, A(x, y)) \qquad \text{(} y + 1 \leqslant A(x, y) \text{ by Lemma 2}$$
$$\text{and } A \text{ is monotonic in its sec-}$$
$$\text{ond argument by Lemma 3a)}$$
$$\leqslant A(x, A(x + 1, y - 1)) $$
$$\text{(by induction hypothesis and}$$

$$A \text{ is monotonic in its second}$$
$$\text{argument by Lemma 3a)}$$
$$= A(x + 1, y) \qquad \text{(by Equation A3)}$$

c. This is a result of the preceding inequalities as follows:

$$A(x, y) < A(x, y + 1) \qquad \text{(by Lemma 3a)}$$
$$\leq A(x + 1, y) \qquad \text{(by Lemma 3b)}$$

∎

LEMMA 4

For all x_1, x_2, and y in $\mathbb{N}$, $A(x_1, y) + A(x_2, y) < A(max(x_1, x_2) + 4, y)$.

PROOF

For convenience, let $m = max(x_1, x_2)$. Then,

$$A(x_1, y) + A(x_2, y) \leq A(m, y) + A(m, y) \qquad \text{(by Lemma 3c)}$$
$$= 2A(m, y)$$
$$< 2A(m, y) + 3$$
$$= A(2, A(m, y)) \qquad \text{(by Lemma 1b)}$$
$$< A(2, A(m + 3, y)) \qquad (A \text{ is monotonic in}$$
$$\text{both arguments}$$
$$\text{by Lemma 3a and 3c)}$$

$$\leq A(m + 2, A(m + 3, y)) \qquad \text{(by Lemma 3c)}$$
$$= A(m + 3, y + 1) \qquad \text{(by Equation A3)}$$
$$\leq A(m + 4, y) \qquad \text{(by Lemma 3b)}$$
$$= A(max(x_1, x_2) + 4, y)$$

∎

LEMMA 5

For all x and y, $A(x, y) + y < A(x + 4, y)$.

PROOF

$$A(x, y) + y < A(x, y) + y + 1$$
$$= A(x, y) + A(0, y) \qquad \text{(by Equation A1)}$$
$$< A(x + 4, y) \qquad \text{(by Lemma 4)}$$

∎

We are now prepared to prove the following proposition which, as we have seen, implies that Ackermann's function is not primitive recursive.

PROPOSITION
For any primitive recursive function f mapping n-tuples to one-tuples there is a positive integer N such that, for each $\bar{x}$ in $\mathbb{N}^n$,

$$f(\bar{x}) < A(N, \Sigma(\bar{x}))$$

where $\Sigma(\bar{x})$ represents the sum of the components of $\bar{x}$. (The sum of the components of a zero-tuple is 0.)

PROOF
Since f is primitive recursive, it must consist of a finite number of combinations, compositions, and primitive recursions of initial functions. We induct on the number of such operations. If no such operations are required to obtain f, f itself must be an initial function. If $f = \zeta$, picking $N = 0$ will fill our needs since $f( ) = \zeta( ) = 0 < 1 = A(0, 0) = A(N, 0)$. If f is a projection, then $N = 0$ will again suffice since $f(\bar{x}) = \pi_j^n(\bar{x}) = x_j \leqslant \Sigma(\bar{x}) < (\Sigma(\bar{x})) + 1 = A(0, \Sigma(\bar{x})) = A(N, \Sigma(\bar{x}))$. If f is the successor function, then $N = 1$ will do since $f(x) = \sigma(x) = x + 1 = A(0, x) < A(1, x) = A(N, x)$, where the inequality is obtained from Lemma 3c.

Now we suppose that f is constructed from initial functions using k applications of combination, composition, and primitive recursion (where $0 < k$), and that the proposition holds for any primitive recursive function constructed from fewer than k applications. Since the output of f is a one-tuple, the last operation in the construction of f must be either composition or primitive recursion. Thus, f can be expressed as either

$$f = h \circ g$$

or

$$f(\bar{x}, 0) = g(\bar{x})$$
$$f(\bar{x}, y + 1) = h(\bar{x}, y, f(\bar{x}, y))$$

where h and g are primitive recursive functions constructed from fewer than k applications of combination, composition, and primitive recursion.

Let us consider the first of these cases, where $f = h \circ g$. In general, the output of g might consist of more than one component, so we should consider g to have the form $g_1 \times g_2 \times \cdots \times g_m$ for some positive m. By our induction hypothesis, there are integers $N_1, N_2, \cdots, N_m$ such that $g_j(\bar{x}) < A(N_j, \Sigma(\bar{x}))$ for all $\bar{x}$ in $\mathbb{N}^n$, as well as an N_0 such that $h(\bar{x}) < A(N_0, \Sigma(\bar{x}))$ for all $\bar{x}$ in $\mathbb{N}^m$. Thus,

$$f(\bar{x}) = h(g_1(\bar{x}), g_2(\bar{x}), \cdots, g_m(\bar{x}))$$
$$< A\left(N_0, \sum_{i=1}^{m} g_i(\bar{x})\right) \qquad \text{(by the choice of } N_0)$$

$$< A(N_0, \sum_{i=1}^{m} A(N_i, \Sigma(\overline{x})\,)\,)$$

(by the choice of N_i and Lemma 3a)

$$< A(N_0, A(M, \Sigma(\overline{x})\,)\,), \text{ where } M = max(N_1, \cdots, N_m) + 4(m-1)$$

(by Lemma 4)

$$< A(N_0, A(M + 1, \Sigma(\overline{x})\,)\,)$$

(by Lemma 3a and 3c)

$$\leq A(N_0, A(max(N_0, M) + 1, \Sigma(\overline{x})\,)\,)$$

(by Lemma 3a and 3c)

$$\leq A(max(N_0, M), A(max(N_0, M) + 1, \Sigma(\overline{x})\,)\,)$$

(by Lemma 3c)

$$< A(max(N_0, M) + 1, \Sigma(\overline{x}) + 1)$$

(by Equation A3)

$$< A(max(N_0, M) + 2, \Sigma(\overline{x})\,)$$

(by Lemma 3b)

Consequently, if we pick N to be $max(N_0, M) + 2$, we know that $f(\overline{x}) < A(N, \Sigma(\overline{x})\,)$, for all $\overline{x}$ in $\mathbb{N}^n$, as desired.

Let us now consider the case in which f is defined from h and g using primitive recursion by

$$f(\overline{x}, 0) = g(\overline{x})$$
$$f(\overline{x}, y + 1) = h(\overline{x}, y, f(\overline{x}, y)\,)$$

Since h and g are constructed with fewer than k applications of combination, composition, and primitive recursion, there exist integers N_1 and N_2 such that $g(\overline{z}) < A(N_1, \Sigma(\overline{z})\,)$, for all $\overline{z}$ in $\mathbb{N}^{n-1}$, and $h(\overline{z}) < A(N_2, \Sigma(\overline{z})\,)$, for all $\overline{z}$ in $\mathbb{N}^{n+1}$. (We can assume that $2 < N_2$.) We must show that there is a positive integer N such that $f(\overline{x}, y) < A(N, \Sigma(\overline{x}) + y)$, for all $(\overline{x}, y)$ in $\mathbb{N}^n$. To this end, we pick N to be any integer greater than $max(N_1, N_2) + 4$, and prove the required inequality by inducting on y. We begin with $y = 0$, in which case we have

$$f(\overline{x}, 0) \leq f(\overline{x}, 0) + \Sigma(\overline{x})$$

$$= g(\overline{x}) + \Sigma(\overline{x})$$

(by definition of g)

$$< A(N_1, \Sigma(\overline{x})\,) + \Sigma(\overline{x})$$

(by the choice of N_1)

$$< A(N_1 + 4, \Sigma(\overline{x})\,)$$

(by Lemma 5)

$$< A(N, \Sigma(\overline{x})\,)$$

(by Lemma 3c and choice of N)

$$= A(N, \Sigma(\overline{x}) + 0)$$

Next we suppose that $f(\overline{x}, y) < A(N, \Sigma(\overline{x}) + y)$ for all $y \leq k$, and show that this implies the inequality for $y = k + 1$. Indeed,

$$f(\overline{x}, k + 1) = h(\overline{x}, k, f(\overline{x}, k)\,)$$

$$< A(N_2, \Sigma(\overline{x}) + k + f(\overline{x}, k)\,)$$

(by choice of N_2)

$$< A(N_2, A(0, \Sigma(\overline{x}) + k) + f(\overline{x}, k)\,)$$

(by Equation A1)

$$< A(N_2, A(0, \Sigma(\overline{x}) + k) + A(N, \Sigma(\overline{x}) + k)\,)$$

(by induction hypothesis)

$$< A(N_2, A(N, \Sigma(\overline{x}) + k) + A(N, \Sigma(\overline{x}) + k))$$
$$(N > 0, \text{Lemmas 3c and 3a})$$
$$< A(N_2, 2A(N, \Sigma(\overline{x}) + k) + 3)$$
$$= A(N_2, A(2, A(N, \Sigma(\overline{x}) + k))) \quad \text{(by Lemma 1b)}$$
$$\leq A(N_2, A(N_2 + 1, A(N, \Sigma(\overline{x}) + k)))$$
$$(\text{by Lemma 3a, 3c, and choice of } N_2)$$
$$= A(N_2 + 1, A(N, \Sigma(\overline{x}) + k) + 1) \quad \text{(by Equation A3)}$$
$$< A(N_2 + 2, A(N, \Sigma(\overline{x}) + k)) \quad \text{(by Lemma 3b)}$$
$$< A(N - 1, A(N, \Sigma(\overline{x}) + k))$$
$$(\text{by choice of } N \text{ and Lemma 3c})$$
$$= A(N, \Sigma(\overline{x}) + k + 1) \quad \text{(by Equation A3)}$$

which is the result we desire.

APPENDIX C

Some Important Unsolvable Problems

The major example of an unsolvable problem given in the text (Chapter 4) is the halting problem. This is probably the most popular textbook example because it is readily presentable in the context of Turing machines, a class of computational devices that has usually been described in a course by the time unsolvable problems are discussed. However, such a presentation has a rather abstract flavor to it and often leaves students with a feeling of irrelevance. Many get the idea that although unsolvable problems exist, one never encounters them in normal situations. They may feel that they can safely attack everyday problems without being concerned by the possibility that the problem being pursued may not have an algorithmic solution.

This, however, is an inaccurate assessment of the significance of unsolvable problems. Such problems surface in a variety of settings. In this appendix we identify two unsolvable problems that occur in real-life situations and discuss some of their ramifications.

C.1 TESTING CONTEXT-FREE GRAMMARS FOR AMBIGUITY

We introduced the concept of a parse tree in Chapter 2. There, our motivation was to show that any string that could be generated from a context-free grammar could also be generated by a leftmost derivation. An important principle used in this argument was that any derivation of a string is associated with a unique parse tree. This allowed us to show that given a derivation of a string that was not leftmost, we could construct the parse tree associated with that derivation and then construct a leftmost derivation for the string from the parse tree.

Because it was not relevant at the time and could merely introduce an element of confusion, we did not mention in Chapter 2 that a given string might be associated with more than one parse tree. (A derivation of a string is associated with only one parse tree, but the string itself may be associated with more than one parse tree.) Consider the grammar

<phrase> → <phrase> or <phrase>
<phrase> → <phrase> and <phrase>
<phrase> → X
<phrase> → Y
<phrase> → Z

that can generate the phrase

X or Y and Z

In fact, it can generate this phrase via two distinct parse trees, as shown in Figure C.1. Note that Figure C.1a corresponds to an interpretation in which the truth of the entire phrase implies the truth of Z, whereas Figure C.1b corresponds to an interpretation in which the entire phrase may be true without Z being true.

Other examples include the common programming structure of nested if–then–else structures, in which an improperly constructed grammar can allow for two distinct interpretations of the structure

if *A* then if *B* then *X* else *Y*

Is *Y* to be executed when *A* is true and *B* is false, or is *Y* to be executed when *A* is false regardless of *B*?

Grammars with such anomalies are said to be ambiguous. Needless to say, it would be a frustrating task to construct a compiler for a programming language based on an ambiguous grammar. Given the preceding if–then–else structure, one would simply not know what machine code to generate. Consequently, one must remove all such ambiguities before attempting to develop a compiler for the language. For example, the ambiguous grammar given earlier could be replaced by either

<phrase> → <phrase> or <term>
<phrase> → <phrase> and <term>
<phrase> → <term>
<term> → X
<term> → Y
<term> → Z

or

<phrase> → <term> or <phrase>
<phrase> → <term> and <phrase>

<phrase> → <term>
<term> → X
<term> → Y
<term> → Z

depending on which of the two potential interpretations was desired.

Unfortunately, grammars for actual programming languages are much more complex than this simple example. Thus, an intuitive analysis can easily (and often does) overlook subtle ambiguities. What is needed is a routine procedure to apply to a grammar that will detect and report any ambiguities involved. That is, we need an algorithm for detecting whether or not a given context-free grammar is ambiguous. However, this is impossible. The problem of determining whether or not a given context-free grammar is ambiguous has been shown to be unsolvable.

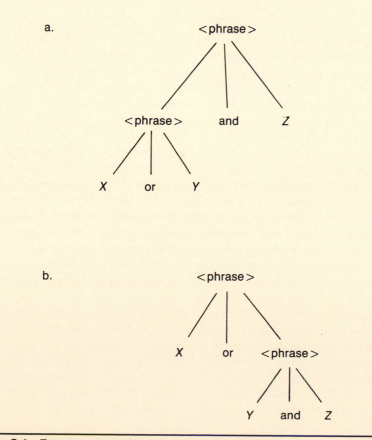

Figure C.1 Two parse trees for the phrase "X or Y and Z"

C.2   PROVING THE CORRECTNESS OF PROGRAMS

As software becomes more complex and is used in increasingly critical situations, its correctness is becoming a dominating issue. Numerous cases have shown that verification by test data simply does not provide the certainty required. What is needed is a way in which the accuracy of a software package can be proven in a rigorous manner. Since such proofs easily become as complex and tedious as the software itself, we would like to develop an automated system for performing them.

Devising such techniques has been the goal of many researchers for several years now, and progress is being made. One significant approach is to formally identify the effect each structure within a programming language has on the state of the program's environment during execution. For example, if some statement about the variable Y could be made before executing the Pascal structure

$$X := Y + 1;$$

then the same statement could be made about $X - 1$ after executing the structure. Thus, if we represent the program's environment as a collection of statements, called assertions, then this observation tells us how the assertions that represent the environment before executing the assignment statement should be altered to obtain the correct set of assertions after execution.

In this manner, the structures in a programming language give rise to environment alteration rules that can be used much like inference rules in a logic system. If, starting with the program's initial environment, we can derive the desired terminal environment by applying the alteration rules proposed by the program, then we can conclude that the program is correct. In turn, the verification of a program becomes similar to the process of proving a theorem, the program's initial environment being analogous to a collection of axioms, the alteration rules being analogous to rules of inference, and the final environment being analogous to a theorem.

This analogy to theorem proving should be enough to raise suspicions that the task of program verification in the general setting might be an unsolvable problem. In general, we would like a system that both verifies correct programs and rejects incorrect ones. However, such a system is an impossibility. Indeed, Gödel's incompleteness theorem implies that such a general purpose system must fail to detect some incorrect programs.

In case you are not prepared to accept the unsolvability of the general verification problem based on this intuitive analogy with theorem proving, let us consider the task of program verification from another perspective. A major component of any program verification process is to show that the program will, in fact, terminate. This, however, is readily identified as the halting problem in disguise. If the programming language involved has the power to compute all the partial recursive functions, as is the case of the simple language developed in Chapter 4, then there is no algorithm for detecting whether or not programs written in that language will halt. Thus, the unsolvability of the halting problem implies that the dream of software engineers, in its most general form, is an impossibility.

APPENDIX D

On the Complexity of the String Comparison Problem

Our goal in this appendix is to show that any solution (using a one-tape Turing machine) to the string comparison problem discussed in Chapter 5 will have a time complexity that is at least a quadratic expression in n, where n is the length of the input strings. (Recall that this comparison problem was to decide whether or not two strings from $\{x, y\}^*$ of equal length are identical. The strings are recorded on the Turing machine's tape with an asterisk separating them.) To accomplish our goal we rely heavily on the concept of a crossing sequence, so let us explain this concept before proceeding.

Given a Turing machine (in which we imagine the tape cells numbered from left to right starting at 1) and a computation of that machine, the **crossing sequence** at tape cell i is a record of the traversals made by the tape head across the boundary between cells i and $i + 1$ during the computation. This record is maintained as a list of states: Each time the tape head crosses the boundary, we record the state of the machine immediately after executing that transition. Thus, if we know that a particular computation started with the tape head over the leftmost tape cell and produced the crossing sequence $q_1, q_2, \cdots, q_n$ at cell i, we know that the first time the tape head passed from cell i to cell $i + 1$ the machine moved to state q_1. Later, when the tape head returned to cell i from the right, the machine moved to state q_2; and so forth. A more detailed example is given in Figure D.1.

We define the length of a crossing sequence to be the number of entries in the sequence. It is easy to see that the sum of the lengths of all the crossing sequences at the various cells on the tape is equal to the number of move transitions executed by the machine (assuming that the computa-

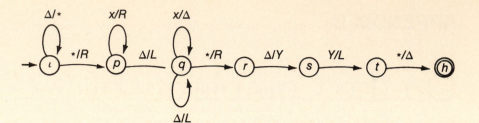

Cell number	Crossing sequence (given initial configuration $\underline{\Delta}xx\Delta\Delta \ldots$)
1	p, q, r, t
2	p, q
3	p, q
4	empty
5	empty
$\vdots$	$\vdots$

Figure D.1   A transition diagram for a Turing machine and the corresponding crossing sequence when accepting the string xx

tion did not end in an abnormal termination). In particular, this sum provides a lower bound for the time complexity of the computation.

Another point to be made is that if w_1, w_2, w_3, w_4 are strings such that $|w_1| = |w_3| = i$, and some Turing machine M accepts both w_1w_2 and w_3w_4 by computations that produce identical crossing sequences at cell $i + 1$—the cell containing the last symbol in w_1 or w_3—then M must also accept the string w_1w_4. The computation performed on cells 1 through $i + 1$ when processing w_1w_4 would be the same as that performed when processing w_1w_2, while the computation performed on cells $i + 2$ and beyond would be identical to that performed when processing the string w_3w_4.

We are now ready to prove that *any solution to our string comparison problem using a (one-tape) Turing machine must have time complexity that is a quadratic expression in* n, *where* n *is the length of the input strings.*

Let M be any Turing machine such that $L(M)$ is the language that consists of all strings of the form $w*w$, where w is a string in $\{x, y, z\}^*$. For each $n \in \mathbb{N}^+$, let W_n be the subset of $L(M)$ that consists of strings of the form $w*w$, where $|w| = n$. We shall show that the average length of all computations of M with inputs from W_n is bounded below by a quadratic expression in n. From this it follows that the time complexity of M is at least a quadratic expression in n. (The worst-case performance of M cannot be faster than the average performance.)

The average number of steps executed by M when accepting a string from W_n, which we write as $A_n(M)$, is no smaller than the sum of the average lengths of the crossing sequences for the cells 1 through n over the same computations. That is, if $a_n(i)$ is the average length of the crossing sequences at cell i over all computations of M with inputs from W_n, then

$$A_n(M) \geqslant \sum_{i=1}^{n} a_n(i)$$

We complete the proof by showing that for each i in $\{1, 2, \cdots, n\}$, there are constants $c_i > 0$ and b_i such that $a_n(i) \geqslant c_i i + b_i$, because we can then extend the above inequality as follows:

$$
\begin{aligned}
A_n(M) &\geqslant \sum_{i=1}^{n} a_n(i) \\
&\geqslant \sum_{i=1}^{n} (c_i i + b_i) \\
&\geqslant min(c_1, \cdots, c_n) \sum_{i=1}^{n} i + \sum_{i=1}^{n} b_i \\
&= min(c_1, \cdots, c_n) \left(\frac{n(n+1)}{2} \right) + \sum_{i=1}^{n} b_i \\
&= \frac{min(c_1, \cdots, c_n)}{2} (n^2 + n) + \sum_{i=1}^{n} b_i
\end{aligned}
$$

which shows that $A_n(M)$ is bounded below by a quadratic expression in n, as required.

Let us turn, then, to the task of showing that for each i in $\{1, 2, \cdots, n\}$, there are constants $c_i > 0$ and b_i such that $a_n(i) \geqslant c_i i + b_i$.

For each i in $\{1, 2, \cdots, n\}$ we note that for at least two-thirds of the 3^n strings $w*w$ in W_n, the computation of M when accepting $w*w$ produces a crossing sequence at cell i of length no more than $3a_n(i)$. (Otherwise, there would be 3^{n-1} strings in W_n that produce crossing sequences of length more than $3a_n(i)$ at cell i, and thus,

$$a_n(i) > \frac{3^{n-1}[3a_n(i)]}{3^n} = a_n(i)$$

which is a contradiction.) Consequently, at least 3^{n-1} strings in W_n lead to crossing sequences of length no more than $3a_n(i)$.

It follows that many strings in W_n lead to the same crossing sequence at cell i. If k is the number of states in M (thus $k \geqslant 2$), then there are at most

k^j different crossing sequences of length j, and therefore at most

$$\sum_{j=0}^{3a_n(i)} k^j$$

different crossing sequences with length no more than $3a_n(i)$. But, this sum is no larger than $(3a_n(i) + 1)(k^{3a_n(i)})$, which is bounded above by $(k^{3a_n(i)+1})(k^{3a_n(i)}) = k^{6a_n(i)+1}$. Thus, there are at least

$$\frac{3^{n-1}}{k^{6a_n(i)+1}}$$

strings in W_n that produce the same crossing sequence at cell i. (There are at least 3^{n-1} strings in W_n with crossing sequences no longer than $3a_n(i)$ and no more than $k^{6a_n(i)+1}$ such sequences.)

We now claim that

$$\frac{3^{n-1}}{k^{6a_n(i)+1}} \leq 3^{n-i}$$

(Otherwise, there would be more strings in W_n that lead to the same crossing sequence at cell i than there are strings in $\{x, y, z\}^*$ of length $n - i$. Thus, there would be distinct strings w_1w_3 and w_2w_3 of length n, with $|w_3| = n - i$, for which $w_1w_3*w_1w_3$ and $w_2w_3*w_2w_3$ would produce the same crossing sequence at i when used as input to M. Consequently, by our observation preceding this proof, M would have to accept the string $w_1w_3*w_2w_3$—a contradiction.)

But, this last inequality implies

$$log_3\left(\frac{3^{n-1}}{k^{6a_n(i)+1}}\right) \leq log_3(3^{n-i})$$

or

$$log_3(3^{n-1}) - log_3(k^{6a_n(i)+1}) \leq log_3(3^{n-i})$$

or

$$(n - 1) - [6a_n(i) + 1]\,log_3 k \leq n - i$$

so

$$a_n(i) \geq \frac{i-1}{6\,log_3 k} - \frac{1}{6} = \frac{i}{6\,log_3 k} + \frac{-1 - log_3 k}{6\,log_3 k}$$

as required.

APPENDIX E

A Sampling of *NP* Problems

In this appendix we identify some of the many decision problems whose associated languages have been shown to belong in the class *NP*, but whose membership or lack of membership in *P* has not yet been determined. (In fact, all the problems listed here are *NP*-complete.)

E.1 FORMAL LANGUAGES AND AUTOMATA THEORY

There are numerous problems related to our study of formal languages and automata theory whose languages are in *NP*. Here are a few of them.

1. When given two nondeterministic finite automata over the same alphabet, respond *Y* if and only if they accept different languages.
2. When given two regular expressions over the same alphabet, respond *Y* if and only if they represent different languages. (You may wish to compare this problem to the preceding one.)
3. When given a context-free grammar and a positive integer k, respond *Y* if and only if the grammar is not an $LR(k)$ grammar.
4. When given a finite collection of deterministic finite automata, respond *Y* if and only if there is a string that is accepted by each of the automata in the collection.

E.2 NUMBER THEORY

The subject of number theory is rich in examples of *NP* problems. Here are just a few.

1. When given three positive integers a, b, and c, respond *Y* if and only if the equation $ax^2 + by = c$ has a solution that consists of positive integers.

2. When given three positive integers *a*, *b*, and *c*, respond *Y* if and only if there is a positive integer *x* that is less than *c* and $x^2 \equiv a(mod\ b)$.
3. When given a finite collection *K* of positive integers and another positive integer *n*, respond *Y* if and only if there is a subset of *K* whose sum is *n*.

E.3   LOGIC

In the text we saw that the satisfiability problem is an important *NP* problem. Here are two related problems.

1. When given a collection of clauses in which each clause contains exactly three literals, respond *Y* if and only if there is a truth assignment that satisfies the entire collection. (This problem is the same as SAT except that the clauses are required to have a uniform size of three. Thus, it is known as 3-SAT.)
2. When given an expression that consists of variables connected by the symbols ¬, ∩, ∪, and → (meaning not, and, or, and implies, respectively), respond *Y* if and only if there is a way of assigning the values true and false to the variables so that the expression is false.

E.4   SCHEDULING PROBLEMS

Numerous *NP* problems that have no known efficient solution are found in the context of developing schedules. Here are two of them.

1. When given a set *T* of tasks, the amount of time required to complete each individual task, a positive integer *n*, and a deadline, respond *Y* if and only if there is a way of assigning the tasks to *n* processors so that the entire set of tasks will be completed by the deadline.
2. Here is an interesting scheduling problem that occurs in the context of database management. Suppose we have a central database that is being manipulated by several remote users. Each transaction requested by a user consists of a sequence of steps that read and write various items of data. As long as the steps from different transactions do not deal with the same item of data or are not interweaved, the validity of the database is not in danger. However, if the steps from different transactions are mixed and happen to manipulate the same data item, the database can quickly become invalid.

   One solution is to require that any transaction be completed before another is allowed access to the database. This results in what is

called a serial schedule of transactions. Although this approach solves the problem, it has the undesirable side effect of needlessly slowing down the system's performance. There are many ways of interweaving the steps of different transactions that do not cause invalid data— even when the steps manipulate the same data items. Thus, to block one transaction's access to the database until another is complete is unnecessarily restrictive.

What is needed is a software package known as a scheduler that receives all requests from the users and schedules their access to the database in a way that allows interweaving (for efficiency) but avoids conflicting requests (for validity). One rather straightforward approach is based on the idea of view serializability. A schedule of transactions is said to be view serializable if each read step in the transactions reads exactly the same value as it would had the transactions been executed in some sequential, nonoverlapping order.

Such a schedule is sufficient to maintain the validity of the database, and thus one may conjecture that a scheduler could be designed based on this idea. The scheduler would allow the various transactions to access the database concurrently as long as the combination remained view serializable. Transactions that would destroy the view serializability of the system would be held back until they could be executed safely.

Unfortunately, no efficient algorithm has been found for testing a schedule of transactions to see if it is view serializable. The view serializable schedules constitute a language in *NP*, but no one has been able to find a polynomial-time, deterministic algorithm for recognizing that language. Thus, whether or not efficient schedulers can be constructed based on view serializability remains an open question.

E.5   GRAPH THEORY

Recall that a graph is a collection of nodes called vertices, some of which may be connected by lines called arcs. The following are only a few of the many *NP* problems posed in the context of graph theory.

1. When given a graph, respond *Y* if and only if that graph contains a path that visits every vertex exactly once and terminates at the same vertex at which it started. (Such a path is known as a **Hamilton circuit;** this problem is known as the **Hamilton circuit problem.**)
2. When given a graph and a positive integer *n*, respond *Y* if and only if the graph contains a clique with *n* vertices. (A clique in a graph is a set of vertices for which any two are connected by an arc.)

3. When given a graph G and a positive integer n, respond Y if and only if G contains n cliques that together contain all the vertices of G.

E.6 SET THEORY

The following are *NP* problems that deal with sets.

1. When given a set X and a finite collection of subsets of X, respond Y if and only if there is a subcollection of those subsets that is pairwise disjoint and whose union is all of X. (This is known as the exact covering problem.)
2. When given a finite set X, in which each element is assigned a positive integer value called its size, and two positive integers m and n, respond Y if and only if there are at least m subsets of X in which the sum of the sizes is no greater than n.
3. When given a finite set X, in which each element is assigned a positive integer value called its size, and a positive integer n, respond Y if and only if there is a subset of X for which the product of the sizes of its members is n.

Additional Reading

There are numerous books available which discuss the material covered in this text in more detail or perhaps from a different perspective. The following is only a partial list. Those listed under "General Coverage" deal with a broader range of topics than those listed under specific headings.

FORMAL LANGUAGES AND AUTOMATA THEORY

Bavel, Z., *Introduction to the Theory of Automata*. Reston, Virginia: Reston, 1983.

Cohen, D. I. A., *Introduction to Computer Theory*. New York: John Wiley, 1986.

Harrison, M. A., *Introduction to Formal Language Theory*. Menlo Park, California: Addison-Wesley, 1978.

Revesz, G. E., *Introduction to Formal Languages*. New York: McGraw-Hill, 1983.

PARSING AND COMPILER CONSTRUCTION

Aho, A. V., Sethi, R., and Ullman, J. D., *Compilers: Principles, Techniques, and Tools*. Menlo Park, California: Addison-Wesley, 1986.

Aho, A. V. and Ullman, J. D., *The Theory of Parsing, Translation, and Compiling*, vols. 1 and 2. Englewood Cliffs, New Jersey: Prentice-Hall, 1972.

Barrett, W. A. and Couch, J. D., *Compiler Construction: Theory and Practice*. Chicago, Illinois: SRA, 1979.

Fischer, C. N. and LeBlanc, R. J. Jr., *Crafting a Compiler*. Menlo Park, California: Benjamin/Cummings, 1988.

Tremblay, J. and Sorenson, P. G., *The Theory and Practice of Compiler Writing*. New York: McGraw-Hill, 1985.

Waite, W. M. and Goos, G., *Compiler Construction*. New York: Springer-Verlag, 1984.

COMPUTABILITY AND RECURSIVE FUNCTION THEORY

Cutland, N. J., *Computability: An Introduction to Recursive Function Theory*. Cambridge, England: Cambridge University Press, 1980.

Machtey, M. and Young, P., *An Introduction to the General Theory of Algorithms*. New York: North Holland, 1978.

Rogers, H. Jr., *Theory of Recursive Functions and Effective Computability*. Cambridge, Massachusetts: MIT Press, 1987.

COMPLEXITY

Garey, M. R. and Johnson, D. S., *Computers and Intractability*. New York: Freeman, 1979.

Wilf, H. S., *Algorithms and Complexity*. Englewood Cliffs, New Jersey: Prentice-Hall, 1986.

GENERAL COVERAGE

Beckman, F. S., *Mathematical Foundations of Programming*. Menlo Park, California: Addison-Wesley, 1981.

Brainerd, W. S. and Landweber, L. H., *Theory of Computation*. New York: John Wiley, 1974.

Davis, M. D. and Weyuker, E. J., *Computability, Complexity, and Languages*. London: Academic Press, 1983.

Denning, P. J., Dennis, J. B., and Qualitz, J. E., *Machines, Languages, and Computation*. Englewood Cliffs, New Jersey: Prentice-Hall, 1978.

Hopcroft, J. E. and Ullman, J. D., *Introduction to Automata Theory, Languages, and Computation*. Menlo Park, California: Addison-Wesley, 1979.

Lewis, H. R. and Papadimitriou, C. H., *Elements of the Theory of Computation*. Englewood Cliffs, New Jersey: Prentice-Hall, 1981.

McNaughton, R., *Elementary Computability, Formal Languages, and Automata*. Englewood Cliffs, New Jersey: Prentice-Hall, 1982.

Sudkamp, T. A., *Languages and Machines*. Menlo Park, California: Addison-Wesley, 1988.

Wood, D., *Theory of Computation*. New York: Harper and Row, 1987.

INDEX